國學擷要

Guoxue Special

Contents

From Cang Jie's creation of Chinese characters to the *Siku Quanshu (Complete Library in the Four Branches of Literature)* and from ancient Buddhist scriptures to today's diverse religions, numerous historical events, cultural practises and treasures of civilisation have combined, creating a priceless resource for the study of Chinese civilisation.

Preface

Retrospection is often a way to pay respect to the past. For this purpose, let us go back to the origins of Chinese culture.

Around 2,500 years ago, a book titled *Erya* gained considerable prominence. It was the first dictionary of the Chinese language, and was compiled and arranged according to the meanings of characters and the taxonomy of things. It consisted of more than 4,300 words arranged in 2,091 entries, which were grouped into 19 chapters. The first character of the name of each chapter was "*shi*," meaning definition. The 19 chapters were definitions of glossary, language, idioms, kin, court, instruments, music, heaven, earth, hills, mountains, waters, grass, trees, insects, fishes, birds, beasts and livestock. Seen from today's perspective, the ancestors defined, explained, expounded and experienced the world around them in those 19 chapters, which demonstrated their ideals of harmony between man and nature.

"The characters *chu* (初), *zai* (哉), *shou* (首), *ji* (基), *zhao* (肇), *zu* (祖), *yuan* (元) , *tai* (胎), *chu* (俶), *luo* (落) and *quanyu* (权舆) mean the beginning." That is the first sentence in the first chapter of *Erya*. Everything began from that sentence. Everything in *guoxue*, from characters, language, myths and epics to axioms and legends, started from the character *chu* (初). It then grew over thousands of years to become the foundation for Chinese culture and spirit, the lingua franca of Chinese descendents who have used it to build solidarity in every corner of the world.

Chinese people have formed a big family because of *guoxue*, which accompanies every Chinese wherever they are. They are lyricists who sing "Kwan-Kwan go the ospreys, on the islet in the river"; they are like Confucius who reflected on "how time passes, like the flowing river"; they are like the idealistic thinker Zhuang Zhou who "wandered between reality and the dreamland; or they are like the poet Du Shaoling who yearned to accommodate all the homeless. They have common games, such as reading aloud, "the basics of the academic should be to probe into the ultimate virtue…," which is the lifelong pursuit of a traditional Chinese gentlemen seeking self-improvement before serving the public. *Guoxue* is the chicken soup for the souls of Chinese, because it can touch the innermost reaches of their hearts.

Guoxue in China has been growing for thousands of years, during which time books and records have been left as milestones. They remain treasures in the cultural legacy of Chinese.

Study of a Nation

Guoxue is a unique appellation in Chinese culture.

The first Chinese scholar to use the term *guoxue* to refer to Chinese culture and scholarship was Deng Shi, who wrote an article titled "*Guoxue Jinglun*" (*A Detailed Elaboration on Guoxue*) in Issue 27 of *Guocui Xuebao* (*Journal of the Quintessence of Chinese Culture*) during the 30th year of Emperor Guangxu's reign (1903). Other experts on Chinese culture subsequently published works on *guoxue*, such as Liu Shipei's *Guoxue* Fawei (On *Guoxue*) and Xu Dishan's *Guocui yu Guoxue* (*Guoxue and the Quintessecnce of Chinese Culture*).

As a general term for traditional Chinese culture and scholarship, *guoxue* has broad connotations and extensions. From recording events by tying knots to today's linguistics and philology, from ancient shamanism and divination to the *Yijing* (*The Book of Changes*), from the "Four Great Inventions" to modern advances in technology and achievements in natural sciences, from primitive aesthetics to works of art and literature, from Confucianism to the *Siku Quanshu* (*The Complete Library in the Four Branches of Literature*), from ancient Buddhist scriptures to today's diverse religions, from the records of primitive tribes to the modern study of ethnology and folklore… all these historical materials and cultural heritages are included in the domain of *guoxue*.

Guoxue is a rich and deep subject in which Chinese people take great pride. Inheriting *guoxue* displays Chinese people's recreation of and adherence to traditional culture.

Origins

Guoxue refers to traditional Chinese culture, including the cultures of its diverse regions and 56 ethnic groups. Regional cultures and ethnic cultures have various representations, forming a whole piciture of traditional Chinese culture.

The word *guoxue* refers to the study of traditional Chinese culture. The term originated from the period when western cultures penetrated into China at the end of the Qing Dynasty (1644–1911). Generally speaking, it refers to the traditional Chinese cultural system centred on Confucian classics, historical records, philosophical writings and literature. It consists of Confucian, Daoist and Buddhist philosophies. Among them, Daoism and Confucianism are the main themes, with Mohism, Legalism and other philosophies included. In contemporary times, Ji Xianlin put forward the concept of "grand *guoxue*," which incorporates all regional and ethnic cultures in China.

The core values of the *guoxue* teachings are benevolence, humanism and an ethical approach to life and the world. In traditional Chinese culture, the core principle of Confucianism is benevolence. In *Lunyu* (*Analects of Confucius*), the word "benevolence" appears more than 70 times. Mencius said, "Benevolence begins with sympathy; righteousness begins with a sense of shame; propriety begins with politeness; wisdom begins with a sense of right and wrong." Benevolence, righteousness, propriety and wisdom are "the four cardinal virtues" inherent in human beings. During the Western Han Dynasty (206 BC–AD 24), Dong Zhongshu added a fifth virtue, "faithfulness," to the mix. Humanism is intrinsic to *guoxue*.

"Equilibrium and harmony," another theme running through the development of *guoxue*, has had substantial influence on national character and customs. Equilibrium refers to the ideal mid-point between two extremes, such as courage, an excess or deficiency of which results in recklessness or cowardice. Harmony means the peaceful coexistence of various elements. According to *Zhongyong* (*Doctrine of the Mean*), "The containment of passions means equilibrium; the rational expression of those passions means harmony. Equilibrium is the origin of the world; harmony is the ultimate aim of the world. The achievement of equilibrium and harmony leads to the orderly arrangement and growth of all things in the world." The path of equilibrium and harmony leads to the coexistence of nature and human society. As the ancient saying goes, "Harmony is the greatest virtue in propriety, as promoted by the ancient emperors." The principle of equilibrium and harmony is the code for human interaction, which can lead to social harmony and, ultimately, global harmony.

The concept of propriety has special significance in China in terms of society and politics. Propriety, which means rituals and codes of conduct that safeguard social order, consists of conduct, rituals, rules, ethics and political thought. Confucius incorporated propriety into his system and regarded it as the core of his political and ethical thought. He said, "Self-abstention and restoration of propriety lead to benevolence." Emperor Wu (reign: 141–87 BC) of the Han Dynasty

(206 BC–AD 220) kept Confucianism dominant while ousting other doctrines. Confucianism became an official philosophy and propriety has remained the prominent feature of traditional Chinese culture, shaping and influencing it and the Chinese character.

With the interaction between Chinese and western cultures, it is natural for Chinese culture to enrich itself by assimilating elements from other cultures. In this new era, *guoxue* has acquired some new features. It is nationalistic, because it focuses on traditional Chinese culture, making it distinctive in the world; it is growing, because its system of unity, formulated prior to the Qin Dynasty (221–206 BC), is vibrant and lasting; and it is modern, because it has contemporary relevance.

The development of *guoxue* incorporates the growth of Chinese philosophy over thousands of years. Therefore, it is the responsibility of today's generation to understand, study and revitalise *guoxue*.

Various Schools

Guoxue originated early and entered its golden stage of development during the Spring and Autumn Period. One Hundred Schools of Thought is a general term used to describe this flourishing period. The most influential of these schools were Confucianism, Daoism, Yin-Yang school, Legalism, Mohism, the school of Logicians and Eclectics, Agriculturalists and Strategists. Many thoughts of these One Hundred Schools of Thought have enlightened later generations.

Confucianism

Confucianism was established by Confucius at the end of the Spring and Autumn Period (770–446 BC). Under his guidance, it became a school following the example of the mythical kings Yao and Shun, the rituals of the Zhou Dynasty (11th century–256 BC) and the teachings of the six Confucian classics. Its focus is "benevolence." It advocates rituals and music, benevolence and righteousness, loyalty and forgiveness, the golden mean, benevolent governance and ethical education. It has remained the mainstream and official philosophy since the Han Dynasty.

Major figures in Confucianism in the Spring and Autumn Period and the Warring States Period (475–221 BC) were Confucius, Mencius and Xunzi. Confucius regarded "benevolence" as the foundation of an ideal personality, which later became the core of Confucianism. He advocated "propriety" as practised during the Zhou Dynasty, and it covered social standards, requirements, norms and codes of conduct that were used to regulate behaviour and settle disputes. He believed behaviour should comply with the propriety of the Zhou Dynasty in all aspects, and this was the embodiment of benevolence. After the death of Confucius, Confucianism divided into a number of schools, namely Zizhang, Zisi, Yanshi, Mencius, Qidiaoshi, Zhongliangshi, Sunshi and Yuezhengshi. Although they had different ideas, they all claimed to be the successors of Confucius. Over time, the Mencius school and Xunzi school became dominant.

Mencius carried Confucius's teachings on "benevolence" forward into his theory of the original goodness of human nature. He believed people were born with four virtues: "benevolence, righteousness, propriety and wisdom." He thought compassion naturally entailed compassionate governance and proposed the idea that "people must be given precedence over the rulers." Xunzi carried the Confucian ideal of "propriety" forward into his theory of the evil of human nature. He thought propriety should be the dominant force in governance, supplemented by law and order.

During the Western Han Dynasty, Dong Zhongshu reformed Confucianism, adding some Daoist and Legalist elements that supported imperial rule. He advocated the divine right of rulers, grand unification and keeping Confucianism as the dominant philosophy, while rejecting other philosophies. His ideas were adopted by Emperor Wu of the Han Dynasty and Confucianism became the orthodoxy in feudal dynasties.

During the Wei (AD 220–265) and Jin (AD 265–420) dynasties, metaphysicists such as He Yan, Wang Bi and the Seven Sages of the Bamboo Grove expounded Confucian classics using Daoist thought.

During the Tang Dynasty (AD 618–907), Han Yu put forward his concept of Confucian Orthodoxy in his *Yuandao (The Original Way)*. It traces philosophical development from King Yao to King Shun, King Yu, King Tang, King Wen, King Wu, Duke Zhou, Confucius and finally to Mencius. He believed this line of succession was the orthodoxy of Confucianism. He said, "Mencius learned from Zisi, who learned from Zengzi. Since the demise of Confucius, all of his disciples have written books, but only Mencius got the orthodox thoughts of Confucius." Han Yu used Confucian Orthodoxy to argue against Buddhist philosophy.

Idealism during the Song Dynasty (AD 960–1279) was Neo-Confucianism, established on the basis of Confucian philosophy but with Buddhist and Daoist elements. Major figures in this school were Cheng Hao, Cheng Yi and Zhu Xi. Zhu Xi represented the culmination of the development of idealism. Building on the foundation of thoughts of the two Chengs, he improved the objective idealist philosophy. The core of his thoughts was that "ideal" was the origin of all things in the world while "air" was the building block of all things in the world. He believed that The Ideal was equal to character in human beings. Divine character was the ideal. Ideal combined with air to form human beings. According to Zhu Xi, The Ideal was supremely good, as was divine character. Air, on the other hand, could be good or evil. He opposed combining divine character with human desire and proposed "keeping divine character and containing human desire," because he thought human desire to be the root of all evil.

During the mid-Ming Dynasty (1368–1644), Wang Yangming opposed Zhu Xi's idea of regarding "heart" and "ideal" as two separate things. He established the subjective idealist theory on the basis of *Shangshu (Book of History/Documents)*. The new thinking was called the "Study of Heart."

Since the Ming and Qing dynasties, western philosophies have penetrated China. After China's defeat in the Opium War in 1840, Confucian philosophers in the Qing Dynasty proposed "Chinese philosophy as the theme and western science as the tool."

Subsequently, China's backwardness drove people to reflect on Chinese culture. The New Culture Movement in 1919 was "anti-establishment, anti-Confucianism and anti-classic Chinese" and advocated cultural reform, a literary revolution, democracy and science. It promoted the vernacular and criticised pure and traditional Chinese culture. If preferred pragmatism to Confucianism, which resulted in the wholesale decline of *guoxue*.

However, Confucianism cannot be removed from the values of the Chinese people. After China's Reform and Opening up period began towards the end of the 1970s, the restoration and revitalisation of Chinese culture based on Confucianism drew more attention. In 1999, Li Ruihuan, member of the Standing Committee of the Political Bureau of the Central Committee of the Communist Party of China (CPC) and chairman of the Chinese People's Political Consultative Conference (CPPCC), addressed the Commemorative Conference on the 2550th birthday of Confucius and the Second Conference of the International Confucian Association. He said, "History over more than two millennia has proved the value of Confucianism. We should study Confucianism with a scientific approach, keeping its essence while discarding the dross." That address set out the modern attitude towards Confucianism.

Since its establishment, Confucianism has become a comprehensive philosophical system through constant reform and development. As the mainstream of Chinese culture, it remains relevant to modern society.

Confucianism is not confined to China. It has widespread influence globally. As early as the first century AD, Confucianism influenced East Asian countries such as Japan, Korea and Vietnam. In the 17th and 18th centuries, Confucianism was known in Europe. It was first brought into Europe by the missionary Matteo Ricci. He wrote, "The most prominent philosopher in China is Confucius, an erudite scholar who was born in 551 BC and died in his 70s. He inspired his compatriots to pursue virtue with his writings, teaching and behaviour. He was abstinent, so he was regarded by his compatriots as the holiest master in the world." There was fervour for Confucius in the 18th century and Confucianism combined with new thoughts formed in Europe since the Renaissance to inspire the Enlightenment. Voltaire was the loudest advocate of Confucianism in Europe. In fact, he was dubbed the "Confucius of Europe." The idealism of the Chengs and Zhu Xi became the foundation for German philosopher Leibnitz's classical philosophy, which he used to fight the "Theology of Revelation" of Roman Catholicism.

Confucianism, as a universal world view and philosophy, is regarded as an integral part of civilisation. As such it is part of humanity's cultural heritage.

Daoism

Daoism (aka Taoism) was one of the most important schools of thought during the Spring and Autumn (770–446 BC) and the Warring States periods (475–221 BC). It was established by the philosopher Laozi and advanced by Zhuangzi. It focuses on *dao* and advocates inaction *(wuwei)* and the harmonious coexistence of man and nature.

Dao is explained in *Laozi* (as Laozi's book, *Daodejing*, is commonly known) as "something established prior to the creation of heaven and earth. It is self-contained and everything else originated from it. It has no name, so I tentatively call it *dao*." *Dao* is the primeval objective matter that can last forever. It has two characters. On the one hand, it is intangible, but is not nil. On the other hand, it contains the possibility of forming all things so it is the foundation for everything in the world. The interaction and interdependence of the two characters is best explained by Laozi. He generalised from several examples that "tangible things provide the interest while intangible things provide the usage." According to him, intangibility is more fundamental than tangibility. The process from intangibility to tangibility is "*dao* begets one, one begets two, two begets three, and three begets everything. Everything goes from yin to yang and achieves harmony." *Dao* is the origin of everything and it begets everything. In addition, *dao* is the guiding principle for movement of everything, from heaven to human beings.

Naturalness and inaction are the main elements of Daoism. It means the reservation of natural characteristics without artificial modifications. The aim is to achieve "action through inaction." This thought can be understood through two aspects. First, everything should follow natural laws. Second, governance should be conducted through inaction and restoration of human nature, which can help solve social problems. Rulers should follow the spirit of nature and simplify rules and regulations so that the people can live their lives undisturbed.

Daoism is plain dialectics. Things always reverse course towards the opposite after reaching an extreme. That is the rule for the movement of *Dao*. All things in the world are interdependent. Opposing characters coexist, such as tangibility and intangibility, easiness and difficulty, long and short, high and low, front and back. It is like a plant, which grows from a tender shoot into a strong plant and then dies. From this principle, Daoism advocates weakness and tenderness and avoids strength, because it believes that weakness brings vitality and space for further development. Strength brings only death. Therefore, the Daoist pursues the virtue of water. Laozi said, "The ultimate virtue is like water, which benefits everything and never competes with others." Water is weak but it can wear away everything hard. "Water is the strongest thing in the world," because it never competes with anything.

Daoism originated with Laozi, who lived at the end of the Spring and Autumn Period. However, the term "Daoism" first appeared in *Lun Liu Jia Yaozhi (Discussing the Essentials of the Six Schools)*, written by Sima Tan, a Western Han historian. During the Warring States Period, Daoism was divided into three schools: Yangzhu school, headed by Yang Zhu and Zi Huazi; Huanglao school, headed by Shen Dao, Tian Pian and Huan Yuan; and Laozhuang school, headed by Laozi, Zhuangzi and Liezi. Different schools had different focuses, either on governance or on self-improvement. The Huanglao school was the dominant among the three and exerted enormous influence on the other schools of thought. At the end of the Warring States Period, the Huanglao school absorbed the other two schools.

After unifying China, Qin Shihuang, first emperor of the Qin Dynasty, adopted Legalism in his governance and burned all the books of other philosophical schools. When the Han Dynasty was established, the country entered a period of recovery, so the early Han rulers favoured the Huanglao school. Then, during the reign of Emperor Wu, the policy of "keeping Confucianism dominant while ousting all other schools" marginalised Daoism. At the end of the Eastern Han Dynasty (AD 25-220), "Huanglao" became associated with the worship of "fairies," so Daoist thoughts became the foundation of the Daoist religion. Figures in Daoism, such as Laozi and Zhuangzi, became deities in Daoism. As a result, Daoist thought continued to exert its influence on art and literature. However, it should be noted there are fundamental differences between Daoist philosophy, which advocates nature and inaction, and Daoist religion, which is a religion with rituals and practises aimed at increasing longevity.

The emergence of metaphysics during the Wei and Jin Dynasties (AD 220–581) injected vitality into Daoism and sparked renewed explanations of the thoughts of Laozi and Zhuangzi. At the time, *Zhouyi (I Ching)*, *Laozi* and *Zhuangzi* were regarded as the "Three Scriptures of Metaphysics." Since then, the Laozhuang school has remained the orthodoxy of Daoism. After the emergence of idealism during the Song Dynasty (AD 960–1279), independent Daoist philosophy ceased to exist.

Among the pre-Qin schools, Daoism did not have a large body of disciples and it has never been adopted as an official philosophy, as Confucianism has. Yet, it has played an important role in ancient Chinese philosophy. Buddhism was influenced by Daoism after entering China. Chan Buddhism (Zen) was inspired in many ways by Zhuangzi. Idealism of the Song and Ming dynasties and Wang Yanming's School of Heart were also strongly influenced by Daoism. With the development of society, Daoism's unique views on the universe, society and life make it an everlasting inheritance of traditional Chinese culture.

Mohism

Mohism was an important school during the period of contention between a hundred schools of thought.

It is recorded that Mozi first learned Confucianism from Zizhang. Discontented with the complicated rituals and extravagant funerals advocated by Confucianism, he established his own school, Mohism, which was introduced in *Mozi (Book of Mozi)*. Mohism had a large body of disciples, most of whom came from the lower classes. The followers continued their work while conducting academic and political activities. Mohists formed hierarchical communes with stringent disciplines. Mohism was highly religious, since it believed in the existence of deities, but it also probed into scientific studies, both practical and theoretical, such as mechanics, optics and acoustics. It is said a wooden axle made by Mozi could carry a weight of 600 *jin* (about 300 kilograms). He pointed out that acceleration came from force. Pinhole imaging was also first discovered by Mozi and his calculus theory predated that of the West. He was called the Democritus of the Orient. His scientific spirit pushed scientific study and practise to a high level in China, thus exerting a profound influence on ancient Chinese science and technology. Mohists regarded Emperor Yu as their model and upheld his diligence, bravery and sacrifice for the common good.

Mohism had 10 premises: universal love, non-aggression, virtuous talent, solidarity, thrift, simple funerals, "non-pleasure," divine will, deities and "non-fortune." In the later Warring States Period, Mohists developed the ancient logic and made great contributions in the field of research on concepts, judgements and reasoning.

Mohism attributed social disorder in the Warring States Period to the lack of universal love among people; therefore, it advocated the establishment of a new interpersonal relationship characterised by universal love and mutual benefit. Universal love is unconditional and undifferentiated, which eliminates blood bonds and class distinctions. Universal love is based on mutual benefit, which is also universal. If people can "love others as they love themselves," their own interests can be unified with universal interests and harmony can be achieved in family, community and country. Mohism proposed the concept of equality for the first time and put it into practise. Universal love means direct love for the country, the community and others, which results in indirect love for themselves. However, such quixotic love was not enforceable at the time.

On the basis of universal love, Mohism advocated "non-aggression." It opposed the invasions of other countries using force, regarding it as unjust. The story of preventing the Chu state from invading the Song state is an example of this ideal. A craftsman named Gongshu Ban (Lu Ban) from the Lu state came to the Chu state to build a ladder for use in sieges. The emperor of Chu decided to invade the Song state using this ladder. Mozi, who was in the Qi state at the time, heard the news and hurried to the Chu state to try to prevent the war. Meanwhile, he sent his disciples to the Song state to help with its defence. After he arrived in the Chu state, Mozi met Gongshu Ban and the Chu state and sought to dissuade them from waging war. To this end, he engaged Gongshu Ban in a simulated siege in the court of Chu, where Gongshu Ban played the offensive and Mozi played the defensive. Mozi defeated Gongshu Ban nine times. In the face of Mozi's supreme wisdom and the hundreds of well-prepared Mohists in the Song state, the emperor of Chu gave up his invasion plan. Mohist "non-aggression" applied only to unjust wars of aggression. Invasions such as those in which Emperor Tang defeated Emperor Jie and Emperor Wu defeated Emperor Zhou were regarded by Mohists as just wars. The idea of "non-aggression" was the most prominent expression of Mohist universal love.

Mohism regarded "virtuous talent" as the foundation for governance. It believed that lack of these talents in government resulted in disorder and decline. Mozi gave the examples of Duke Wen of Jin and Duke Huan of Qi to illustrate the importance of talent. Duke Wen came back to his homeland after 19 years in exile and appointed people with virtuous talents to top positions, which made the dukedom of Jin a great power. Duke Huan appointed the capable Guan Zhong and thus became a famous leader of the Spring and Autumn Period. The Mohist principle of appointment was promotion of talent regardless of background and class and to leave no room for nepotism and cronyism. That was in direct opposition to the hereditary system of the time, in which slavery was a cornerstone of society.

Solidarity required compliance with the will of rulers, which unified people's opinions and set the standards for judgement, so stability could be maintained in the face of hostilities among separatist realms.

"Thrift" was directly opposite to luxury. A "simple funeral" was the expression of thrift. "Non-pleasure" opposed the enjoyment of music by rulers, because Mohists thought the manufacturing and playing of instruments constituted a waste of manpower and, therefore, was not good for the people.

"Divine will" and "deities" were the religious thoughts of Mohism. "Non-fortune" opposed the "god-given fortune" proposed by Confucianism, because Mohism believed humans were the determining factor of society.

In the pre-Qin period, Mohism existed as the direct opposite of Confucianism. However, after the unification of China by the Qin Dynasty, culture was also unified and the contention of a hundred schools ceased. After the establishment of the Han Dynasty, many schools were revitalised, but Mohism was not, since it was regarded as unfit by the ruling class. Over the two millennia from the Qin to Qing dynasties, Mohism went into decline and stagnation, but Mohist spirits lingered on, as shown by poetry and novels glorifying the spirits of knighthood and brotherhood. Mohism, which has kept its influence among grassroots Chinese, has been as powerful and significant a contributor to Chinese culture as Confucianism and Daoism.

Legalist School

The Legalist school was among the most influential schools during the pre-Qin period. The Legalist school took the socio-historical outlook that human beings were basically selfish and indolent as the theoretical basis for their proposed reforms. They advocated the rule of law, the clear promulgation of laws and heavy penalties for law breakers. They believed the goal of making a state wealthy and militarily powerful should be achieved through agriculture and war. They upheld the centralisation of power and proposed a comprehensive set of theories and methods for the governance of a country.

The Legalist school can be divided into the legalists of the Qi state and the legalists of the three states established after the split of the Jin state. The Legalist school of the Qi state originated in present-day Shandong Province. Their philosophy can be summarised as "Equal Weight between Rituals and Laws." On the one hand, they advocated Legalist reform and emphasised the real effect of governance by the rule of law. On the other hand, they emphasised that ethics and morals played the role of value orientation in running a country. They established the common values of rituals, righteousness, chastity and sense of shame, and defended the rituals, ritual music and the patriarchal clan system.

In 403 BC, the three families of Han, Zhao and Wei divided the Jin state. These three states were known collectively as the "Three Jin states." The Legalist school of the Three Jin states refers to the Legalist thought that was formed in the region of the Three Jin states during the Spring and Autumn Period and the Warring States Period. The main characteristics of their philosophy were valuing agriculture and restraining commerce, running the country according to the rule of law, emphasizing rigorous penalties for breaches of law, rewarding farming and military conquest and negating rituals, ritual music and moral teaching. The main representative scholars were Li Li and Wu Qi in the early Warring States Period; Shang Yang, Shen Buhai and Shen Dao in the mid Warring States Period; and Li Si and Han Fei in the late Warring States Period.

Legalist thought can be divided into the three parts: "Law," "Method" and "Power." Law refers to the codified standards of a regime. It is open and visible. Shang Yang was representative of this concept; he believed that a political system and decree were both instruments to make the country powerful and bring benefits to the people.

Method refers to the means with which a monarch controls his ministers in accordance with the law. Unlike the law, the method is not visible but hidden. Shen Buhai was representative of this concept. He believed that, in order to consolidate the centralised power of a monarch and to avoid usurpation by the ministers, a monarch must master the art of controlling his ministers.

Power refers to the regime. It includes authority and influence. Shen Dao was representative of this concept. When he discussed the importance of power, Shen Dao said, "If the sage emperor Yao had been a commoner, he would not be able to govern three people. But the tyrant Jie could put the empire into chaos when he was the Son of the Heaven. From this, I know that it is important to hold the position of power and that the wisdom of a sage is not worthy of admiration." He advocated that a monarch could "hold the law and the position of power" and "rule the country with inaction."

During the late Warring States Period, Han Fei summarised the philosophy of Shang Yang, Shen Buhai and Shen Dao and proposed a philosophy that centred on the rule of law and combined law, method and power. Han Fei was from the declining aristocracy of the Han state, and spoke with a stutter. But he was versatile and agile in thought.

Han Fei's philosophy was the essence of the thought of the Legalist school. He believed that in order to consolidate absolute monarchy, law, method and power were all indispensable. If there was no written law, it was impossible to rule the people and guard against corruption. But if attention was only paid to written laws, and a monarch did not have the ability to rule the officials, he would not be able to prevent his ministers developing their own power. Law and method both had to take "holding power" as their premise. Han Fei's ideas were adopted by the Qin state, and laid the ideological foundation for Qin Shihuang to "sweep all over China and unify it."

The Legalist school believed human society progressed and history advanced constantly. They opposed the doctrine that "affirmed the ancient and negated the present" and advocated aggressive reform. The issues to be resolved in different times were also different. The ways to solve problems also changed with the times. As the ages changed, social life and political systems changed together. The proposition of "back to the ancients" would not work. Shang Yang proposed that "people should neither imitate the ancients nor follow the present." Han Fei further developed Shang Yang's ideas and proposed that "a state that does not change its rule when the times change will end up in turmoil." People should not follow the beaten track, nor should they regress.

The Legalist school believed that human beings were selfish in nature and naturally indolent, that they sought advantages and avoided disadvantages, and that they liked noble titles and official salaries and hated penalties and punishments. The Legalist school took the historical outlook of evolution and development and the theory of human nature that human beings "liked benefits and detested harm" as their theoretical basis and proposed a complete series of theories and approaches on the governance of a country that aimed to make the country wealthy and militarily powerful, all while maintaining an absolute monarchy.

Legalist thought advocates "running a country by law." First, the making of a law should not violate heavenly principles. It should conform to the basic principles of nature and society. The actual conditions of common people should be taken into consideration as much as possible. When the standards of the law are set up, specific legal provisions should also be formulated. Too abstract and ambiguous standards should never be proposed because they would make a law that ends up just being empty words. A law should be easily understandable, have some stability and should not be changed lightly.

Second, the "clear promulgation of law" was stressed in the application of a law. It meant that a law should be open so that common people could understand it and choose their behaviour in accordance with the standards in the legal provisions. Also, it would help to prevent officials bending the law for personal gain. In addition, "awards and punishments should be rigorously carried out" on the basis of "clear promulgation of law."

The Chinese idiom "Building Trust by Moving a Wooden Pole" refers to an incident that occurred in 359 BC. Shang Yang erected a nine-metre wooden pole in the market and announced that whoever moved this wooden pole to the North Gate would be rewarded with 10 gold pieces. But at the time, the country was full of mistrust. People thought it was a trick and nobody took it seriously. So Shang Yang raised the reward to fifty gold pieces. Eventually someone moved the wooden pole to the north gate, and was rewarded as promised, so Shang Yang won the trust of the people. Later political measures and decrees all could be implemented smoothly and successfully in the Qin state and the country grew powerful.

Third, the Legalist school stressed that stern or even cruel means be taken to punish criminals as a deterrent. The doctrine of severe punishment included implications in two aspects: One is more punishment and less reward. This meant that, of the "two handles" of punishment and reward in the governance of a country, punishment should be taken as the main instrument. Main efforts should be made to let punishment play its role. The other is heavier punishment imposed on lesser crime, or using violence to prevent violence.

Fourth, the legalists also proposed that anyone who committed a crime, regardless of status, should be punished according to the law. Later, Han Fei specifically proposed that "the law does not protect the powerful" and advocated that "the punishment of wrongs do not turn aside from a court minister while the reward of goodness will not leave out a commoner." Such Legalist thought initially embodied the concept that all people were equal in the eyes of the law.

The theoretical foundation of the rule of law played a significant role when Qin Shihuang conquered and united six other states and established a feudal country with centralised rule. It became the ruling ideology of the Qin Dynasty. But in the Western Han Dynasty, intellectuals opposed Legalist thought because the Qin Dynasty fell due to its tyrannical politics. Emperor Wudi of the Han Dynasty adopted Dong Zhongshu's suggestion and practised the policy of "suppressing the hundred schools of thought and making Confucianism the state ideology."

Independent Legalist schools gradually disappeared. However, rulers secretly accepted and adopted many of the principles of Legalist thought as complementary when they applied Confucianism in governing the country. They employed imperial grace and punishment in parallel. At the same time, Legalist scholars of the Western Han Dynasty also continuously reformed Legalist thought. The merger of Confucianism and Legalism was embodied in the laws of the Tang Dynasty (AD 618–907) when Legalist thought was incorporated into the system of Confucian learning.

Military Theory During Pre-Qin Period

Focusing on the philosophy of war, military operations and commands, militarists and their theories form an important school among the various schools of thought in the Warring States period. Representative figures of this school include Sun Tzu (Sun Wu) and Sima Rangju from the end of the Spring and Autumn Period, and Sun Bin, Wu Qi, Yu Liao, Wei Wuji and Bai Qi from the Warring States Period, and Zhang Liang and Han Xin from the beginning of the Han Dynasty. Today, the works of this school that are available include *Huangdi Yinfujing (Yellow Emperor's Talisman Classic)*, *Liu Dao (Six Arts of War)*, *San Lü (Three Strategies of War)*, *Sunzi Bingfa (Art of War by Sun Tzu)*, *Sima Fa (Art of War by Sima)*, *Sun Bin Bingfa (Art of War by Sun Bin)*, *Wu Zi*, *Weiliaozi* and *Jiang Yuan (Garden of Generals)*. While they differ from each other in some way, the theory of each militarist is a summary of war and the command experience at that time, and therefore were widely influential in the pre-Qin period.

The school of militarists was a product of the intense turmoil and social change in the Spring and Autumn and Warring States periods. As a school with a complete ideological system, it officially came into shape at the end of the Spring and Autumn Period, with Sun Tzu as its representative figure and his *The Art of War* the universally acknowledged classic of ancient military science. In fact, Sun Tzu's *The Art of War*, together with Carl von Clausewitz's *On War*, are the representative works of eastern and western military science. In the early stages of the Warring States Period, all schools of thought were fighting for attention, discussing topics covering politics, economics, culture and military affairs. In this period, the representative militarists included Wu Qi and Sun Tzu, who, based on the nature of the wars for hegemony at that time, summarised characteristics and laws of war into militarist masterpieces, such as *Wuzi* by Wu Qi and *The Art of War* by Sun Bin. By the end of the Warring States Period, after a long period of fighting for hegemony, the major purpose of war had been to unify the country. Wars in this period were more devastating, being fought on a bigger scale. *Weiliaozi* is a summary of the thoughts and strategies of war during this period. After the Qin Dynasty unified China, the collision among various schools gradually disappeared because freedom of thought was restricted. As with other schools, the militarist school was also abandoned and rejected and then gradually disappeared, along with its unique ideological system, views and methods.

As to the sects within this school, *Hanshu (History of the Han Dynasty)* has made a clear classification: the Yin-Yang militarists, the skill militarists, the tactical militarists, and the situation militarists.

The tactical militarists were masters in defeating the enemy by employing military strategies. Stressing the research of military strategies, this sect summarised the war and leadership of that time and integrated the thoughts of the other three sects. This group's thoughts, which cover strategic and tactical principles, abundant military dialectical thought, and a philosophy of commanding and military operations, are the core of militarist theories.

The situation militarists stressed research into tactics, discussing the mobility of military actions and the flexibility of the application of tactics. The famous battle of wits between Sun Bin and Pang Juan is a practical example of the military theories of this sect. Sun Bin, the descendant of Sun Tzu, the great militarist, was a Qi national, while Pang Juan, a national of Wei, was also a general commanding Wei forces. They were both students of Guiguzi and were both serving the Wei state. Being jealous of Sun's talent, Pang secretly framed Sun, who was punished for treason by having his kneecaps removed, rendering him disabled. Pang then tried to trick Sun into revealing his military strategies by urging him to write a book, after which Pang intended to have Sun killed. But, alerted to Pang's plot by a servant, Sun pretended to become mad to avoid being killed and was later able to flee to the Qi state with the help of the Qi envoy. There he became a military counsellor. In the Battle of Guiling, Sun employed the tactic of besieging Wei to rescue Zhao, and thereby managed to resolve the crisis faced by the Zhao state while inflicting a massive blow on the Wei army and thus the vitality of the Wei state. In the Battle of Maling, Sun reduced the number of cooking stoves the Qi lit day by day, successfully fooling Pang into believing the Qi force was weakening and luring the Wei army into an ill-judged attack. In the end, Wei was defeated and Pang Juan was killed at the Maling Path. This was the turning point where Wei lost the power to expand and the Qi and Qin states became the two great powers.

The Yin-Yang militarists, building their military theories on the theory of yin and yang and the five elements, applied astronomical, meteorological and geographical knowledge to military operations. By studying the relationship between wars and weather and geographical conditions, they aimed to identify the best timing and location of military campaigns.

The skill militarists studied weapons and military skills to focus on the training of soldiers, building elite troops, and military equipment. They combined the physical training of soldiers with the use of weapons, and strengthened military drills and coordination during actual combat. As the representative figure of this sect, Wu Qi is famous for his training of the elite soldiers of Wei. Only those who could travel 100 *li* (50 kilometre) within half a day while wearing armour and carrying a crossbow with a draw weight of 12 *dan* (360 kilograms), 50 arrows, a dagger-axe, a sword and provisions for three days qualified to join this army. According to *Wuzi*, in 389 BC, Wu Qi, with 50,000 soldiers, 100 chariots and 3,000 horses, defeated the Qin army, which had 500,000 soldiers. This battle has become a famous case study in Chinese war history in how to defeat an enemy despite having an inferior force.

The core principle of militarists' war theories is to treat war with caution. Militarist theories are a summary of war and strategies, and militarists are not against wars. In fact, they consider wars significant to state affairs. But they have made clear that war is not the answer to every problem. In their opinion, wars, closely related to a nation's destiny and people's lives, have to be treated with caution; launching a war blindly is folly, and should be done only after all precautions and careful preparations have been made.

As for strategies and tactics, militarists advocate subduing an enemy without going to war; in short, achieving the greatest victory at the minimum cost. Knowing oneself as well as one's enemy is also stressed, which means only with deep understanding of oneself and the enemy can a war be won, by launching attacks when the enemy is unprepared and appearing where is not expected. In addition, militarists value quick battles that can bring the biggest victories within the shortest time. Last but not the least, surprise attacks are also employed to win a war.

As to their thoughts on how to run an army, militarists argue, on the one hand, soldiers need to be educated by political morality to build obedience on the soldiers' side and trust between soldiers and commanders, so that military orders will be effectively carried out; on the other hand, military discipline involving strict rules of reward and punishment are needed to achieve concerted action. Militarists also stress the selection of commanders and the training of soldiers. As the director and planner of wars, commanders are of great significance. Militarists require commanders to be wise, true, benevolent, valiant, and rigorous. The quality of soldiers is important to the result of wars. The strength of an army lies in its quality instead of quantity. Therefore, intensive training of soldiers and frequent drills are necessary. A harmonious relationship between commanders and soldiers is also a necessity for combat effectiveness and victories.

As an important component of the thought and culture of ancient China, the militarist theories of the pre-Qin period have been widely applied to various fields, such as military affairs, politics, economics, foreign affairs and sports. Inspired by these profound minds, people today are also infusing fresh blood into militarist theories while making use of them.w

One Hundred Schools of Thought Contend

As the first ideological emancipation movement in the history of China, and an important stage of the academic, cultural, ideological and moral development, the contention of numerous schools of thought in the Spring and Autumn Period played a significant role in promoting social and historical development at that time and in later periods. The doctrines formed during that period enriched Chinese thought and culture, but also, as a framework of the ideological and theoretical system of Chinese civilisation, laid a foundation for Chinese culture. They have had a huge influence on the psychology, habits, and behaviour of future generations of Chinese people, giving rise to a unique cultural tradition of the Chinese nation.

The Spring and Autumn Period was a time when society was undergoing great changes, and numerous schools of thought came into being. The exponents of these schools wrote books, gathered disciples, gave lectures, and argued with each other; there was rivalry over academic issues among the various schools that came to be known as "one hundred schools of thought contend." The most influential of these schools were Confucianism, Daoism, Yin-Yang school, Legalism, school of Logicians, Mohism, Eclectics, Agriculturalists and Strategists. The struggle between Confucianism and the Mohist school paved the way for the birth of other schools, all of which reached their peak in the middle and late Warring States Period.

The productive forces had been significantly improved during the Spring and Autumn Period, especially the widespread use of ironware which reclaimed many wastelands. As a result, the handicraft industry, commerce and towns also prospered. With the growing strength of various vassal states, the imperial family of the Zhou Dynasty declined along with the destruction of the traditional social order. The vassal states were engaged in wars of annexation and sought hegemony, with their main efforts devoted to political, economic and military reforms; this gave rise to a free social environment in the ideological and cultural fields, so that scholars could freely travel to promote their ideological propositions.

The emergence of the class of "*shi*," or intelligentsia, and its active involvement in the political arena, was an important foundation for the contentions between various schools of thought. During the Western Zhou Dynasty, schools were fully controlled by the government, whereby the officials were also teachers. To learn, people had to study with relevant officials. For example, to study law, it was necessary to learn from officers who were in charge of land and people. Moreover, only children from imperial and noble families were eligible to enter schools; common people were not allowed to master knowledge. With Emperor Ping of Zhou moving his capital to the east, however, the emperor's status declined, resulting in the "collapse of the rites and music."

Some aristocrats had to live among the common folk, for they had lost their source of income and had to earn their own living. As they were well educated, they took advantage of their knowledge and used it as a means of subsistence. When the schools were no longer under the control of the government, emperors lost their power, and the running of academic institutions was relegated to common people. Consequently, private schools flourished, and those who had been ineligible to receive an education in the past were also able to join the ranks of intellectuals.

One private school of this kind, which advocated education for all, was founded by wConfucius. As long as a student gave Confucius a quantity of bacon as tuition fee, he could be enrolled, which expanded the scope of education. Confucius had 3,000 disciples, among whom 72 were conversant with the Six Classical Arts (rites, music, archery, riding, writing and arithmetic). These men were the so-called "*shi*," who had a wide range of social ties and great social standing. While they widely enrolled students and wrote books, they were also active in the political arenas of various states, greatly contributing to the emergence of the various schools of thought in that period.

The emergence of various schools vying against each other also resulted from the fact that the heads of vassal states provided for scholars and treated them courteously. To make their states rich and build up their military might so as to strive for supremacy, the vassal states, in addition to strengthening their political, economic, military power, also needed intellectuals for counselling. Thus Emperor Zhao of the Yan state during the Warring States Period build the Jieshi Palace to accommodate wise men, while Duke Wen of the Wei state befriended himself to Zi Xia, Tian Zifang, and Duan Zimu and made them his tutors.

Duke Huan of the Qi state was another example. He created the Jixia Academy at the west gate of his capital Linzi to enlist the service of scholars of various schools to write books and debate on politics. The nobility most famous for providing for scholars were the "four gentlemen of the Warring States Period"—Tian Wen of Qi, Zhao Sheng of Zhao, Huang Xie of Chu, and Wu Ji of Wei. These four dukes maintained an army of 4,000 scholars in their residences. They were known to be "wise and faithful, tolerant and benevolent, and respectful to the learned, exerting a great influence over society."

Wu Ji of Wei, in particular, went out of his way to seek hermits across the country with the result that men of virtue were vying to offer their services to him. Princes and dukes also tended to adopt a tolerant policy towards the intelligentsia, allowing academic freedom. In the Qi state, although Daoism was the mainstream, the state did not discriminate against scholars of other beliefs. Instead, it incorporated teachings of diverse nature, and allowed scholars the freedom to come and go. As stated in *Huainanzi*, a work of eclectic learning, "good governance calls for one hundred schools of thought": each school had its strengths and drawbacks, so it was advisable for the vassal states to summarise their political pros and cons based on the teachings of each school to further consolidate their regime. The tolerant attitude assumed by princes and dukes towards scholars played a crucial role in promoting the contention of various schools of thought in the Warring States Period.

The struggle between Confucianism and the Mohist school was seen as the prelude to the contention of various schools. The Mohist school was the first one to oppose Confucius and Confucianism publicly. Although Mozi studied under the tutelage of Confucian teachers, he was later disgusted by the elaborate and prolonged funerary rites advocated by Confucianism and founded the Mohist school. *The Book of Mozi* records many stories about the disputes between Confucianism and Mohism. A conversation between Wu Mazi and Mozi is one such example. Wu said to Mozi, "You are doing righteous things, but people do not agree with you nor help you, nor do the spirits protect and bless you. However, you still insist on what you are doing. This shows you are insane."

Mozi replied: "Suppose you have two servants. One would do something when he knows you are present, but when you leave, he would stop. The other would keep doing things no matter whether you are present or not. Which one do you prefer?"

Ma said, "I like the second one."

"Then you also like insane people," said Mozi.

Another story in the book involved the dialogue between Mozi and Gong Meng. Gong believed that a gentleman should not offer his council voluntarily. He should give his opinions when asked, otherwise, he should remain silent, like a bell that rings only when struck. Mozi argued that if a country is facing imminent disaster, with swords drawn and bows bent, a gentleman—if he is likened to a bell—must speak out even without being struck.

Mozi's critique of Confucian ideas was very sharp. Once he found loopholes in the logic of Confucian scholars, he would refute them with their own arguments. In the face of criticism of the Mohist scholars, later Confucian scholars also fought back. Mencius attacked the universal love advocated by Mozi, stating, "Young Zhu is only concerned about himself and ignored the monarch; Mozi is only concerned about universal love, and ignored his father. Ignoring one's monarch and father is the behaviour of beasts."

There were also many debates between Confucianism and Daoism, and between Confucianism and Legalists. In the process of mutual criticism and debates, these philosophers made progress together which contributed to the development of ancient Chinese culture, and constitutes a glorious history of ancient China.

The contention also helped each school to influence and learn from each other. Daoist teachings were the philosophical basis at the Jixia Academy, but the thought of the Legalist school was also incorporated. "All things should abide by law, and law is formulated with power, and power stems from Dao." Therefore, "laws" are closely linked with Dao.

Yinwenzi records, "Everything is attributed to oneness, and all matters are measured by law," which means "oneness" is "Dao." The interaction of Confucianism with Legalism finds its best expression in Xunzi. Inheriting the political doctrine of Confucius with "rites" as the core, Xunzi incorporated legalist elements in his political ideas, making the two doctrines complementary. He noted, "Respect for rites and the learned can make one an emperor; abiding by the law and loving the people can make one a supreme leader." The ideas of morality, propriety, law, art, filial piety and righteousness described in the *Lü's Spring and Autumn Annals* are blended with those of Confucianism, Mohism, school of Logicians, and Legalists, an important manifestation of the confluence of various schools of thought.

Four Branches of Literature

*S*iku Quanshu *(The Complete Library in the Four Branches of Literature)*, completed in 1782, is the world's longest series of books. Comprising the four traditional divisions of Chinese learning—Confucian classics, historical records, philosophical works and literary works—*Siku Quanshu* contains 3,503 titles bound into more than 36,000 books with a total of 853,456 pages.

Siku Quanshu includes almost all classic works written before the mid-Qing Dynasty. The series preserves many rare classic works and corrects errors and mistakes in them, leaving a precious legacy to later generations. *Siku Quanshu*, which survived so many years of war and turmoil, still serves as a precious resource for research into historical events and cultures.

Guoxue is a broad and profound academic creation. It is based on the *Siku Quanshu*, which is divided into four branches and covers the arts, history, philosophy, sciences, medicine and other fields. The books were rigorously, scientifically and subtly compiled. Its principle of classifying and categorising displays the scientific basess of ancient Chinese literature, which was a project of compiling and preserving ancient books, which popularised folk culture and turned ancient books into national treasures sought after by collectors. The seven imperial libraries built to house the *Siku Quanshu* contributed to the development of modern library science. With the *Siku Quanshu*, book collecting was widely promoted, displaying the dignity and value of traditional Chinese culture.

All Chinese scholars studying ancient China base their research on the *Siku Quanshu*.

Foundation of Guoxue

The Complete Library in Four Branches of Literature, which has been in existence for more than 200 years, represents the richest and most comprehensive record of traditional Chinese culture. The sources of almost all of our academic disciplines, including Chinese history, philosophy, science, engineering and medicine, can be found in this project. Almost all emerging disciplines can find soil here for their survival, and nutrition for their development.

Work started on the *Siku Quanshu (The Complete Library in Four Branches of Literature)* in 1772 during the reign of Emperor Qianlong (1735–96) of the Qing Dynasty (1644–1911) and took one decade to complete. It is one of the largest such projects ever undertaken by a government. The project was so-named because its contents are divided into four categories: Confucian classics, historical records, philosophical works and literary works. The edition in Wenjinge, one of the seven pavilions built specifically to house copies of *Siku Quanshu*, contains a 3,503 ancient texts in 79,337 volumes, bound into more than 36,000 books.

The name *"Siku"* (*Siku=Sibu*, the four traditional divisions of a Chinese library: Confucian classics, history, philosophy and arts and sciences) originates during the early Tang Dynasty (AD 618–907). As the four categories determine the main classifications of ancient books, they contain basically all the books from the past, hence *Siku Quanshu* represents the "complete book."

In the early years of Emperor Qianlong, a scholar named Zhou Shuinian suggested collating all known Confucian writings. In November 1772, Zhu Yun from Anhui Province raised the problem of the scattered writings in *Yongle Dadian (The Great Encyclopedia of Yongle)*. This came to the attention of Emperor Qianlong, who ordered the writings to be compiled, along with all the officially engraved books by scholars of various provinces collected at Wuying Hall, to create the *Siku Quanshu*.

The vast project was completed in four stages. The first stage was to collect copies of all the books, which took seven years, from 1772–78.

The second stage was sorting. Emperor Qianlong ordered the construction of seven pavilions modelled on the Tianyige Pavilion, the national book repository, to house the works. In December 1781, the first transcribed copy of *Siku Quanshu* was completed and presented to the emperor. It took three more years to copy the second, third and fourth editions of the book, which were placed in Wenyuange, Wenyuange, Wensuge and Wenjinge, four pavilions North China. Three more manuscripts were transcribed from July 1782–87; they were kept in Wenzongge, Wenhuige and Wenlan'ge in southern China. Each manuscript was bound into 36,300 volumes and placed in 6,752 caskets. All seven sets bear seals of the emperor.

The main sources of the books for *Siku Quanshu* were the imperial palace, government collections, various localities and the writings from the *Great Encyclopedia of Yongle*.

The court appointed an official to make suggestions as to which books should be copied, engraved or kept. Those that should be transcribed were considered good enough for the *Siku Quanshu*; those that should be engraved were deemed to be the best ones and must be copied into *Siku Quanshu* and widely circulated among the people. The books considered to contain substandard writings were not to be included in *Siku Quanshu*; their titles were recorded in the general table of contents. There were 6,793 writings of this kind collected in 93,551 volumes, nearly double the number included in *Siku Quanshu*. Works selected for copying and engraving had to be chosen from the best editions. Once a book was chosen as a master copy, it also needed to go through a series of processes. In one of those processes, proofreaders would attach slips of paper in the book with preliminary revisions and comments and submit it to the compiling official. The official would than either agree or revise the comments with red ink. He then submitted his comments or notes to the chief editor, who would either accept the proofreader's or the compiling officer's ideas. The final edits would be submitted to the emperor for review.

The third step was to transcribe the master copy. Copyists were chosen from among those who had failed provincial civil service examinations but who had excellent handwriting skills. Almost 4,000 copyists were employed for the task. Effective measures such as meting out rewards and punishment in a fair and strict way ensured smooth work of this huge project.

The fourth step was proofreading, the final part of a critical process. To ensure the progress of proofreading, *The Regulations of Rewards and Punishments* was established. Any copied book must be proofread by first- and second-tier editors before being submitted to the emperor. This accountability system played an important role in guaranteeing the quality of *Siku Quanshu*.

Alongside the project itself, a series of related works were also compiled: *Siku Quanshu Huiyao (The Cream of the Complete Library in Four Branches of Literature)*, *Siku Quanshu Zongmu (The General Table of Contents of the Complete Library in Four Branches of Literature)*, *Siku Quanshu Jianming Mulu (A Concise General Table of Contents of the Complete Library in Four Branches of Literature)*, *Siku Quanshu Kaozheng (A Textual Research of the Complete Library in Four Branches of Literature)* and *Wuyingdian Juzhenban Congshu (A Collection of Rare Versions of Wuying Hall)*. These works can be seen as the by-products of the compilation of *Siku Quanshu Huiyao* is the essence of *Siku Quanshu*, containing 473 books in 19,931 volumes. The 100-volume *A Textual Research of the Complete Library in Four Branches of Literature* is a collation of the books that should be copied and engraved by the scholars who compiled the *Siku Quanshu*, thus having a high reference value for collating ancient texts. *A Collection of Rare Versions of Wuying Hall*, printed with wooden movable type, consists of 138 books of *Siku Quanshu* that should be engraved. Jin Jian, the chief editor of *A Collection of Rare Versions of Wuying Hall*, decided to use wooden movable type because it was less costly and more practical than other types. He also wrote a book on the process of using the wooden movable-type printing process and included it in *Siku Quanshu*. The book is considered an important record in the history of printing and has been translated into German and English.

The success of the compilation of the *Siku Quanshu* depended on the stable social environment at the time. At the time it was being compiled, there was no disruption from wars, and scholars were able to concentrate on their work with no distractions. Emperor Qianlong was actively involved in the project, from formulating a detailed plan, selecting books and master copies, to copying and proofreading. The court also set up a Siku Quanshu Office headed by a director and several deputy directors. Princes, secretaries of grand councils, cabinet ministers and other high-ranking officials were responsible for the compiling affairs of the office. Under the office were the Compiling Department, Copying Department and Supervision Department. The Compiling Department was responsible for the collation of all the books, the Copying Department was in charge of transcribing and proofreading, and the Supervision Department was responsible for printing and binding the books at Wuying Hall. Three hundred sixty people were employed at the office. Of particular importance was the fact that the office was home to the most talented people in the country, many of whom were hired by breaking conventions, such as Shao Jinhan, Yu Ji, Zhou Yongnian, Dai Zhen and Yang Changlin. Before being admitted to the office, they had to be members of the Imperial Academy and at least successful candidates in the imperial examinations at the provincial level. This concentration of first-rate scholars created more favourable conditions for the success of the project.

In the 200 years since the *Siku Quanshu's completion*, China has suffered countless episodes of unrest and turmoil, and the work also experienced many vicissitudes. The copy kept at Wenyuange was destroyed when the British and French troops captured Beijing in 1860, and burned down the Old Summer Palace. The manuscripts kept at Wenzongge and Wenhuige were destroyed during the Taiping rebellion (1850–64). The Wenlange Library in Hangzhou collapsed during the Taiping army's capture of Hangzhou for the second time, in 1861, and the *Siku Quanshu* manuscript kept there was lost. Later, the Ding brothers, who were book collectors, rescued and recopied the manuscript but only a quarter of the original was recovered. In 1881, the restored version was placed back in the renovated Wenlan'ge. In the Republic of China period (1912–49), the version underwent another large-scale restoration, with most of the contents being restored.

As a result, only three and a half sets of the *Siku Quanshu* exist today. The copy at *Wenyuange*, which is well-preserved and used to be kept at the Forbidden City in Beijing, is now kept in the National Palace Museum in Taipei. The copy at *Wensuge*, now kept in the Library of Gansu Province, was almost sold to the Japanese in 1922. In recent years, Gansu and Liaoning provinces have been discussing whether this manuscript should be returned to Shenyang but have not yet reached an agreement. The Chinese Government moved the copy kept at Wenjinge in the Chengde Imperial Summer Resort, currently the only one kept in its original casket, to the National Library of China in the 1950s. The damaged version at *Wenlange* is now kept in the Library of Zhejiang Province.

In October 1966, when Sino-Soviet relations were very tense, Marshal Lin Biao, to protect *Siku Quanshu*, ordered the copy at Wensuge to be secretly sent from Shenyang to Lanzhou, where it was hidden in the Gobi Desert. Authorities in Liaoning have demanded the return of the copy, saying the manuscript should be kept at its original place. However, Gansu Province is building a library specifically to protect the book. So the stewardship of this copy is still being debated.

In the early years of the Republic of China, the Commercial Press, Commercial Press in Taiwan and Shanghai Ancient Book Publishing House all made copies of *Siku Quanshu*. In 1999, Digital Heritage Publishing in Hong Kong, Shanghai People's Publishing House and the Chinese University of Hong Kong all developed and issued electronic versions of the Wenyuange copy of Siku Quanshu on the Chinese mainland and in Hong Kong.

Since its birth, this work, as a symbol of the national foundation, has become a model for the lifelong pursuit of Chinese and Asian scholars.

Confucian Classics

The Confucian classics category in the *Siku Quanshu* contains the Confucian classics and philological studies, including *The Book of Changes, Collection of Ancient Texts, Book of Songs, Book of Rites, Spring and Autumn Annals, Book of Filial Piety,* and books on music, etymology and semantics. Philological studies are classified into textual exegesis, lexicon and a dictionary of rhyming words. The Confucian classics category is the foundation of the Confucian culture. Over a long period of time, these 13 key works of Confucian literature gained canonical, or classical status.

The meaning of Chinese character *"jing,"* or "canon," comes from the horizontal lines in weaving. A piece of cloth cannot be sturdy unless the horizontal lines link up with the vertical lines; therefore horizontal lines play a very important role and later came to refer to the exemplary, authoritative and most valuable writings, which were selected through history and could endure for all ages.

Legend has it that Fuxi, the ancestor of the Chinese people, created the Eight Trigrams by observing the heavens and the earth. These were developed into the Sixty-Four Trigrams by his descendants. In ancient times, monarchs handled their state affairs by reading the commentaries on various combinations of the Eight Trigrams, which evolved into *Yijing (Book of Changes)*. The ancients attached great importance to history, especially the deeds of emperors, so they recorded their deeds to pass judgment on what is right and wrong. To this end, they appointed the "Left Historian" and "Right Historian," the former being in charge of recording the words of the monarch, which later became *Shangshu (Book of History Documents)*, and the latter being responsible for documenting the deeds of monarchs, which were collected into the *Chunqiu (The Spring and Autumn Annals)*. After King Shun and King Yu, rulers of all dynasties sent officers to various localities to collect poems and folklore so monarchs would be able to keep abreast of the sufferings of the people. That resulted in *Shijing (Book of Songs)*. Legend has it that during the reign of the Yellow Emperor (2697–2599 BC), primitive music was invented. After that, whenever a regime changed hands, the victor would use music to celebrate his success, thus, *Yuejing (Book of Music)* came into being. With the emergence of class-based society, etiquette and rites developed, such as the three rites of "heaven, earth and man," and the five rites of "good omen, ill omen, army, guest and wedding," created by King Yao and King Shun. These practises gradually became formalised as *The Book of Rites*.

However, *Liujing (The Six Classics)*, as these six books were known, was not compiled to a unified standard at the time. It was not until the Western Zhou Dynasty that The *Six Classics*, or canons, were compiled in a unified format, thanks to the revision undertaken by Emperor Wen of Zhou and the Duke of Zhou. *The Six Classics* were so respected during the Western Zhou Dynasty that they became school textbooks and were regarded as criterion for princes and dukes. During the Eastern Zhou Dynasty, many scholars, including Confucius, studied *The Six Classics*.

Confucius studied *The Book of Changes* and *The Spring and Autumn Annals* from the historians of the Lu state; *Li (The Book of Rites)* from Laozi; *Yue (The Book of Music)* from Chang Hong and *Shi (The Book of Songs)* from the senior members of Chang's family. Confucius hoped that monarchs would adopt his doctrines, but after travelling around the country for 14 years and failing to have his ideas adopted, he became frustrated and returned to the Lu state to teach at a private school he established, and to revise *The Six Classics*. He traced the ritual laws of the Xia, Shang and Zhou dynasties, and recorded the ritual ceremonies from Yao and Shun to Duke Mu of the Qin state. He also standardised the music for "court hymns" and "ode" parts in *The*

Book of Songs. He selected 310 poems out of 3,000 to be included in *The Book of Songs.* Based on the history of the Lu state, he chronicled the Spring and Autumn Period, starting from the Duke of Yin to the 14th year of the Duke of Ai.

The Six Classics were used by Confucius either as his lecture notes or textbooks. *The Book of Changes* was used for philosophy; *The Book of Songs* was for singing; *Collection of Ancient Texts* was for teaching Chinese; *The Spring and Autumn Annals* was used to teach the modern history of the Lu state; *The Book or Rites* was a textbook for cultivating one's moral character and *The Book of Music* was for singing and gymnastics.

After Confucius died, his 72 disciples, as well as Xunzi and Mencius, actively and widely spread Confucianism. But in the chaotic years of war, the benevolence advocated by Confucian thought had little appeal to rulers. When Qin Shihuang unified China, he ordered the burning of all Confucian classics. Five of the classics were targeted for destruction, with only *The Book of Changes* spared on the grounds it was a book about sorcery. When the Qin Dynasty was overthrown and General Xiang Yu entered Xianyang in Shaanxi Province, the capital of Qin, he burned the city for three months. The National Library of Qin was destroyed and along with it, the only existing copy of *The Book of Songs.*

The Han Dynasty was established in the wake of Qin, and Confucian scholars were again able to live in a relaxed political atmosphere. In the period of Emperors Wendi (203–157 BC) and Jingdi (188–141 BC), what was now known as the *"Five Classics"* were restored to some extent. By the time the young and energetic Emperor Wudi came to power, the Han state had become very prosperous. To establish a unified ideological system, the emperor, who admired Confucianism, banned all other schools of thought, and only set up official posts for specialists in the *"Five Classics,"* thus, Confucianism flourished and became the official school of learning and was linked with wealth and position.

Zheng Xuan, born in Gaomi in Shandong Province, was a leading Confucian expert. Conversant with Confucian classics both in modern and pre-Qin scripts, Zheng comprehensively revised the Confucian texts from after the Han Dynasty by integrating the doctrines of various schools of thought. The notes he made for the *"Five Classics"* became authoritative and the criterion for scholars in later generations.

The research of Confucian classics became a social trend and was increasingly linked with fame and position. Explanations to and collations of Confucian classics became indispensable tools, so they were also gradually included in the ranks of the "classics." *The Spring and Autumn Annals* with commentaries by Zuo Qiumeng, Gongyang Gao and Gu Liang are all essential books for its study. *Zhouli (The Rites of the Zhou Dynasty)* recorded the ideal system of bureaucracy by people of the pre-Qin period; *The Book of Rites* explains and supplements the *Yili (Book of Etiquette)*, thus it is considered as a reference book for *The Book of Etiquette.* Since rulers attached great importance to these two books, especially after Zheng Xuan made annotations to them, they gradually acquired the status of classics during the early Tang Dynasty.

The Analects is a record of Confucius's words and deeds, and is also considered a classic work. *The Xiaojing (The Book of Filial Piety)* was written by later generations of descendants of Confucius, so it also attracted the attention of rulers and became a part of the classics.

Shisanjing (The Thirteen Classics of Confucianism) were established and engraved in stone during the reign of Qing Emperor Qianlong. They also became the subjects to be studied at the Imperial College. The Confucian classic category of *Siku Quanshu* is also based on these 13 works. The canons in the Confucian classics category occupy a high position in academic history and have important academic and literary value.

Historical Records

History books in China can be classified into five types. Official history books record the achievements of emperors, stories of dynasties, biographies, and accounts of economy, military, culture and geography. *Ershisi Shi (Twenty-Four Dynastic Histories)* were mostly written by court officials. Anecdotal history books record individual events from beginning to end, the outlook of an era, or the private account of a family. Incidental history books, which are sometimes difficult to distinguish from anecdotal history books, refer to accounts of one or several dynasties that are neither annals nor biographies. Unofficial history books were privately compiled. Legendary history books record folklore, customs, anecdotes and legends.

The character *"shi" (history)* written on ancient "oracle bones" represented a hand holding a book. In ancient times, historians were responsible for the recording of significant events and collecting documents, but also for matters related to worship and communication between rulers and deities. *The Siku Quanshu* includes volumes of stories of the success and failures of historical characters.

The styles of history books include biographies, annals, chronicles, comprehensive, dynastic and specific. Biographical histories began with *Shiji (Historical Records)* by Sima Qian during the Western Han Dynasty. It centres around historical figures, using *"benji," "shijia"* and *"liezhuan"* to record the stories of emperors, nobles and significant figures, ethnic groups, using *"biao"* to summarise years, lineage and characters, *"shu"* and *"zhi"* to record laws and regulations. This style was followed by successive dynasties.

Annals arrange events along a timeline. Chronicles originated from *Tong jian Jishi Benmo (General Chronicle)* compiled by Yuan Shu in the Southern Song Dynasty. This style centres on historical events, with each event comprising a self-contained chapter written along a timeline.

Comprehensive history books record the history of dynasties. One example is *Historical Records,* which records the three millennia from the legendary Yellow Emperor down to Emperor Wu of the Han Dynasty. Dynastic history books record the history of one dynasty. All volumes in the *Ershisi Shi (Twenty-Four Dynastic Histories)* except *Historical Records* are dynastic, such as *Hanshu (History of Han).* History books on specific disciplines and professions focus on subjects such as economic history, philosophical history or literary history.

The branch of historical records in the *Siku Quanshu* is divided into fifteen categories: official history, annals, chronicles, anecdotal history, incidental history, statements, biographies, abridged history, accounts, timeline, geography, officialdom, orders, contents and comments.

People in the pre-Qin period created a splendid culture and passed down stories orally. Characters, which appeared in or even prior to the Shang Dynasty, began to be used to record events and historian began to write histories. *Shangshu* contains many historical documents written during the Shang and Zhou dynasties.

The Spring and Autumn Annals is the earliest surviving historical text arranged on annalistic principles. Originally the national history of the Lu state, this 18,000-character book records history from 722–481 BC. Originally written by historians of the Lu state and later compiled by Confucius, this concise history records events among the states, including wars, alliances, usurpations, methods of worship, disasters, folklore and customs. It accurately records the succession of the 12 emperors of the Lu state. Solar eclipses recorded in the book correspond with records from western scholars, proving the reliability of the book. "Spring and Autumn" subsequently became the generic term for history books and the name for the historical period.

Later, there appeared other books of various styles that recorded the history of the Spring and Autumn Period and the Warring States Period. *Zuo Zhuan (Chronicles of Zuo or Commentary of Zuo)* is a highly detailed annalistic history. The author was Zuo Qiuming, as certified by both Sima Qian and Ban Gu. As an exegesis of Spring and Autumn, it records the history of the imperial family of Zhou and the contention of dukes, covering all social classes and thus representing a supreme achievement of the pre-Qin period. It records popular contemporary narratives, which set examples for later practical writing, so it is also of great literary value.

In addition, there are dynastic history books compiled for specific states, such as *Guoyu and Zhanguoce (Strategies of the Warring States).* *Shanhaijing (The Book of Mountains and Seas)* records geography and legends. Books of philosophers record their thoughts, political opinions, and comments on historical events.

During the Qin and Han dynasties, *Historical Records* by Sima Qian and *History of Han* by Ban Gu, two masterpieces, appeared. *Historical Records,* which contains 130 volumes and 520,000 characters, records the three millennia from the Yellow Emperor to Liu Che, Emperor Wu of Han. It set the standard for annalistic history over the next 2,000 years. With its clear and vivid narrative, it embodies high literary value. *History of Han,* which contains 100 volumes and 800,000 characters, is a detailed account of the history of the Western Han Dynasty, setting a precedent for dynastic biographical history books in later dynasties. It gives down-to-earth accounts of historical figures of all classes and became a model for later biographies.

After those two masterpieces, there appeared many biographies between the Han and Tang dynasties, such as *Sanguozhi (History of Three Kingdoms)* and *Houhanshu (History of Later Han).*

History of Three Kingdoms contains 65 volumes, in which *Weishu (The History of Wei)* contains 30 volumes, *Shushu (The History of Shu),* 30 volumes, and *Wushu (The History of Wu),* 20 volumes. Since it was written by Chen Shou, an official of the Jin Dynasty (AD 265–420), a successor of the Wei state, the book regards the Wei state as the official predecessor of the Han Dynasty. The book is one of the earliest four histories, the other three being *Historical Records, History of Han and History of Hou Han. The History of Three Kingdoms* employs concise and beautiful language in its characterisation, thus achieving both historical and literary value.

History of Hou Han, a dynastic history of the Eastern Han Dynasty, was compiled by Fan Ye, a historian of the Southern Dynasties. It records events in the 195 years from AD 25–220. Fan Ye was the first historian to write biographies of women. It is worth noting that the 17 prominent women in his book include Cai Yan, a talented woman who did not conform to the propriety of feudal society.

In the first hundred years of the Tang Dynasty, eight history books appeared, including official histories such as *Jinshu (History of Jin), Liangshu (History of Liang), Chenshu (History of Chen), Zhoushu (History of Zhou), Beiqishu (History of Northern Qi)* and *Suishu (History of Sui)* as well as privately compiled histories, such as *Nanshi (History of Southern Dynasties)* and *Beishi (History of Northern Dynasties).* Since then, biographies have been compiled for each subsequent dynasty.

Shitong (On History), written by Liu Zhiji, a Tang Dynasty historian, discusses the styles and compilation of history books and comments on previous history books. The content of the book can be divided into historical theory and historical comments. Historical theory refers to an introduction of styles, compilations, and systems of historians. Historical comments are about historical events, records, and accounts. Liu Zhiji preferred direct accounts based on fact over indirect accounts based on suppositions. He was strongly opposed to a state monopoly of history. *On History* is a comprehensive overview of ancient Chinese historical study and put forward a systematic historical theory, thus it became a milestone in the field of history up to the Tang Dynasty.

After Sima Qian put forward the theory that "history should study the reasons for historical events," a number of such history books, seeking to probe into causes and give advice to rulers, appeared since the middle of the Tang Dynasty, such as *Tongdian (General History)* by Du You, *Tongzhi (General Records)* by Zheng Qiao, *Wenxian Tongkao (General Study of Historical Documents)* by Ma Duanlin and *Zizhi Tongjian (General Mirror for Better Governance)* by Sima Guang. Those are the representative works of history and historical study in this period. The best among them is General Mirror for Better Governance.

General Mirror for Better Governance is an annalistic comprehensive history of 294 volumes which records the history from the early Warring States Period to the end of the Five Dynasties. Sima Guang invited Liu Shu, Liu Pan and Fan Zuyu onto his team, which had a clear division of labour. They first made a list of contents, which served as the basis for the whole book. Discrepancies were settled before the text was finalised. The book is a detailed account of history written in concise language.

Since the Tang and Song dynasties, ethnic groups, such as Qidan (aka Khitan), Nuzhen (aka Jurchen)and Mongols, have entered into the inland of China establishing the Liao, Jin and Yuan dynasties, each of which is recorded.

In the early and mid-Ming Dynasty, historical studies were in decline. However, during the transitional disorder from the Ming to the Qing Dynasty, historical study showed vigour and vitality. Thinker and writer Li Zhi advocated that history should serve as the foundation for philosophy. Later, Huang Zongxi, Gu Yanwu, and Wang Fuzhi advocated that history should be studied so that the rules of social development could be found and social problems could be solved.

Qing rulers employed scholars to compile history books in order to consolidate their government. *Mingshi (History of Ming)* is the last of *The Twenty-Four Histories*. This biography was complied by Zhang Tingyu under the auspices of Qing rulers. It records the 277-year period from 1368–1644. Scholars during the Qing believed it to be the most rigorous among final several books of *The Twenty-Four Histories*. It is second only to *Songshi (History of Song)* in terms of length.

History serves a dual purpose: to record the past and to inspire the future. China is the only nation whose history has been recorded continuously. In a larger scope, those history books have served as a bridge between China and the rest of the world. As Chinese civilisation is an integral part of the world, so Chinese history is a part of world history.

Philosophical Works

The branch of philosophical works was divided into 14 subcategories: Confucianism, Militarism, Legalism, Agriculturalism, Medicalism, Astronomy, Arithmetic, Art, lineage, Eclectics, Reference, Novels, Buddhism, and Daoism.

The branch of *zi (philosophical works)* in *the Siku Quanshu* is a collection of philosophical books. In ancient China, *"zi"* is a term for men of virtue, knowledge or status. As writing materials were expensive and characters were hard to learn, only people of high social classes could receive an education. *"Zi"* gradually became a respectful form of address for influential figures of various schools of philosophy.

Ancient Chinese believed that a man should first cultivate virtue before writing books to establish his school of philosophy. Learned gentlemen strove to leave books of their thoughts for posterity in order to establish their fame, such as Feng Hou, Li Mu and Yi Yin. Their words were recorded by people living during the Warring States Period. Later, Yu Xiong, who served as an advisor for Emperor Wen of the Zhou Dynasty, had his words recorded in the book *Yuzi*, the first book incorporating *"zi"* in the title. In the Spring and Autumn Period, Lao Dan, who was a mentor of Confucius and the author of *The Daodejing*, became the first of the 100 philosophers.

After Emperor Ping moved his capital from the west to the east, his authority rapidly declined as dukedoms engaged in wars of annexation and conquest. During this great social transition, various schools of philosophers wrote books to promote their thoughts, including those of Confucius, Mozi, Laozi and Sunzi.

During the Warring States Period, prominent figures continued to emerge. Mencius was a follower of Confucianism. Zhuangzi expounded Daoism. Mozi conducted stoicism. Yin Wenzi studied the agreement of name and fact. Agriculturalists advocated that good governance came from better use of farmland. Zouzi thought that rulers should pay attention to natural phenomenon. Shen Buhai and Shang Yang advocated that law and order was necessary for governance. Gui Guzi wanted to succeed through debates. Shijiao summarised all schools of thoughts while Qingshizi put together all street sayings. Various schools of philosophers were active in proposing their own thoughts. Even Qin Shihuang failed to put an end to those thoughts. Under the auspices of Emperor Cheng (33–7 BC) of Western Han, Liu Xiang summarised those schools in the book *Qi Lüe (Seven Summaries)*, which contained 180 schools. In the Wei and Jin dynasties, even some overblown words and sayings were printed in books.

Liu Xin innovated by collecting all books of various schools since the Zhou and Qin dynasties into *Zhuzi Lüe (Summary of All Schools)*. The practise was later adopted by Ban Gu and *"zi"* became the generic term for this type of book.

Although there are large numbers of books in this category, their contents are easy to follow. They are branches of the "Five Classics." Some of them conform to the "Five Classics", such as *Liji—Yueling (The Book of Propriety—Months)*, taken from the first chapter of *Lüshi Chunqiu—Shier Yueji (Lü's Spring and Autumn Annals—The Twelve Months)*, and *Liji— Sannian Wen (The Book of Propriety—Three Years)*, taken from *Xunzi—Lilun (Xunzi—On Propriety)*. Others are against the "Five Classics," such as the words of *Xia Ge, Dai Jinren, Liezi* and *Huannanzi*. However, even the classics contain some absurd stories. The emperor of Dongping asked Emperor Cheng of Han for *Zhuzi (Schools of Philosophy)* and *Historical Records*, but Emperor Cheng refused to do so, probably because that both books contain strategies and tactics that might be used in military operations.

The essence of various schools of philosophy is also reflected in their styles. *The Book of Mencius and Xunzi* are full of aesthetic value; *Guanzi* and *Yanzi* are written in concise words on the basis of reliable facts; *Liezi* is splendid in style; *Zouzi* contains rich content written powerfully; *Mozi* and *Sui Chaozi* are thought-provoking accounts written in a plain style; *Shizi* and *Yu Liaozi* give simple theories written in down-to-earth words; *He Guanzi* is full of profound reflections; *Guiguzi* is hard to comprehend; *Wenzi* and *Yinwenzi* are compact and persuasive; *Shenzi* is full of complex analysis; *Han Feizi* uses a large number of similes; *Lü's Spring and Autumn Annals* has a compact organization; *Huainanzi* is comprehensive in content.

During the Tang Dynasty, the system of four categories, namely, classics, history, *zi* (philosophy) and collection, was established. Ji Yun adopted this practise when compiling the *Siku Quanshu*.

The branch of *zi* contains a wide variety involving all aspects of society, including entertainment and religion as well as everyday life. Therefore, it is the crystallization of ancient Chinese civilisation and wisdom.

22

Literary Works

The branch of literary works in the *Siku Quanshu* includes five categories: songs of Chu, personal collections, general collections, critical comments and poems. These categories include all books in ancient China except novels and plays.

Essays can contain various schools of thoughts and be written in various forms. Classics, history and zi are about one particular school at a specific time. Therefore, the branch of literary works was created to collect those book series.

During the Han Dynasty, Liu Xin collected many books to compile Seven Summaries, in which there is a part called *"Ji Lüe (Collection)*," which is the origin of the term *"ji" (collection)*. Zhi Yu of the Jin Dynasty compiled Wenzhang *Liubie (Schools of Essays)*, which started the trend of compiling collections. In the Qi Period (AD 479–502) in the Southern Dynasties, Wang Jian compiled *Qi Lüe (Seven Summaries)*, which is the predecessor of "the branch of literary works." In the Liang Period (AD 502–557) of the Southern Dynasties, cataloguist Ruan Xiaoxu compiled *Qi Lüe (Seven Records)*, creating categories such as "classics," "biographies," "philosophers" and "collections." When Zhangsun Wuji in the Tang Dynasty compiled *Suishu—Jingjizhi (Classic Volumes, History of Sui)*, the names of the four branches were fixed. His branch of literary works consisted of songs of Chu, individual collections and general collections, which set the model for later compilers. After reforms and innovations by several compilers, the style was finally established and then adopted by Ji Xiaolan when he compiled the *Siku Quanshu*.

During the Han Dynasty, Liu Xiang collected poems by Qu Yuan and Song Yu and compiled *Chu Ci (The Songs of Chu)*. As the style of poetry changed after the Han Dynasty, *The Songs of Chu* was treated as a separate category. Qu Yuan, an upright official who suffered exile, wrote *Li Sao (Encountering Sorrow)*, which consisted of eight poems. Later, Jia Yi, Dongfang Shuo, Liu Xiang and Yang Xiong admired the literary excellence of Qu Yuan and imitated his style. Later scholars wrote notations and comments for *Songs of Chu*, such as *Chuci Zhangju (Cantos and Lines of the Songs of Chu)* by Wang Yi, *Chuci Buzhu (Notations on the Songs of Chu)* by Hong Xingzu and *Chuci Buzhu (Notations on the Songs of Chu)* by Zhu Xi, which are all necessary references. The branch of literary works includes all those commentaries.

At the end of the Han Dynasty, all works of an author were compiled as a collection, which is useful for scholars to study the thoughts of an author. Those collections that have remained are truly excellent ones, such as the collections of essays by Sima Xiangru, history by Sima Qian, the unique style of Yang Xiong in the Western Han Dynasty, and Kong Rong, prominent figure of the "Seven Leading Writers of Jian'an Period" in the Eastern Han Dynasty and Cao Zhi in the Three Kingdoms Period (AD 220–280). From the Tang Dynasty, literature began to serve practical purposes. The eight leading writers of the Tang and Song dynasties, led by Han Yu and Liu Zongyuan, were the mainstream at the time. In the Yuan Dynasty, Yao Sui began to reform the style of the end of the Song Dynasty. In the early Ming Dynasty, the grand style of Song Lian and Liu Ji was the norm. During the Qing Dynasty, Hou Fangyu established the "Tongcheng Style."

General collections include works of a number of authors. After Jian'an Period of the late Han Dynasty, many poems and essays appeared, so Zhi Yu of the Jin Dynasty selected the best ones and compiled Liubie, the first general collection. General collections include only the best works of several authors. Later, when general collections themselves strove to be all-inclusive, selected collections emerged. The best examples of general collections are *Zhao Ming Wenxuan (Selected Essays of Zhaoming)* compiled by Xiao Tong, *Yutai Xinyong (New Poems of Yutai)* by Xu Ling, Wenyuan Yinghua compiled in the Song Dynasty, and *Quan Tangshi (General Collection of Tang Poems)* compiled by Peng Dingqiu.

The Han Dynasty was the period when essays flourished without literary criticism. Later, critics emerged and flourished. Ji Xiaolan, during the Qing Dynasty, collected those critical works, because he thought it could help distinguish excellent works from mediocre ones. The best critical works are *Wenxin Diaolong* by Liu Xie, *Shi Pin (Comments on Poetry)* by Liang Zhongrong, *Liuyi Shihua* by Ouyang Xiu, and Zhongshan Shihua by Liu Pan. In ancient times, *"ci"* and *"qu"* (two forms of poetry) were regarded as unworthy for collection. However, Ji Xiaolan believed them to be integral and included them in a branch of literary works. Examples are *Dongpo Ci (Poems by Dongpo)*, *Fangweng Ci (Poems by Fangweng)* and *Jiaxuan Ci (Poems by Jiaxuan)*.

Essence of Five Constant Virtues

The Five Constant Virtues, benevolence, righteousness, propriety, wisdom and faithfulness, are essential elements of *guoxue*. Human beings should possess and practise these five virtues for individual development and social progress.

As the core of the Chinese ethical value system, the Five Constant Virtues ran through the development of Chinese ethics. The Chinese ancients found different people often held different opinions about the same thing based on their different experiences and interests. Therefore, the concept "benevolence" was put forward to encourage people to be more tolerant of other's views. Benevolence is not only the most basic and loftiest moral principle, but also the general moral standard. It became an important component of modern humanism.

Righteousness is another moral principle as important as benevolence. Righteousness, as the view of life and value and the sense of responsibility and dedication, displays Chinese people's lofty morals. Propriety is also an important traditional virtue, which has become an embodiment of how civilized an individual, a society or a nation is; the inheritance of propriety is essential to the building of a harmonious society. Wisdom, which can be extended from the moral to intellectual aspects, blended scientific and humanistic spirits. Faithfulness requires people to keep their word, which is a recognised value and basic moral standard of the Chinese nation.

As five moral standards put forward by ancient Chinese thinkers, the Five Constant Virtues in *guoxue* still have great significance in modern society.

Five Constant Virtues

The Five Constant Virtues of Confucianism, benevolence, righteousness, propriety, wisdom and faithfulness, have practical significance, which indicates that Confucianism can be adapted to modern life. This is just the essence of Chinese culture. Confucianism has exerted the most influence on Chinese culture, so the Five Constant Virtues play a pivotal role in shaping Chinese thought.

Using words to record the essence of 5,000 years of Chinese cultural achievements resulted in the classical writings of traditional Chinese culture. The rich cultural heritage contained within these works convey abundant truths and lessons about how people should conduct themselves in the world. At the core of this type of thought are the concepts of benevolence, righteousness, propriety, wisdom and faithfulness. These five virtues of Confucianism, known as the Five Constant Virtues, are central elements in China's several-thousand-year-old value system. In contemporary society, the study of these Five Constant Virtues can bring people inspiration and enlightenment.

Confucius initially proposed "benevolence, righteousness and propriety" as central virtues. Mencius later added wisdom and Dong Zhongshu contributed faithfulness. After the Han Dynasty, the Five Constant Virtues permeated the whole of the development process of ethical thought which was taking place within Chinese culture. They became the ideas most central to the traditional Chinese value system. Passing through further development during the Song and Ming dynasties, the ideas behind the Five Constant Virtues were gradually perfected.

There was also a profound historical background behind the development of the Five Constant Virtues, one which was based in the societal background as well as the ideological and cultural background that existed during the time Confucius lived. This was a volatile era that saw many changes. The most striking feature of society during this era was that social and political ruling power devolved from the declining Zhou Dynasty imperial family and was spread amongst various feudal princes and then further down to the level of senior officials. The feudal system that was headed by the Zhou imperial family was but a shadow of its former strength, and to derive personal benefit, people representing different interests and cultural factions all strived to find ideological justification inside morality. They used moral constraints as a method to help them achieve their political goals.

Because of the breakdown in social institutions and cultural order that was taking place at the time, Confucius sought to use the propriety of the Zhou Dynasty to bring about changes, in the hope of revitalising the Zhou systems and institutions. Confucius was dissatisfied with the social realities that he saw around him, and he viewed the Zhou Dynasty as an ideal society. The propriety of the Zhou Dynasty was an important means by which he would re-establish an ideal society.

The era that Confucius lived in was the first cultural high point in ancient China. Political and economic progress occurred alongside the emergence of the broad development and discussion of thoughts and ideas which characterised the situation known as "One Hundred Schools of Thought Contend." This spurred great development in the areas of cultural thinking and theory. Thinking about ethical and moral principles occupied an important place within this development process. Confucius was the first thinker of this new era, and he was also the last thinker of the prior era. In China's history of intellectual thought, he was a link between the past and future.

The establishment of Confucius's ideology of benevolence was closely connected to the birth and maturing of the social environment of the Lu state. Lu state was a fief of the Duke Dan of Zhou, and it was the cultural centre of the slave system that existed at that time. It preserved a large number of Zhou Dynasty classic writings. Confucius extensively read these classic books on culture and history. From this reading, he gained a clear sense of history and a deep understanding of the traditional religious and moral thought that had existed since the late Shang and Zhou dynasties, forming his own characteristic ideology of benevolence. He persevered in his efforts even though he knew success was unlikely, and he dedicated his life to the propagation of this ideology which centred around ordinary people and the uniform foundation of "benevolence." Ultimately, this ideology of benevolence became the main body of traditional Chinese thinking. Confucianism also became the school of thought which had the deepest and most extensive influence.

Although the five virtues have different connotations, they are all related. Among them, benevolence is the core virtue. Being the highest of principles, it is also the ultimate type of care and concern that can be bestowed upon human beings, human nature and life. It should be our ultimate aim, and it is the most supreme moral principle. Righteousness refers to how, when there are conflicting interests and values between oneself and others or between an individual and a group, appropriate limits on choices and behaviour should be maintained. Propriety refers to external forms of cultural propriety, which take the spirit of benevolence and righteousness and incorporate it into everyday societal behaviours in the form of observable actions. The pursuit of wisdom must be carried out within the limits of not going against human nature and not harming the fundamental interests of benevolence. That is to say, one cannot depart from the spirit of benevolence and the principle of righteousness. Faithfulness is based on sincerity and the genuineness of the other four virtues.

All in all, borrowing their forms, transforming their substances, and being entrusted with the spirits of new eras, the five moral categories of Confucianism, benevolence, righteousness, propriety, wisdom and faithfulness, remain a valuable cultural resource that can still be used to promote moral and cultural progress in the modern era.

Benevolence

Benevolence, the core of Confucianism, has played a critical role in the cultural and social development of the Chinese nation. For the past 5,000 thousand years of human civilisation, the meaning of benevolence has developed from a traditional theory into a moral standard which has gone beyond the original thinking of Confucius.

The Five Constant Virtues of the Confucian school are the elements at the core of China's value system, and the concept of benevolence is at the core of the Five Constant Virtues. As the Song Dynasty scholar Zhu Xi said: "The Five Constant Virtues are at the centre of benevolent action, and benevolence is at the centre of the Five Constant Virtues." An ancient form of the character for "benevolence" was composed of the body of a person and a heart, expressing the meaning that benevolent people have unified hearts and bodies as well as unified ideas and behaviour. Benevolent people conduct themselves in the world and get along with others with kindness that stems from both the body and soul.

As a result, the virtue of benevolence is consistent with the harmonious unity of opposites, including the sky and the earth, the body and heart, the self and others, and people and things.

From examining the form of the Chinese character for benevolence (仁), we can see that the character is made up of the characters for person (人) and two (二). It can be seen as signifying two people close enough to be as one, which can be understood as representing the way that two people get along with each other.

Many records that deal with the idea of benevolence appeared during the Spring and Autumn Period. The Chinese character for benevolence first appeared in *Shangshu (The Book of Documents)* where it was used to indicate good morality. This character also appeared in two places in *Shijing (The Classic of Poetry)*, which is the earliest existing anthology of Chinese poems. Moreover, in both of its appearances in *Shijing*, benevolence was used together with the word "beauty." From the abundance of the Spring and Autumn Period materials that dealt with thinking on benevolence, Confucius made choices about which to accept and which to reject. Refining and summarising, he identified a fixed scope for the idea of benevolence, turning it into a virtue that stood out from all the other virtues and endowing it with abundant meanings.

Chapters and sentences about "benevolence" recorded in *Lunyu (The Analects)* give the best expression to Confucius's thinking on benevolence. On one occasion, a student of Confucius named Zi Zhang asked, "What exactly is 'benevolence'?" Confucius replied, "Benevolence is carrying out the five virtues of courtesy, magnanimity, faithfulness, diligence and kindness." He explained, "A heart that is not wanton is called courtesy. A heart that is not narrow is called magnanimity. A heart that lacks deception is polite. A heart free of indolence is diligent. A heart with no harshness is kind. If a person is not benevolent, he cannot be called a person."

Confucius's thinking on the concept of benevolence possessed very strong practical characteristics. He focused his attention on society and reality, paying close attention on how to achieve all round development. In pursuit of the lofty concept of benevolence, it is unacceptable to do things that run against the most supreme moral rules.

The important concept of benevolence that lies at the centre of the Confucian ideological system is abundant with different connotations. How can people achieve benevolence? What ways and methods can people use to embody benevolence in their deeds and actions? Deep and profound, it relates to things both small and large, from the cultivation of the ideal character in individual people to the ideal political policy of a country. It is also reflected in systems for the cultivation of ideal personalities that exist in the areas of every type of thought and behaviour that are part of the lives of individuals and groups.

The Confucian school of thought applied theories about benevolence to the arena of politics, forming the theory of benevolent governance. This had important influences on the development of Chinese political thought. On the foundations of the Confucian theory of benevolence, Mencius proposed his famous theory of benevolent governance. This theory sought to take the theory of benevolence and apply it to specific areas of governance. It specified the practise of benevolent government, opposed domineering political rule, brought peace and tranquillity to political affairs, and allowed the common people to live and work in peace and contentment. Mencius raised a few very down to earth propositions, the points of which centred around improving the livelihood of the people and strengthening moral cultivation. If benevolent government is practised, then it will be possible to govern the affairs of the land. If benevolent government is not practised, then it will be very difficult to govern the affairs of the land. Mencius felt that as long as benevolent governance was practised, even a small territory was enough to constitute a viable kingship.

Mencius once said to Emperor Hui of Liang, "Your majesty should give a humane government to the people, be careful in punishing crime, make the taxes light; plough the fields deeply and hoe them well. Then all the strong and healthy people can in their leisure time cultivate filial piety, sibling affection, loyalty and sincerity. These people will be victorious even in the face of strong troops." He emphasised how benevolent governance had the ability first to unify the country and then to govern it. He advocated using benevolent governance to win the hearts and minds of the people with virtue and kindness. He opposed using domineering measures to make people submit by force. He criticised violence and opposed war. These were the basic starting points of the Confucian school's theory of benevolent governance. Followers of the Confucian school believed that the livelihood of the people was the basis for the state. Through satisfying the basic needs of the common people, a country would become stable and easy to govern.

After Confucius, the seedlings of his philosophy were watered and tended to by members of the Confucian school. Over the successive dynasties, they endured for more than 2,000 years. They finally developed into the towering trees of the Confucian school of thought as well as China's Confucian centred traditional culture. As a result, the development of the concept of benevolence and the rooting of rules and rituals within this concept can be said to be Confucius's greatest contribution to Chinese culture.

In China, the tale of the Justice and Benevolence Hutong was once an often told story. Once upon a time, there were two neighbouring properties, and a dispute broke out between the residents of the two places over land boundaries. One family involved in the dispute had a family member who was working as an official in the capital who was influential and powerful. The family wrote him a letter explaining the details of their land dispute with their neighbours. They hoped to make use of his power and influence in resolving the matter. This official was both honest and enlightened, and was unwilling to throw his power around in order to resolve his family's private affairs. When he wrote back to his family, he included a poem that expressed his attitude towards their request: "This letter has travelled for miles just for the sake of a wall. Why not give up a few metres? The Great Wall of China still exists, but the Emperor Qin Shihuang who built it has long since vanished from the earth." When the family received this poem, they all understood what the official was suggesting, and they acted according to his suggestion. They not only ended their dispute with their neighbours, but they also took the initiative in conceding a strip of land. When the first family conceded the land, the other family was deeply moved. After some discussion, they also decided to concede a strip of land. In this way, a strip of land was created by both families. As it happened, the area was lacking a north to south road, and so they built a *hutong* in this space. Though the identity of the person who gave this alley the name "Justice and Benevolence *Hutong*" is unknown, locals have been calling it this for several hundred years.

Benevolence is the centre and the core of the Confucian school of thought, and it has had a profound impact on the course of development of Chinese culture and society. Through 5,000 years of human civilisation, the different eras of history have developed into the present day. The concept of benevolence has gradually evolved beyond the traditional meaning attached to it in the Confucian school of thought, which can be understood through quotations like, "A man of benevolence, wishing to establish his own character, also establishes the character of others, and wishing to be prominent himself also helps others to be prominent." It has reached new heights in the modern age. These heights are reflected in ideas such as "serving the people."

Righteousness

Righteousness, as an important moral standard of Confucianism, connotes friendship, equity and appropriateness. Benevolence requires appropriateness so righteousness conforms to the moral standard of benevolence. Righteousness can also be defined as moral conduct.

According to the Han Dynasty *Shuowen Jiezi* (the first Chinese dictionary arranged according to radicals), the character for righteousness (義) is an associative compound character. It is formed from the components "I" (我) and "sheep" (羊). "I" implies that the character's meaning is inseparable from the self and that one uses the ideas of the self to distinguish right from wrong. Sheep were once commonly used as sacrificial animals. The sheep component of this character thus carries the meaning of sacrifice. Looking at the character as a whole, we can interpret the components as expressing the meaning of self sacrifice. As a result, the general meaning of the righteousness has to do with actions or principles that are consistent with morality.

As a category within Confucian ethics, the basic connotations of "righteousness" include dignity, friendship, camaraderie, goodness, fairness, justice, and appropriateness. The Song Dynasty Confucian scholar Zhu Xi wrote, "Righteous actions are guided by appropriateness." Benevolence is taken as the standard for appropriateness, and things that are consistent with benevolence can be considered appropriate. Therefore, righteousness can be understood as a code of ethics that is consistent with benevolence. It can also be explained as behaviour that is consistent with justice or a code of ethics. More specifically, righteousness encapsulates respect among brothers, respect for elders, respect for superiors, respect for virtue, fairness, justice, selflessness, preventing people from doing bad things, and respecting and protecting private property as well as opposing encroachments, annexations of territory and unjust wars, among other things.

Confucius was the first to put forth the idea of righteousness. He used righteousness as a moral standard to judge the thoughts and behaviour of people. Confucius also made a connection between righteousness and bravery, saying in the *"Yang Huo"* chapter of *The Analects* that, *"A junzi* (Chinese equivalent of a gentleman), having valour without righteousness, will be guilty of insubordination; the lesser man having valour without righteousness, will commit robbery." Confucius also said, "He who fails to be ready to take up arms for a just cause should not be deemed brave."

During the end of the Warring States Period, the great army of the Qin state proceeded to the Yan state after capturing the Zhao state. Jing Ke, a warrior of the Yan state, went to the Qin state on a diplomatic mission. When he was presenting the severed head of the traitor Qin general Fan Yuqi and a map of the Zhao state to the emperor of Qin—the man who would later becom Qin Shihuang—Jing Ke pulled a dagger out from the folds of the map and rushed toward the emperor. Although he was ultimately unsuccessful, people ever since have been telling the story of Jing Ke's bravery and heroic self sacrifice.

Yan Zhenqing, a man of faithfulness, displeased Lu Qi, who was a treacherous and selfish official of the imperial court. When Li Xilie started an armed revolt against the imperial government, the emperor listened to the advice of Lu Qi and sent Yan Zhenqing to coax Li Xilie into surrendering. Yan Zhenqing went to the location of Li Xilie's army where he spoke out of justice and denounced Li Xilie. As his shame turned to anger, Li Xilie threatened to have Yan Zhenqing burned to death. As he was beside the blazing fire, Yan Zhenqing picked up his pen and wrote the words, "The name of he who acts with faithfulness will remain immortal."

These two classical stories are both widely told within China. Capable of evoking both praise and tears, these tales of self sacrifice for the sake of country and overall national interests deal with the themes of loyalty and righteousness.

Both righteousness as well as the idea that there is a distinction between righteousness and profit are important core concepts in Confucian ethics. In *The Analects*, a *junzi* is defined as a man of ideal and noble character. The *junzi* values righteousness, while the small man values profit. In the eyes of Confucius, a *junzi* puts righteousness before all else and puts profit last. Confucius's concept of righteousness and profit warns people about how to deal with the relationship between righteousness and profit when confronting the prospect of personal gain. The precise relationship is that "profit should be gained through righteousness"—that is to say, righteous techniques should be used to gain profit in a reasonable way. Confucius's concept of righteousness and profit also warns people that they must keep righteousness in mind in the face of profit. When pursuing personal gain, one must always stop and think about whether this gain complies with morality and righteousness. Only personal gain that is consistent with morality and righteousness should be pursued. One should give a wide berth to personal gain that runs counter to morality and righteousness.

Although the Confucian school of thought places much importance on the distinction between righteousness and profit, it does not completely oppose the reasonable pursuit of profit. Confucius said that "wealth and status are the desires of every man." However, the Confucian school of thought emphasised that in the pursuit of profit and the free pursuit of individual development, a line must be drawn at some point. This line separates the righteous from the unrighteous. One cannot use unrighteous methods to chase after profit.

Mencius went a step further in explaining the concept of righteousness. He believed that righteousness had to be the precondition for both faithfulness and resoluteness. He placed righteousness among the highest moral standards of the Confucian school of thought. Righteousness and benevolence are representatives of morality. These two virtues made up the core morality in China's feudal era, that is to say, they were "the pinnacle of benevolence and righteousness." As stated in the *"Li Ren"* chapter of *The Analects,* "When the virtuous man is out in the world, he does not set his mind for or against anything; what is right, he will follow. [. . .] The mind of the virtuous man is conversant with righteousness; the mind of the small man is conversant with profit." As stated in the *"Li Lou 1"* chapter of *Mengzi (Mencius):* "The great man does not think beforehand of his words that they may be sincere, nor of his actions that they may be resolute; he simply speaks and does what is right."

Mencius saw righteousness as a standard for distinguishing right from wrong, a yardstick for evaluating the degree to which leaders are able to practising benevolent government, and a principle for guiding the conduct and moral cultivation of the common people. He felt that righteousness was the most important of all of values, and so he prized righteousness and disdained profit. In everything, he advocated being guided by righteousness instead of profit. As recorded in the *"Liang Hui Wang 1"* chapter of *Mengzi,* "Superiors and inferiors will try to snatch this profit from each other, and the state will be endangered." In the *"Wen Yan"* chapter of *The Book of Changes,* there are two sentences, "What is called 'the advantageous' is the harmony of all that is right," and, "Benefiting all creatures, the virtuous man is fit to exhibit the harmony of all that is right." As a fundamental concept of moral philosophy, "righteousness" refers to the rules of moral conduct that the general public of a society regard as being appropriate and proper. The principle of righteousness is often given expression in the form of laws, and it can also be regarded as a definite precondition for the existence of laws in society.

Moreover, the ideas of righteousness and duty have the meaning of doing things that one ought to do, as not doing these things are considered unrighteous. This is what is meant by the idea of "being willing to pay any price in pursuit of righteousness." One of the important tasks involved in promoting moral and cultural progress is establishing a society's concept of righteousness as well as the cultivation of citizens' awareness and conviction in this righteousness. Nowadays, on one hand, the concept of righteousness needs to be endowed with new connotations, which among other things include social equity, impartiality, and public welfare. On the other hand, people's awareness and conviction of justice must also be called forth anew, a process which we can also view as establishing a sense of morals and justice in members of the public as well as allowing them to adopt moral positions based on ethical principles.

Righteousness has become a type of outlook on life as well as a set of values. For example, when either kinship or friendship develops into their consummate form, righteousness will be a component. With the presence of righteousness, friendships of all types are pure and long-lasting. With the presence of righteousness, friends don't betray other friends and parents don't abandon families. Righteousness is the responsibility and dedication that intrinsically exists in life.

In spite of the fact that the precise definition of righteousness varies from society to society and era to era, there is a universality and continuity that spans concepts of righteousness of all societies and eras. As human contact becomes increasingly frequent, human beings will also have more common views on areas relating to morals and principles. Those morals and principles that are widely accepted as being appropriate will compose a brand of righteousness that will govern the behaviour of people in that society and era.

Propriety

Propriety, a moral standard and a code of conduct in Chinese society, plays an important role in shaping the spirit of the Chinese nation. With social reform and progress, propriety has been endowed with new meaning, adapting to correct times.

In Chinese, the word "propriety" originally referred to a person's manners and actions carried out during religious ceremonies as is recorded in *Shouwen Jiezi*, "Propriety refers to worship, by following propriety, one will receive good fortune." From this we can see that propriety originally had nothing to do with hierarchical ethics. But as time went by, propriety developed into a part of everyday life; an external way to cultivate one's internal morality. Propriety dictates and acts as a guide for how one should conduct oneself in public. Confucius's *The Analects* says, "If one does not understand propriety, how can one know how to conduct oneself?"

Before Confucius, China already had a well established propriety system which had come to being in the Xia, late Shang and Zhou dynasties. The essence of social status that was attached to propriety came about no later than the late Shang Dynasty but didn't become a set of concrete regulations until the early Zhou Dynasty. After Emperor Wu of Zhou overthrew the Shang Dynasty he began to reformulate the country's propriety system based on that of the previous dynasty's. By the time the Duke of Zhou took the throne, the Zhou Dynasty propriety system was relatively complete.

The Zhou Dynasty was famous for its strict abidance to propriety. By the Spring and Autumn Period, however, the power of the imperial family began to decline, the county's hierarchy with it, and as rulers throughout the country began to gain power, they began to overstep their power and eventually China's system of propriety collapsed. But due to the propriety system of the Zhou Dynasty, the literati and scholars of the time constantly strove to uphold and revive it.

During the Spring and Autumn Period there were a number of people who discussed propriety, but it was Confucius who was at the forefront and made it into a system. He dedicated his whole life to teaching his disciples about propriety and he mentions propriety 75 times in *The Analects*. He talked about the importance of propriety in conduct and for ruling a country. In Confucian thought, everyone should adhere to the social ethics expected of his class and status in order to maintain social order and the hierarchal structure of society; in this way and only this way, can a ruler successfully govern a country.

Propriety incorporates the ideas of hierarchy and ethics. In terms of hierarchy it refers to fame and status, i.e. the Confucian relationship between "ruler and subjects, father and son." In terms of moral ethics, propriety includes ideas on filial piety, kindness, politeness, obedience, respect, harmony, benevolence and righteousness. As an ideology, Confucius believed propriety is inseparable from benevolence. Confucius said: "If a man is not benevolent, what good is it if he adheres to propriety?" He put forward the idea that "one should not try to control man's behaviour with law as this is only an external, superficial form of control; it is better to use propriety as this is an internal physiological change, which is better for social order." This idea broke away from the Zhou Dynasty idea that "propriety should not be enforced on the masses." This saying does not mean the masses do not need propriety, but that they are restricted by a lack of time and money to preoccupy themselves with it.

What it really means is that the propriety used by the noble class is not suitable for use by the masses. Propriety varies and is not merely one set of rules that should be obeyed by everyone. Each person should follow the propriety seen fit for his social and political status, otherwise their actions will be deemed as improper.

Taking for example the *Bayi* dance which was a ritual dance restricted to the imperial class. Ministers were only allowed to conduct the dance with four groups of eight people, but when certain ministers attempted to conduct the ritual dance with eight groups of eight people, as was conducted by the emperor, Confucius said it went against propriety. There were propriety rules like this for all types of ceremonies differing depending on the status of those conducting the ritual. In homes, propriety differed depending on whether it was between father and son, husband and wife, or between siblings. Only by adhering to this system of propriety could social and family order be maintained.

During the Warring States Period, Mencius said that benevolence, righteousness, propriety and wisdom were the core moral ethics. Xunzi placed even greater importance on propriety and focused on its origin and social use. He believed that propriety defined everyone's position in society under various circumstances, whether between rulers and subjects, old and young, rich and poor. Propriety centred around social relations, and the structure of society was born out of this.

From this it is easy to see the relationship between Confucian propriety and modern sociology. Confucian propriety was not merely a form of etiquette, as this merely outlines the rules for social interaction. Propriety in the Confucian sense is rooted in social relationships and changes depending on the relationship. Therefore, propriety in the pre-Confucian dynasties changed as society and social relationships changed. Confucianism advocated rule by propriety and its various forms to maintain social and political order. This is the exact opposite of the Legalist school of thought, as promoted by Han Fei, which advocated the rule of law regardless of social or political status.

In pre-Qin China, the Confucians and Legalist were in a constant argument over who was right. When China began to enact law according to propriety, the way the law worked saw a huge change and began to rely entirely on the idea of propriety. Law and punishment became a way to uphold propriety and thus strengthened its legal quality. This close interwoven relationship between law and propriety is the essence and main characteristic of feudal China's law system.

Throughout the course of history, propriety as a guide for moral ethics has had an important effect on the Chinese way of thinking and culture. At the same time, as society has developed, new meanings have been given to propriety and it is constantly undergoing change and development itself.

Since the Republican era, the Chinese propriety system has been constantly simplified and has utilized certain western ideas. Propriety now has already lost its originally hierarchal elements and is merely an ethical code which should be applied to everyday life. But this doesn't mean we have escaped the confines of propriety. In fact we only need to do away with the unnecessary parts of the Confucian ethic code yet still uphold the more important Confucian ethics. In the world's eye, China is a cultured and open country. Propriety helps strengthen a country's image.

Wisdom

A person can be considered wise if he or she is good at learning and thinking. A wise person is not only knowledgeable, but also smart and intelligent. So Confucius said, "A wise man won't be confused." A *junzi* should not only be benevolent, but also be wise. Wisdom is as important as benevolence because the eagerness to learn promotes the growth of benevolence.

The word "wisdom" was originally used to describe knowledge of the heavens and earth. Wisdom refers to truth and is of course related to benevolence and righteousness. In Confucian ethics, wisdom is regarded as one of the core ethical qualities.

Wisdom relies on intelligence, the ability to discern right from wrong, and the ability to uphold benevolence and righteousness. The key to wisdom is this sense of right and wrong. Confucius created the structure and standard for moral wisdom based on the examples of wise people before him such as Emperor Yao, Xia Yu and Tang of the Shang Dynasty.

Wise is he who can discern a person's character. Confucius said that knowing oneself was the moral prerequisite to being a *junzi*. The ability to understand and care for others was built on the basis of benevolence. Confucius believed "wisdom," "benevolence" and "bravery" were the three key virtues one should possess. He described the three as, "The benevolent do not worry, the wise are never perplexed and the brave are not afraid." In actual fact, Confucius stressed that benevolence was the most important attribute: "The wise like water, the benevolent like mountains. The wise are active while the benevolent enjoy peace and quiet. The wise may live happily, but the benevolent live longer."

Mencius was the first to quote "benevolence, righteousness, propriety and wisdom" together. He affirmed the importance of propriety and wisdom in the Confucian system of ethics by talking about the control of actions and the acknowledgement of morals. In the end, the four qualities of benevolence, righteousness, propriety and wisdom merged to form a complete system of ethics.

By the Han Dynasty, the Five Constant Virtues (benevolence, righteousness, propriety, wisdom and faithfulness) had been defined with wisdom being one of them. The belief that the quest for knowledge and increasing intelligence was an important value reflected in the importance placed on knowledge and wisdom.

Confucian thought dictates that man has the ability to understand things, and everything can potentially be understood by man. There is nothing that can't be understood, only things we haven't yet understood. Man is constantly learning more about himself and the world he lives in as this knowledge is collected and passed down. Today we use this idea of wisdom to promote the search for knowledge and truth.

A wise man is one who has knowledge and is adept at thinking. But a wise man is not just clever; there is a difference between clever and wise. A *junzi* should not only be benevolent but also wise. Benevolence and wisdom are supplementary as knowledge can promote benevolence. As part of the requirement for benevolence, wisdom can be broken down into five parts; extensive learning, questioning, reflection, discerning and perseverance. Socrates once said: "Virtue is knowledge." If one can form the correct outlook on life and moral outlook based on knowledge, then man's moral foundation will become more solid.

Confucius once said, "Those born with knowledge rank first, those who gain knowledge later come second, and those who learn during difficulties are third. Those who encounter difficulties and still don't learn are fools." This can be said to be the core of Confucius's theory of knowledge. From this we can see that Confucius believed there were two ways to gain knowledge; you either are born with it, or learn it.

Confucius's thought on gaining knowledge includes thoughts similar to modern day dialectic. Confucius said, "Study as if one can't get enough, as if one is afraid to forget it" and "When I am with two likeminded people, there is at least one that I can learn something from." Confucius himself spent his whole life gaining knowledge and summed it up saying, "I try to remember all I have studied, I never feel satisfied with my level of study, I never get tired of teaching others; what do I have to regret?"

Confucius and Mencius were educators. Confucius advocated "education for all without discrimination" which makes him a pioneer for universal education. The "Four Confucian Subjects" and the "Six Arts" embodied the Confucian ethic system and so can be said to have been a complete model for quality orientated education. The Confucian education ideology was centred around moral ethics as opposed to material gain. There are a number of Confucian sayings regarding education and study that are still used today, such as "If one studies without reflecting, one will become confused; but only reflecting and not studying is no good either," "Anyone with knowledge worth learning can be your teacher" and "Teaching and studying are supplementary." These Confucian sayings are still applicable today.

Today, "wisdom" in China has evolved from moral wisdom to scientific wisdom in order to build a harmonious society, which is in essence still the goal of Confucianism; "benevolence."

Faithfulness

Faithfulness requires people to abide by the fundamental principles for behaviour, that is, being honest and not deceiving others. Faithfulness is one of the requirements for benevolence and is necessary for moral cultivation. Being honest is a moral standard and basic virtue universally recognised by the entire Chinese nation.

The Confucian principle of faithfulness was developed by scholars such as Confucius and Mencius based on the honesty and sincerity of people before them such as Emperor Yao and Xia Yu.

The Confucian ideal of faithfulness involves keeping one's word, upholding the truth, keeping one's promises, being devoted to one's duty and assuming responsibility. The opposite of faithfulness is saying one thing and doing another, deceiving, going back on one's word and not taking responsibility. Without faithfulness, people would constantly trick and deceive one another and society would turn ugly.

When looking at the origin and development of "faithfulness" we have to look at Confucius. Confucius made faithfulness one of the four core principles he taught to his disciples along with knowledge, character and loyalty. Faithfulness became one of the key prerequisites for a junzi. In addition, Confucius believed that faithfulness was essential for governing the country.

"Zi Gong asked about governing. Confucius said, 'The people should have enough food, the country should have a large enough army, and the people should have faith in their ruler. Zi Gong went on to ask, 'If you had to give up one of these, which would it be?' Confucius said, 'The army.' Zi Gong then asked: 'And if you had to give up a second?' Confucius said: 'The ample supply of food. People will always die, but a country is nothing without faithfulness.' " From this passage we can see that according to Confucian thought, faithfulness was the root to good governance.

Confucius said that faithfulness was the outward display of benevolence. He believed one should "be careful in one's work and be trustworthy" and that this was an integral virtue. Confucius also said that "If one is sincere, one will be appointed to work." In *Daxue (The Great Learning)* it is also recorded that a sense of justice and sincerity are the key to cultivating a moral character.

One of Confucius's students, Zi Xia, also pointed out that "When with friends, one must speak sincerely." Faithfulness merely requires people to abide by the fundamental principles for behaviour, that is, being honest and not deceiving others. Faithfulness is one of the requirements for benevolence and is necessary for moral cultivation. Thinkers throughout history have constantly striven to remind later generations of the importance of faithfulness and the danger of going back on one's word.

It was Mencius who put forward the principle and method of sincerity. He said that sincerity came from within and that only through cultivating one's character and self reflection could one become sincere. He also believed that the only way moral behaviour could be effective was if it was sincere. From this we can see the importance of sincerity in the path to attaining benevolence and a moral character.

During the Spring and Autumn and Warring States periods, Duke Xiao of Qin conducted political reforms according to Shang Yang's proposals. The law had been changed but not yet public announced and Shang Yang was afraid the public would not believe him when he publicised it. He placed a large wooden pole in the market in the capital city Xianyang. He then announced he would give 10 pieces of gold to anyone who could take the pole to the northern city gate. At first no one believed him and daren't try. He then announced he would give fifty pieces to anyone who could do it. At that point one man stepped forward and transported the pole to the northern gate and received fifty pieces of gold from Shang Yang. After gaining the masses trust, it was easy for him to publicise the new law which helped make the country strong.

Another story concerning faithfulness comes from *Zuo Zhuan*. After encountering danger, Chong E had to flee his home. None of the other states would offer him refuge, but when he went to the Chu state, he was warmly received. The ruler of Chu asked him, "If later you become ruler of Jin, how will you repay me?" Chong E replied, "If I become ruler of Jin there's no point me giving you gold or jewels as you're not short of these, and I won't have anything rarer to give you. Instead, if we even meet on the battlefield, I will retreat 15 kilometres." Later Chong E became Duke Wen of Jin. Five years after, the two met on the battlefield and the Duke kept his word and retreated almost 50 kilometres to repay the Chu ruler.

A market economy society relies heavily on social and individual faithfulness. Western market economy societies place great emphasis on ensuring social and individual faithfulness. They use both law and traditional cultural and religious beliefs regarding honesty to ensure this moral faithfulness. Confucian thoughts on faithfulness can also be used in the same way to ensure social faithfulness in China.

Modern day "Confucian businessmen" place great emphasis on faithfulness. The modern Chinese have developed and perfected the traditional Chinese ethic of faithfulness to make it more relevant for modern society.

33

Elites in Chinese history relied upon and interpreted Chinese nationalities' strong will and wisdom to manage their nations. They are the matchless representatives of each period of Chinese history, which grows brighter with each passing day.

Preface

Chinese people love bamboo. It is said that a nobleman can eat without meat, but a man of virtue cannot live without bamboo. Chinese history is intertwined with bamboo. The straight and upright spirit of bamboo is admired by the Chinese and something they aspire to.

Chinese history was recorded on thin bamboo strips that were handed down from generation to generation. The spirit and soul of the Chinese nation is near at hand when we unfold these bound bamboo strips today. Heroes, noblemen and men of virtue created dynasties and a unique civilisation. They were Chinese history's elites, who shouldered the historical responsibility of advancing the nation's development. Their quest to acquire knowledge, to study the rules of social development and their practical work reflect the wisdom that ensured national development. The humane spirit and inclusive souls of the Chinese nation are revealed in their virtues, but also in their kindness.

Sorting out the history of the Chinese' spiritual development is like viewing the inner lives of the dynasties' heroes and noblemen. Their dedication to the overall national interest and their heroic make the 5,000-year history of the Chinese shimmer with vitality.

People make history. The personal beauty of human beings and their stories are the world's most brilliant beacons. The stories of China's heroes help people get closer to modern Chinese, as with relatives, good friends, sisters and brothers. The essences of their efforts, whether passed down or inherited, showcase the dignity and brilliance of the Chinese civilisation.

Through tides of time ebb and flow, historical heroes remain important ethical models, like guiding stars that give people direction, while illuminating the ground of history. History gives us our roots.

Overall National Interest

For ancient Chinese, their world was ordered according to the collective wisdom of Chinese culture and civilisation. The 18th century French thinker Francois Voltaire recognised this wisdom, saying, "China is the oldest nation in the world. It is second to none in ethics, morality and state governance." Harlan Cleveland, a government official in the United States in the 20th century, said, "Many of the essentials of management and leadership were lauded a long time ago, and most were recorded in Chinese."

In ancient China, emperors succeeded by skilfully employing their wisdom and ability and by proving the truth of the statement that: "Those who harness talent win the world." They drew upon the wisdom of competent people, who were encouraged to enter public life, to manage regimes that were expected to last forever. They assisted rulers in achieving hegemony, employing their acute political senses, passion and visions. Faithful and capable officials embodied the national mentality of the Chinese people, a product of countless generations. In contrast to passive hermits or pedantic scholars, these people of insight were resourceful, and they could manoeuvre among various political groups with skill and ease, even in troubled times. They were wise people, whether they served as senior governments officials or in civilian roles.

Jiang Ziya (1156–1017 BC), the forefather of Chinese counsellors, helped King Wen (reign 1105–1056 BC) of the Zhou destroy the Shang regime, laying a solid foundation for the 800-year rule of the Zhou Dynasty (11th century–256 BC). Yingzheng (220–210 BC), king of Qin (221–206 BC), put an end to 500 years of continuous wars and turmoil and became the First Emperor in China: Qin Shihuang. Liu Che, Emperor Wu of the Han Dynasty (206 BC–AD 220), adopted a series of reforms and strengthened the rule of the Western Han Dynasty (206 BC–AD 25); Emperor Taizong of the Tang Dynasty (AD 618–907), has been extolled in ancient and modern times for seeking talent with eagerness; Zhuge Liang (AD 181–234), the virtuous prime minister of the Shu State during the Three Kingdoms period (AD 220–280), did his utmost in battles to help the Shu-Han regime; Wang Anshi (1021–86), prime minister of Emperor Shenzong (1067–85) of the Northern Song Dynasty (AD 960–1279), overcame conservative opposition and carried out reforms; Genghis Khan(1162–1227) of the Yuan Dynasty (1271–1368) relied on Yelu Chucai; Liu Ji (1311–75), founder of Ming Dynasty (1368–1644), won peace; Emperor Kangxi (reign: 1661–1722) rule over a prosperous era of the Qing Dynasty (1644–1911).

People sometimes view history as a "mirror," a tool that allows us to view society from all aspects. But history also resembles a stage on which all play their own roles. From a historical perspective, virtuous emperors and capable officials guide the country in the tide of historical development. They ensured national security and protected the national interests.

I Set Stage; You Pull Strings

Panxi Town, located in Baoji City's Chencang District, in Northwest China's Shaanxi Province, is famous for its rich historical and cultural heritage. According to historical records, the story of King Wen of Zhou seeking worthy persons, and Jiang Ziya, also known as Jiang Taigong, angling for fish occurred here.

King Wen of Zhou, though surrounded by civilian officials and military officers, did not limit his search for a man of both literary and military capacity to plan the strategy that would allow the king to establish a well-managed state, find an opportunity to overthrow the Shang regime and to revenge their insults. One day, he went hunting and met an old man fishing by the Panxi River (today's Panxi Town). The grey-haired old man looked to be in his 70s or 80s. It was strange that he spoke to the fish: "Come to swallow the bait. Come to the bait, if you will." On taking a closer look, the king noticed the old man's fishhook was straight rather than hooked, free of bait and was dangling high above the water's surface. King Wen, puzzled, decided to chat with the old man who would become known as Jiang Shang or Jiang Ziya.

In talking with Jiang, King Wen found him to be far-sighted and learned. Jiang was proficient in astronomy, geography, politics and in military affairs. He was particularly clear and logical in assessing current political situations. He did not think the Shang regime would last long. He believed sagacious leaders should overthrow it, and establish a new regime that would allow common people to live a comfortable life. Jiang's remarks touched the heart of King Wen. He realised Jiang was exactly the sage he was seeking to help him topple the Shang regime. King Wen then sincerely addressed Jiang: "We have expected you for a long time. Please come and help us to govern the country!" and invited Jiang to share his carriage on his return to the court.

Jiang was initially given the title of imperial master, the highest military rank. Later, he was promoted to the post of prime minister, managing the political and military affairs of the whole country. When King Wen's father, Taigong Jili, was on the throne, he looked for sages like Jiang. In this sense, Jiang was addressed respectfully as Taigong Wang (anticipated by Taigong). Later, people simply left out the character Wang, and referred to Jiang as Jiang Taigong. Jiang was truly a pillar of society. As the prime minister, he helped King Wen consolidate his political situation and improve his military effectiveness. They developed the economy, allowing people to live and work in relative peace and contentment. But they also conquered neighbouring tribes and expanded their territory, thus weakening the Shang regime. By his later years, King Wen had enlarged his territory, incorporating all of the native places of the Zhou's ancestors in the west (today's Shaanxi and Gansu provinces), Licheng in today's Shanxi Province in North China, Qinyang in today's Henan Province in the east (near Zhaoge, the capital city of the Shang regime), and the valleys of the Yangtze, Hanshui and Rushui rivers in the south. King Wen then controlled two-thirds of China's land area, laying a solid foundation for the Shang's ultimate demise.

Discovering Talent, Admitting Mistakes

The world has no lack of talented people, but there may be a lack of eyes to discover them. Emperor Wu of the Han Dynasty (156–87 BC) was exceptional in his regard for talent: anyone could be recruited, regardless of origin or background, so long as they were talented. This gave Emperor Wu a large reservoir of talent to employ, which earned him a reputation as the wisest among Han Dynasty men. Zhu Maichen, Zhufu Yan, Sima Xiangru and other great names in Chinese history were immediately made proper use of by Emperor Wu once they displayed their talents no matter how frustrated they used to be. This shows Emperor Wu, a great statesman, also had a great mind. The most successful cases of Emperor Wu making proper use of personnel are Bu Shi, Sang Hongyang, Wei Qing and Jin Ridi.

Bu Shi was an honest and sincere man who made a fortune by herding sheep. When his younger brother grew up and married, Bu Shi generously gave all his property to his brother except for 100 sheep. Bu Shi, as an expert of breeding sheep, increased his flock to more than 1,000 after ten years of hard work. Bu Shi made another fortune, while his brother lost everything due to mismanagement. Bu Shi helped his younger brother again and again by giving him his own property. When the emperor sent an expedition to conquer the Huns, Bu Shi donated his property to help the cause. The emperor sent a messenger to ask Bu Shi what he wanted in return. Bu Shi answered that he had no requirements since every man has a share of responsibility for the fate of his country. After hearing the messenger's report, Emperor Wu was greatly impressed by Bu Shi.

A year later, King Hunye of the Huns surrendered, and Emperor Wu gave a great reward, which then led to an empty treasury and migration of the poor. Bu Shi again offered timely help by giving the governor of Henan 200,000 coins to help the refugees. When Emperor Wu read the list of rich people who have helped the poor, he saw Bu Shi's name again and this reminded him of Bu Shi's donation to the cause of the expedition. Then Emperor Wu gave Bu Shi a handsome reward, but Bu Shi returned all of it. Emperor Wu considered Bu Shi an honest and sincere old man and offered him an official post. However, Bu Shi had no interest in this, either, so Emperor Wu had to lie to Bu Shi, telling him that he wanted Bu Shi to herd sheep for him in the royal garden. This time Bu Shi agreed. One year later, when Emperor Wu visited, he was impressed by the good quality of the sheep raised by Bu Shi. To the emperor's surprise, Bu Shi gave him a lecture on running a state, saying that governing people was like herding sheep: just follow routine and drive away the bad to protect the group from negative influences. Emperor Wu then offered Bu Shi an official post. Bu Shi performed excellently in this position and was promoted all the way to the position of senior censor.

Compared to Bu Shi, the origin of Jin Ridi was even worse. Still, his role in the Han Empire was more significant than that of Bu Shi's. Originally a Hun, Jin became a slave in charge of keeping horses at the age of 14 after his careless father, King Xiutu, surrendered to the Han. One day, Emperor Wu wanted to review the royal horses during a feast; Jin Ridi and some other slaves were asked to lead the horses in the review. When the slaves passed Emperor Wu, they all cast furtive glances at him except for Jin Ridi. Instead, Jin looked steadily forward. In addition to this, Jin was handsome and his horse was plump and sturdy, which caught the emperor's attention. Emperor Wu believed Jin to be trustworthy and prudent. So Jin ended up as Emperor Wu's advisor on national policy. Emperor Wu proved to be right in his reading of the man: Jin Ridi made no mistakes in his positions, and even saved the emperor's life once. When Jiang Chong was caught framing the crown princess, his whole family was exterminated; Mang Heluo, a member of his clique, fearing implication, conspired to kill Emperor Wu. Jin sensed something was wrong, so he spied on Mang and foiled his plan. When Mang was cornered and tried to kill the emperor, Jin stopped him and called for the guards. In this way, Jin saved the emperor and prevented a tragedy.

These two cases amount to sound evidence of Emperor Wu's capability for discovering and managing talented individuals. This is why he had the help of such individuals and was able to lead the Han to prosperity.

In his later years, Emperor Wu made some mistakes in governing the country and felt the necessity in making a change, so he issued an edict in 89 BC, admitting his mistakes in adopting a warlike policy, exhausting the people and draining the treasury. He turned down Sang Hongyang's suggestions of enhancing military power at borders, reduced corvee and developed agriculture by promoting new farming methods and improving farm tools and technology. These policies brought social stability, restored feudal order and aided economic development, laying a solid foundation for the prosperity seen during Emperor Zhao (87–74 BC) and Emperor Xuan's (73–49 BC) reigns. Usually, under an autocratic monarchy, regardless what an emperor does, most ministers tend to sing the ruler's praises to protect themselves or to win promotions. When Emperor Wu realised that to be a good ruler, he had to win the hearts of his subjects, he admitted his mistakes and changed policies. This is proof of his great wisdom and vision.

As one of the outstanding rulers in Chinese history, Emperor Wu was also a visionary strategist and statesman. He ascended the throne at the age of 16, and during his reign of 50 years, he won several significant battles against the Huns and sent several missions to the western region. In doing so, he enhanced Han's ties with the outside world and expanded Han territory. Politically, he carried out legal reforms to strengthen centralization; economically, he promoted agricultural development. He established a prosperous empire that could rival the Roman Empire and made it a centre of world civilisation.

Serve Country with Loyalty, Repay Sincere Invitations

A couplet was penned: "Conquer the Sichuan area; arrange eight battle arrays; capture the enemy 7 times in 6 forays; light up 49 lamps in Wuzhangyuan," reflecting gratitude for 3 invitations. This is a true moment from the life of Zhuge Liang, the virtuous prime minister of the Kingdom of Shu (AD 221–280) of the Three Kingdoms period. Zhuge Liang (AD 181–234), also called Kong Ming or Wo Long, came from Yinan, Shandong Province.

Unlike most people, Zhuge Liang did not rigidly linger over isolated thoughts or phrases in his reading of books, but tried to understand their overall meaning. He was ambitious and concerned about the country's well being. He carefully observed and analysed social affairs and accumulated a rich understanding of governmental management and military operations.

In AD 207 when Zhuge Liang was 27, Liu Bei made three personal calls on him in Longzhong, Xiangyang, to ask for advice about unifying the country. Zhuge Liang gave an insightful analysis of the situation, *Longzhong Dui (Conversation at Longzhong)*.

Liu Bei, after hearing Zhuge Liang's brilliant and thorough analyses, suddenly saw the light. He felt that Zhuge Liang was a rare talent, so he earnestly invited him to leave his abode in the mountains and help him complete the great cause of rejuvenating the Han Dynasty. Zhuge Liang accepted his invitation. When Cao Cao made an expedition to the south the following year, Zhuge Liang cooperated with Zhou Yu and Lu Su, becoming an ally, and personally went to the Kingdom of Wu in the lower reaches of the Yangtze River to drum up support, resulting in the victory of the Battle of Red Cliff. Consequently, the three kingdoms organised a tripartite balance. Zhuge Liang subsequently helped Liu Bei take four prefectures in Jingzhou and served as a senior military counsellor to him. Soon afterwards, he led an army to Shu, present-day Sichuan Province, to help Liu Bei hem in Chengdu on all sides. As a result, Liu Zhang's rule was overthrown and Liu Bei captured Yizhou. Zhuge Liang, promoted to the rank of general, soon defeated Cao Cao's army and seized Hanzhong.

In 225, to consolidate his rear, Prime Minister Zhuge Liang conducted an expedition to the south. When he was ready to withdraw troops after accomplishing his mission, the leader of the Southern Yi people, Meng Huo, mustered the defeated soldiers to attack the army of Shu. Zhuge learned Meng was a brave soldier with a strong will, but treated people honestly, so he was popular with the Yi. He was even admired by many Han people. As a result, Zhuge decided to win him over.

But, though Meng was brave, he was not good at directing military operations. In the first battle, when he saw the army of Shu retreating, he thought Zhuge Liang was not his match and chased him only to rush into an ambush. Meng was sure that Zhuge Liang would put him to death, so he said to himself that he would die like a hero and not disgrace his people. Unexpectedly, Zhuge Liang untied him and persuaded him to pledge allegiance to Shu with good words. Meng arrogantly refused to accept his defeat and Zhuge Liang's words. Instead of obliging him, Zhuge Liang asked him to look at his camps.

Meng carefully observed the camp, finding that there were mainly elderly and wounded soldiers there. So he said: "I did not know your actual situation; so you have won the battle. Now I know you better after seeing your camps. It's not difficult for me to win next time!" Without further explanation, Zhuge Liang let go of Meng with a smile. He was convinced that Meng would launch a surprise attack at night so he immediately devised an ambush. That night, Meng snuck deep into Shu's camps with 500 men. Since they encountered no one, Meng was secretly pleased, believing that success was just around the corner. Suddenly, hidden troops ambushed and captured Meng again.

After being captured a couple of times, Meng became more prudent. He led all his troops to retreat to the south bank of the Lu River. When the Shu army arrived at the river, they could not cross it because they had no boats. Zhuge Liang ordered his men to build some rafts and sent a few soldiers to pretend crossing the river. As soon as the enemy shot arrows at them from the other side of the river, they would immediately turn around but then start to cross the river again. At the same time, Zhuge sent two detachments to cross the river in narrower parts upstream and downstream and had the city where Meng Huo was entrenched.

Consequently, Meng was captured a third time. Still, Zhuge Liang did not kill him; again he let Meng go after entertaining him cordially. Some soldiers did not understand Zhuge Liang's approach, thinking their chief was too lenient with Meng. But Zhuge Liang explained: "If we want to completely put down the rebels of the south, we have to make use of men like Meng Huo. If he would willingly serve the court with all the armies in the south, it is worth 100,000 troops. If you take the trouble of dealing with him now, you will not have to come here again to fight."

Thus, Meng Huo came to admire Zhuge Liang from the bottom of his heart. To persuade all the tribes to pledge allegiance to Shu, he invited the various tribal chiefs to fight against Shu alongside him. They were all lured into an ambush and became captives of Shu. Word came out of the Shu headquarters that Meng and other chiefs might feel free to go, so the leaders all asked Meng to make a decision as to what to do. With tears in his eyes, Meng said: "Since ancient times, I have not heard a case in battle where a man was caught seven times and freed each time. The prime minister is doing everything humanly possible for us; so I am too ashamed to go back." Finally, Meng and other chiefs surrendered to Shu and obeyed the orders of Zhuge Liang.

After that, Zhuge Liang appointed minority leaders to manage the locals, with relations between the Shu regime and minority groups improved. At the same time, he also carried out internal reforms, appointed talented people to important posts, paid attention to agricultural production and water conservancy construction and strengthened military discipline, alleviating crisis in the Shu kingdom.

All Palaces Opened,
All Officials Paid Respects to Emperor

During the Zhenguan Period (AD 635–700) of the Tang Dynasty, many outstanding persons came forward. Wei Zhen, originally an important advisor to Prince Li Jiancheng, was appointed as a supervisory official who often discussed state affairs at the centre of the palace court, as curator of the imperial library and to other positions with the rank of prime minister. Wei Zheng was upright, honest and blunt. He would clearly state what he felt to be correct. Even when the Emperor Taizong flew into a rage, he remained calm and unflinching. The emperor liked him, yet he also feared him.

Once, when the emperor was discussing state affairs at court, he was sitting up on his chair, and his hands were lightly touching the handrails of the chair. He displayed a solemn and mighty air, striking fear into the hearts of his servants. Then he coughed softly, clearing his throat, before asking the ministers: "Dear ministers, many of you are eloquent and experienced scholars. Why are you jittery and even disordered in court?"

Wei Zheng knew why and stepped forward, saying, "His Majesty, you have a mighty figure and you show a serious expression and fire-eating manner at the imperial court. Together with the strict court, we are all flurried. Next time, when you are in the court, please slightly reduce your display of power. You should pocket your pride and treat us in an amiable manner. In this way we can speak freely." The emperor was complacent in the dark, yet felt embarrassed. However, on second thought, such heartfelt words were rare, so he didn't lose his temper. He entrapped Wei Zheng with an issue always on his mind. "What you said reminds me...I've been thinking of 'wise emperor' and 'fatuous emperor,' an issue much heard in the talk of ancient people. What's your take on the difference?"

Wei Zheng was ready. He approached slowly and answered, "His Majesty, an emperor who can embrace opinions from all walks of life is a wise emperor. Yet, an emperor who takes sides and even partially believes in the voice of villains is a fatuous emperor. Those like Emperor Yang (reign AD 604–617) of the Sui Dynasty (AD 581–618) are fatuous emperors. Only wise emperors can be free from mistakes and win the support of all. That said, fatuous emperors invariably lose all reputation and allow a state to perish. Your Majesty, you're advised to remain prudent." Such dissuasion discomforted the emperor; yet, this was but a tip of an iceberg in Wei's history of dissuasion.

Wei Zheng was upright and outspoken in criticising Emperor Taizong, because he sought to bring lasting political stability to the country and contentment to the people. The emperor didn't scold him, but still trusted him. In the 17th year (AD 643) of the Zhenguan Period, when Wei Zheng was seriously ill, the emperor constantly dispatched people to deliver medicine and food to him, to take care of him and to report on his condition. He even visited Wei's home twice, taking a prince and Princess Hengyang on his second visit. Wei Zheng returned this respect to the emperor with difficulty. The emperor comforted Wei Zheng sadly and let him rest to regain his health and asked in tears what his requirements were. Wei Zheng said with difficulty, "I am not concerned with petty things. What I care about is the rise and fall of the country." As a high official of the Emperor Taizong, Wei Zheng spared no effort in performing his duties.

Emperor Taizong was deeply grieved after Wei Zheng died. He suspended court affairs for five days to express condolences and ordered Wei be buried as a first-rank official. He even painted the portrait of Wei Zheng in the Lingyan Pavilion where he often went to express condolences and inscribe poems to commemorate Wei Zheng. Once, standing before Wei Zheng's portrait, he exclaimed, "With copper as a mirror, you can see whether you're well-dressed; with history as the mirror, you can know the rules behind the waxing and waning of a country; with people, you can take note of your mistakes. The death of Wei Zheng deprived me of a mirror." It was because the emperor's adoption of personnel policies of seeking talents, discovering able people and putting them at suitable posts while not sticking to one pattern that he enlisted many exceptional talents during the Zhenguan Period.

Apart from his open-minded acceptance of dissuasion, Emperor Taizong also advocated thrift and simplicity and led by example. He lived in a palace built during the Sui Dynasty after his enthronement; most of the houses were very shabby. Most monarchs of a new dynasty always scaled up development projects and built new palaces. But to cut back on expenditures, Emperor Taizong didn't approve construction in the first year of the Zhenguan Period. He also strictly banned elaborate funerals and ordered officials above the fifth rank and near-royals to abide by the order. He seriously prohibited officials' luxurious extravagances. In the first year of the Zhenguan Period, an atmosphere of upholding thrift took shape and a host of ministers famous for their frugalness appeared. Dai Zhou, minister of revenue, lived in a dilapidated house and didn't have a sacrificial place after his death. Famous minister Wei Zheng didn't have a central room in his house. The popularization of thrift played an active role in reducing the country's and individuals' burdens and promoting the restoration and development of the society and economy.

During his 23-years of reign, Emperor Taizong pursued the principle of managing the country well, worked to make the country prosperous and forged ahead with determination so that the Tang Dynasty rapidly reached the well-governed state where society was stable, people lived and worked in contentment, national strength became more evident and a political environment rarely seen in traditional society was formed. Emperor Taizong initiated the most prominent time of national peace and order in China's traditional society known as the Zhenguan Period, becoming the most eminent representative among China's monarchs of all dynasties as a result.

When Bold, Brilliant Men Exist
The Moon Always Shines Brightly

It is easy to take the world with military force, but difficult to rule it in the same way. The eventual establishment of the Mongol empire can be attributed to Genghis Khan's military talent and Yelu Chucai's assistance in political management.

After he smashed the Jin army in May 1215, Genghis Khan stopped his troops in Huanzhou and summoned the most talented people from the Liao and Jin kingdoms to his palace. At that time, Yelu Chucai was young but looked mature and experienced. He was eight feet tall, with a big head, loud voice and a beautiful long beard. At a glance, this young man impressed Genghis Khan. The khan said, "I defeated the Jin Kingdom for your revenge." Yelu Chucai replied, "From the generations of my father and grandfather, our people were held as hostages to serve the Jin Kingdom. Once we become the subjects of the kingdom, how can we not be loyal or hold a grudge against the emperor?" Touched by Yelu Chucai's personal integrity and lofty attitude, Genghis Khan decided to keep him as an adviser in his house.

After Genghis Khan returned to Lu Lian riverside, one of his trusted bowyers, a man from Tangwuxi, boasted of his own skills and challenged the young new adviser by saying, "The country is going to war. What is the interest in bringing pure scholars like Yelu Chucai?" Yelu replied calmly, "It is true that bowyers are required to make a bow, but for ruling the country, it needs a capable man." Genghis Khan trusted him even more after hearing that story. That trust was so deep that Genghis Khan immediately stopped his invasion to the west when Yelu Chucai, who also joined the expedition, warned him that killing would only bring more disasters. When he was dying, Genghis Khan highly recommended Yelu Chucai to his sons.

Genghis Khan was seriously ill and confined to bed in July 1227. He knew his time was coming and called his third son, Ogedei, and fourth son, Tuo Lei, to his bedside, where he told the brothers to be close with each other. He also shared his strategy for conquering the Jin Kingdom: "The strongest army of the Jin Kingdom is based in Tongguan, a place with mountains in the south and near the Yellow River on the north. It is difficult to conquer frontally, but if you seek to borrow the road from the Song Kingdom, since the Song and Jin Kingdoms have been enemies for generations, the Song Kingdom will agree to lend the road as required. In that way we can send troops to invade the Tang and Zheng states (both in today's Henan Province) and even Bianjin City (the capital of the Jin Kingdom). When Jin is in imminent danger, they will transfer the army based in Tongguan and, at that time, we can win by defeating the exhausted army after its long trip." He also said, "After I die, do not announce the news to avoid it being known by our enemy. When the emperor, soldiers and civilians from Western Xia State go out of town at a particular moment, destroy all of them immediately." After all the military arrangements, Genghis Khan, ended his magnificent and colourful life full of achievements. Following Genghis Khan's last will, his body was returned to his birthplace in Mongolia and buried on the Mountain of Burkhan. His tomb was buried deep to the north and flattened by thousands of horses. A later generation then built the "white room on earth," now known as "Genghis Khan s Tomb."

Devoting Myself to the World Without Personal Gain

After 200 years of ups and downs, the Ming Dynasty (1368–1644) was riddled with crises during the Jiajing Period (1522–66). Yan Song and his son took this oppurtunity to do evil, taking bribes and perverting justice. Against such a background, the head of the cabinet Prime Minister Zhang Juzheng, a man of humble birth, was pushed to the front of history's stage. With extraordinary courage and wisdom, Zhang reorganised the ruling laws and regulations, consolidated national defence and implemented the *Single Whip Law*, which commuted all taxes and labour obligations into silver payments, helping the dying Ming Dynasty regain vigour and vitality. Zhang Juzheng is known as an "outstanding prime minister" for his tremendous achievements in history.

Zhang Juzheng (1525–84) was born in Jiangling, Jinzhou (now Hubei Province). In the first year of Emperor Longqing (reign: 1567–72), as an old minister of Emperor Yu, Zhang Juzheng joined the cabinet and participated in state affairs by working as a vice-minister of the Ministry of Personnel and was grand scholar at the Pavilion of the Imperial Library. In April that year, he was promoted to director of the Ministry of Rites and grand scholar at Wuying Palace. Zhang Juzheng did not seek glory in his personal career; instead, he oversaw defence and consolidation of the border areas with the support of Prime Minister Xu Jie and Gao Gong, an official with a key position in the cabinet.

Through his analyses of the social reality, Zhang Juzheng understood that an empire's weakness was caused by malpractise within the government. To this end, Zhang decided to start his reforms by overhauling the government, aiming to establish "a rich and prosperous country with strong military forces." He required the supreme ruler of the feudal society to hold the financial strings tightly and exercise economy in daily life. Zhang mentioned to Emperor Wanli (reign: 1572–1620) many times the need for "costs saving and loving your people in order to maintain the source of the country." He also sought to clamp down on imperial spending on luxury items. In the seventh year of Wanli, Emperor Shenzong asked the Ministry of Revenue for 100,000 taels of silver for the renovation of the Guanglu Temple, but Zhang spoke against the project, saying in a statement: "At present, we are barely self-sufficient. If natural disasters like droughts or floods happen, how can we support the victims?" He urged the emperor to "avoid all unnecessary expenditures." As a result, not only was the request for 100,000 taels of silver rejected, even the budget for lights and flower lanterns for decorating the palace during the Lantern Festival was withdrawn. Zhang Juzheng also succeeded in suspending the renovation of Ciqing Palace, Cining Palace and Wuqing Palace, cutting monetary rewards, cutting the royal budget for clothes and reducing weavings from the Susong and Yingtian weaving centres. The consumption of luxury goods by the feudal rulers was finally under firm control.

Zhang Juzheng applied the same frugality to himself. It was customary to award his position a banquet after compiling and editing the written records of the late emperor. However, Zhang Juzheng rejected the banquet, saying, "One banquet normally cost hundreds of pieces of gold; it is also a way to save money to cancel it." He urged Emperor Wanli to attend lectures during the day rather than at night to save on the cost of providing lights and fires. Zhang Juzheng not only performed his official duties honestly when overhauling the government and seeking savings, he also applied strict requirements to his family members. Once, when his son returned to Jiangling for examinations, Zhang asked his son to pay for the transport himself. On his father's birthday, he asked the servant to ride a donkey back to his hometown with a birthday present to join the celebration. In the eighth year of Wanli, Zhang's second brother, Zhang Jujing, became seriously ill and needed to return to his hometown. Zhang Lu, the governor of Baoding made an exception and issued a "Kan He" (a certificate for using posts where couriers changed horses or rested) for him. Zhang Juzheng returned the certificate immediately, and attached a letter, saying that when implementing the country's laws and regulations, one cannot set an indecent living example himself.

For the Ming Dynasty, Zhang Juzheng was indeed a rare talent in national administration. When facing cruel internal fighting inside the cabinet and with his political career at stake, he wrote one line, "Willing to devote myself to the world while considering no personal gains and interests." He did what he said. In addition, his implementation of the regulation known to the later generations as the *Single Whip Law*, to a certain extent, eased burdens on the general public and mitigated imminent class contradictions, playing a positive role in the development of history.

Heroic Legends

"**Y**ou marched out on a long journey but never returned, with swords and bows, fighting to your last breath. Your bravery and heroism will never fade, so you will become deities after death.…" This lament by the great ancient poet Qu Yuan memorialised the death of soldiers.

With the passage of time, many of the compelling scenes of war that have long inspired the imaginations of the Chinese people are fading into history. However, heroic figures and their legends will never fade or be forgotten by posterity. On the contrary, their spirit of "righteousness in peacetime and sacrifice in troubled times" has been the indispensable anchor of Chinese culture.

Su Wu, the Chinese envoy to the Western Regions, suffered hardships near the North Sea but remained loyal to the Western Han Dynasty (206 BC–AD 24); Yue Fei during the Southern Song Dynasty (1127–1279) was unyielding in his defence of his country against Jin (1115–1234) aggression; Zheng Chenggong, a hero in the late-Ming and early Qing Dynasty (1644–1911), led bravely, and Taiwan was returned to the homeland after 38 years of Dutch rule; Lin Zexu, at Humen Estuary, safeguarded the dignity and interests of China.

……

Many other national heroes have demonstrated their bravery at critical moments in the country life, winning the praise of later generations.

General Huo Qubing of the Western Han Dynasty fought against the Huns several times and finally ended Hun threats to the Western Han Dynasty; Yu Qian, a Ming Dynasty minister of war, won the War of Defending Jingshi (today's Beijing) and brought safety to the Ming; Politician Shi Kefa of the late-Ming Dynasty was captured yet remained loyal to the Ming.

Guan Tianpei of the late-Qing Dynasty sacrificed himself in the war against British invaders and made contributions to maintaining national sovereignty.

There have been many heroes in Chinese history. They have sacrificed for the nation and persevered through hardships. They symbolise the cohesion of the Chinese nation and have won the respect of the people.

Remaining Loyal to Han while Exiled with Sheep at the North Sea

Su Wu came from Duling (today's Xi'an in Shaanxi Province). He was honest, upright and daring. In 100 BC, Han Emperor Wu sent Su Wu as an envoy to the Western Regions. Upon receiving the emperor's order, he led his deputy Zhang Sheng, his retainer Chang Hui and a team of more than a hundred from Chang'an to the court of the king of the Huns. However, as Su Wu was about to return, an incident occurred that was to thrust him into a historical spotlight. The roots of the incident date back to before Su Wu left Chang'an. Wei Lu, a Han official, defected to the Huns whose king made him a prince. Wei Lu's subordinate, Yu Chang, who was discontent with Wei Lu, planned with Zhang Sheng to kidnap the Hun king's mother and take her back to Han territory, but the plot was thwarted by an informer, and Yu Chang was arrested. The king was furious and ordered Wei Lu to investigate. Zhang Sheng, fearful of being given away by Yu Chang, told Su Wu the whole story, which made Su Wu nervous, because he feared the incident might destroy the improving relationship between the two peoples. Sure enough, Yu Chang gave Zhang Sheng away. The angry Hun king demanded the Han envoy to defect. When Su Wu was brought in front of the king, the patriotic envoy attempted to commit suicide with a sword. The king respected this act of loyalty and asked Wei Lu to persuade Su to switch sides.

After Su Wu recovered, the king had him and Zhang Sheng witness the trial of Yu Chang in order to frighten them into defecting. However, despite the use of both threats and persuasion, Su Wu remained adamant. Seeing that Su Wu would never defect, Wei Lu reported the fact to the king who then put Su Wu in a big cellar without food and water. Su Wu managed to stay alive by eating snow mixed with felt for several days. Amazed by Su Wu's perseverance, the king sent him to a no-man's land on the coast of the North Sea to shepherd rams. He told Su Wu he could return home only when the rams (male sheep) gave birth to lambs. Su Wu had to steal fruit from the dens of voles because he had no reliable source of food. Despite hardships, he kept his envoy's mace, though the yak tails on the mace peeled off completely.

Five years passed before Prince Yuqian, the king's younger brother, went to the North Sea to hunt and spotted Su Wu spinning nets for hunting and mending bows. He thought highly of Su Wu, so he left him a large supply of clothes and food. Three years later, Prince Yuqian became critically ill. He sent Su Wu many horses, livestock, vessels and tents before he died. Unfortunately, people from Dingling stole the livestock, so Su Wu fell back into poverty.

In 99 BC, Li Ling led 5,000 troops to attack the Huns north of Juyan Lake, only to be surrounded by 80,000 Hun troops. After a desperate battle, Li Ling surrendered to the Huns, who was at first ashamed to meet his friend Su Wu. However, after the Dingling people stole Su Wu's livestock, their relationship resumed. The king asked Li Ling to bring Su Wu round to defecting. Li Ling went to the North Sea and entertained Su Wu. Then he began to persuade him, "If you can never return to Han and suffer from the hardship in this barren land, who will know your loyalty to the Han Dynasty?" Li Ling told Su Wu about the "death and exile of his family and dozens of innocent ministers have been executed with their families." Your fate is still uncertain, so why on earth do you remain loyal to such a dynasty?"

Su Wu answered, "My father and I were both promoted to high positions by the emperor, so we owe his majesty a great debt of gratitude. Today, I'm honoured to have this opportunity to sacrifice for the nation and I'm most willing to do so." After several days of attempted persuasion, Li Ling failed to bring Su Wu around, so he bade him farewell in shame and asked his wife to send Su Wu dozens of cattle and sheep. In 87 BC, Li Ling told Su Wu about the death of Emperor Wu. Su Wu was extremely sad and wailed towards the south. In 85 BC, the king of the Huns died and his kingdom fell into disorder. The new king was unable to fight the Han Dynasty, and he sent envoys to the Han to seek peace. The new Han Emperor Zhao sent envoys in return, demanding the release of Su Wu. The Huns deceived the envoys and told them Su Wu had died. However, the Han envoy learned the truth: Su Wu was still alive and caring for livestock at the North Sea. When he paid audience to the king of the Huns, the envoy said, "You Huns should not try to cheat the Han Dynasty if you really want to make peace. Our emperor shot down a wild goose at the imperial garden and found a cloth fastened to one of the legs. The words on it say Su Wu is still alive." The king apologised to the envoy and released Su Wu."

Su Wu went to the land of the Huns as an envoy at age 40 and spent 19 years hardship there. On the day of his return to Chang'an, all the residents of the city came out to welcome him. They were all deeply moved when they saw the bare mace in Su Wu's hands.

Rank, Honour As Dust
Conducting Expeditions Day and Night

Yue Fei (1103–1141) came from a poor farming family in Tangyin, Xiangzhou of Hebei Xilu (today's Henan Province). He studied *Zuoshi Chunqiu (Zuo's Spring and Autumn)* and military strategies and also mastered martial arts. At 19, he joined the army to fight Liao invaders. When the Jin army invaded the ancient Central Plain in 1126, he rejoined the army and fought against the invaders. It was said that Yue's mother Yao tattooed his back with four characters meaning "repay the country with supreme loyalty and patriotism," which became his lifelong motto.

Yue Fei was quickly promoted for his bravery. Yue was highly appreciated by deputy commander Zong Ze "as intelligent and as brave as famous ancient generals" in the battle against Jin invaders. In 1126, Kaifeng was occupied, Emperors Hui and Qin were captured and the Northern Song Dynasty (960–1127) ended. In 1127, Zhao Gou (Emperor Gaozong) ascended the throne and moved the capital to Lin'an. Yue Fei submitted a proposal to the emperor to recover the lost territory, but was demoted. Then, he followed General Du Chong to defend Kaifeng again.

In 1129, General Wuzhu of Jin invaded southward and Du Chong fled Kaifeng and surrendered to Jin. As a result, the Jin army crossed the Yangtze River and took Lin'an, Yuezhou (today's Shaoxing) and Mingzhou, forcing Emperor Gaozong to escape to the sea. Yue Fei led an insurgent army to fight inside the occupied territory and won six consecutive victories. Later, he rescued the besieged Changzhou with four victories. In 1130, he ambushed and defeated Wuzhu at Niutou Mountain, reclaimed Jiankang and forced the Jin army to retreat to the north. In July, he was promoted to general in charge of the garrison in Tongzhou and Taizhou, commanding more than 10,000 troops, which he turned into the disciplined and valiant Yue Army.

In 1133, Emperor Gaozong awarded the banner "Yue Fei the Loyal" to Yue Fei for his achievements in wiping out bandits. In April the next year, he marched northwards, defeated enemies and recovered six counties and was promoted to commander-in-chief of the Qingyuan army. In 1135, he suppressed an uprising led by Yang Yao and then strengthened his Yue Army with the 50,000–60,000 troops who had surrendered.

In 1136, Yue Fei conducted second northward expedition and recovered Yiyang, Luoyang, Shangzhou and Guozhou. However, he was isolated without reinforcements or provisions. He retreated to Ezhou (today's Wuchang in Hubei Province) and wrote the poem *Man Jiang Hong*:

Rage bristling under the cap,

I lean against the railing;
The rushing rain has ceased.
Lifting my eyes towards the sky,
I let out a battle cry;
My blood is boiling.
Thirty years: rank and honour, just so much dust;
Eight hundred leagues: travelling with the moon and clouds.
Do not let it slip away;
When a young man's head turns grey,
Regret will be too late.

The national insult
Is yet to be avenged;
Your servant's shame:
When will it be erased?
Let us ride the long chariots
To crush those mountain strongholds.
Glorious quest: to feast on the flesh of the invaders.
We laugh and chat and quench our thirst with Tartar blood.
Let us start
To take back our rivers and mountains,
And report to the Heavenly Palace.

In 1139, Emperor Gaozong and Minister Qin Hui negotiated peace with the Jin Dynasty and the Southern Song agreed to render tribute to the Jin, which infuriated Yue Fei. The next year, General Wuzhu broke the peace treaty and launched another southward expedition. Yue Fei was ordered to mount a counterattack and recovered Zhengzhou and Luoyang. Wuzhu decided to unite all its forces to attack Yancheng, where Yue Fei was stationed. Yue Fei ordered his son Yue Yun to attack the enemy's front. He told his son, "If you cannot succeed, you will be executed." Yue Yun fought vigorously and took over Zhuxian County. Wuzhu was forced to withdraw from Kaifeng.

In Zhuxian County, Yue Fei strengthened his troops and prepared for an expedition across the Huanghe River. At the time, Emperor Gaozong and Qin Hui only wanted peace with the Jin, and they issued 12 consecutive golden orders of withdrawal. Yue Fei was unable to resist his grief and indignation. He sighed, "Ten years of efforts are about to be in vain. All territory recovered is going to be lost again. The dynasty may never rejuvenate and prosperity may never be restored."

Yue Fei was removed from military command and appointed a deputy privy councillor. Yue Fei's execution came to be a prerequisite for peace with Jin. Qin Hui made a false charge of treason against Yue Fei and put him in jail. On December 29, 1142, Yue Fei was poisoned at Fengbo Pavilion in Lin'an on groundless charges at age 39. His son Yue Yun and Lieutenant Zhang Xian were also executed. Yue Fei's case was redressed, and he was posthumously granted the title of Prince of E by Emperor Ningzong.

Yue Fei was a military strategist and tactician. He imposed strict discipline on his troops. His military philosophies, deployment strategies and tactics could be seen from his letters, memorials to the emperor and poems, which were compiled into book *Yuewumu Yiwen (Selected Essays of General Yue Fei)*.

Leave a Loyal Heart
Shining in Pages of History

When the Southern Song Dynasty (1127–1279) was in its death throes, Wen Tianxiang unremittingly resisted Yuan (1271–1368) invaders. Even when the Southern Song Dynasty was conquered, he remained loyal and sacrificed for his nation.

Wen Tianxiang (1236–83) came from Luling in Jizhou (today's Ji'an in Jiangxi Province) and obtained the first rank in the imperial examination in 1256.

In January 1276, Empress Dowager Xie appointed Wen as prime minister and privy councillor and asked him to negotiate with the commander of Yuan troops Bo Yan. But Bo Yan detained Wen, intending to use Wen's prestige to conquer the Southern Song. But Wen would have died rather than surrender, and was escorted north. Wen managed to escape from his escorts and returned to Fuzhou in May 1276 and was appointed as right-side prime minister by Emperor Duanzong (1276–78). At the time, Empress Dowager Xie had already surrendered to Yuan troops, who occupied Lin'an.

Wen continued to resist Yuan invaders in collaboration in Zhangzhou and Meizhou in Fujian Province. In the summer of 1277, Wen led troops to attack Jiangxi, Ganzhou and Jizhou and recovered many counties and towns. Li Heng, Yuan governor of Jiangxi, lodged a counterattack from Xingguo County and defeated Wen. Then, Wen retreated to Xunzhou (today's Longchuan, Guangdong Province). In the summer of 1278, Wen heard the government-in-exile was stationed in Yashan, so he wanted to go there, but was refused by Zhang Shijie. Wen had to retreat to Chaoyang County. In the winter of that year when Yuan troops stormed the place, Wen retreated to Haifeng, only to be captured by Zhang Hongfan, a Yuan general.

After an unsuccessful suicide attempt, Wen was escorted to Yashan by Zhang Hongfan, who ordered Wen to write a letter to persuade Zhang to surrender. Wen said, "I cannot protect my parents. How can I ask others to betray theirs?" Wen wrote the poem *"Guo Lingdingyang" ("On Crossing the Lonely Ocean")*. The last two sentences of the poem, "All men are mortal; let me leave a loyal heart shining in the pages of history," moved Zhang.

Yuan Emperor Shizu, or Kublai Khan (1260–94) ordered Zhang to escort Wen to Dadu (today's Beijing) and put him under house arrest in the Huitong Mansion. The emperor sent the former prime minister of Southern Song Liu Mengyan and former Emperor Gongdi (1274–76) of the Southern Song, who had surrendered to the Yuan, to persuade Wen Tianxiang to give up. But Wen became furious as soon as he saw Liu; he knelt facing north and wailed to the emperor, "Please return, your majesty." Emperor Shizu was enraged and ordered others to bind Wen's hands, shackle him and throw him into the Ministry of Defence jail.

The trial was presided over by Boluo, the Yuan's prime minister. At the hall of the Privy Council, Wen stood upright and gave Boluo a salute. Boluo asked Wen if he had anything to say. Wen answered fearlessly, "It is unavoidable that one dynasty rises while another falls. There must be some loyalists who die for their country. I would like to die loyal to the Song Dynasty!" Boluo was infuriated and said, "You'll be jailed!"

Wen was jailed for three years. He received a letter from his daughter Liuniang and knew his wife and two daughters were now maids in the imperial palace. The letter sent a message: "surrender for family reunion." Wen expressed his agony and great pain in the letter to her daughter, saying: "Who has no passion for their families? However, it is righteous for me to sacrifice, which is my destiny." Wen wrote many famous poems, including the third volume of *"Zhinan Houlu" ("The Latter Guide")* and *"Zhengqi Ge" ("The Song of Righteousness")*.

In December 1282, Emperor Yuan Shizu awarded Wen a senior position and attempted to persuade him to defect. Wen said, "I'm a prime minister of Song. Now that the country has perished, I only want to die quickly." The emperor was infuriated and ordered the execution of Wen. On the following day, Wen was escorted to Caishikou, the place of execution. The executioner asked him, "If you say something, maybe you will be spared." Wen said austerely, "Nothing!" He then knelt down southwards and said, "I have fulfilled my duty to my heart's content!" He died with composure at age 47. After his death, a poem was found in his pocket, "Confucius required benevolence and Mencius required righteousness. One achieves benevolence only through being righteous. What is the point of learning the teachings of sages? From now on I shall have no regrets."

My Wish Is not to Attain Titles But Peace on Coast

During the early Ming Dynasty, a batch of Japanese pirates came to loot the coast of China. Some local officials, gangsters, merchants and criminals colluded with Japanese pirates so that they pillaged the coasts of Zhejiang, Fujian and Guangdong without restraint. In 1553, large numbers of pirates, led by their heads Wang Zhi and Xu Hai, landed in Zhejiang and Jiangsu provinces and harassed dozens of cities such as Chongming, Shanghai, Taizhou, Wenzhou, Ningbo and Shaoxing.

To protect themselves, people living on the coast began to fight the pirates. Among them, Qi Jiguang was the most outstanding general and a national hero.

Qi Jiguang (1528–87) came from Dengzhou of Shandong. He was eager to learn, especially religious scriptures and history. In 1544, he became a commander in Dengzhou at 17 and began to defend the area against Japanese pirates, whose looting infuriated the young man.

In 1555, as pirates became more rampant and aggressive, the government had no choice but to transfer Qi Jiguang from Shandong to Jiangsu and Zhejiang. Qi Jiguang was appointed as a general in Ningbo, Shaoxing and Taizhou, places infested by Japanese pirates. Fighting side by side with Qi Jiguang were Tan Lun and Yu Dayou. Tan Lun later became the immediate superior of Qi Jiguang and gave him support.

Once in Zhejiang, Qi Jiguang and Yu Dayou encircled and annihilated the Japanese who had landed in Longshansuo through three successful battles. But, Qi Jiguang noticed discipline among the Ming troops was slack. At the end of one battle, a soldier came to report an achievement with a skull, while another soldier came crying, "It is the head of my brother, who was injured…."

Qi decided to organise a new, more disciplined army. He went to Yiwu in Zhejiang to enlist new soldiers. He rejected all the sly, timid and roguish candidates and handpicked 3,000 muscular, daring, persevering and agile peasants and miners to form a new army. After months of training, it grew into a disciplined and brave army that was later regarded as benevolent troops. Qi led this army across battlefields in Zhejiang and Fujian and won numerous victories, earning himself the nickname of "Tiger Qi" by pirates. The people called his troops the "Qi Army."

In 1559, Qi Jiguang joined forces with Tan Lun to suppress pirates who were pillaging Taizhou. After a series of battles, they drove the pirates to South Bay in Taiping (today's Wenling in Zhejiang Province). The pirates stuck to the hills on the coast and put up a stiff resistance. Qi and his younger brother Qi Jimei were directing the battle at the front. They both shot an arrow and killed the two heads of the pirates. The pirates were frightened, cowering; the Qi Army swarmed to the hilltop. All pirates were either slain or fell into the sea and drowned.

Later, Qi led his army in combating pirates in Fujian. Hengyu, a small island off the northeast coast of Ningde, had been occupied by more than 1,000 pirates for three years. Qi dispatched his soldiers to reconnoitre the landform, waterways and tides of the island before formulating tactics. He asked each soldier to carry a bundle of hay and throw the hay into the water to pave a path for the troops. The battle ended in victory, with the pirates killed, captured or drowned in the sea.

Qi won numerous battles at Niutian, Lindun, Pinghaiwei, Xianyou and Xinghua. In 1566, he suppressed Wu Ping, a pirate who occupied Nan'ao Island and colluded with Japanese pirates. Finally, the Japanese pirates that had attacked the southeast coast for decades were annihilated.

Qi Jiguang directed dozens of battles against pirates over a decade. His great achievements were and are still glorified by the Chinese people. His effective strategies and tactics in those battles became a valuable legacy for the Chinese in resisting aggressions.

Strait Will Be Crossed, Land Belongs to Emperor

Zheng Chenggong was born in Hirado, Japan, in 1624, the eldest son of Zheng Zhilong. In August 1646, Qing troops occupied Zhejiang and Fujian provinces. Zheng Zhilong surrendered. At the time, Zheng Chenggong, a young admiral at the age of 22 advised his father not to do so, but to no avail. Infuriated, he fled to Nan'ao Island and organised an army of several thousand to fight against the Qing troops and controlled the sea off the coast of Fujian, Zhejiang and Guangdong.

The Qing Dynasty failed to persuade Zheng to defect. Zheng remained adamant and broke off relations with his father.

Zheng Chenggong established a navy in Xiamen and united forces with anti-Qing general Zhang Huangyan. They led a navy of 170,000 troops to attack Nanjing along both a land route and a waterway. However, Qing troops tricked him with a false surrender and Zheng retreated to Xiamen. Qing troops blocked all supplies to Zheng's troops. Facing difficulties, Zheng decided to take Taiwan as a base for further development.

Taiwan has been part of China since ancient times. Zheng had been to Taiwan with his father when he was young and grew acquainted with the miseries of the people there; so regaining Taiwan was one of his ambitions. He made up his mind to act and ordered the preparation of ships and provisions.

At this moment, He Tingbin, an interpreter working among the Dutch troops, went to Xiamen to see Zheng Chenggong; there, he gave him a map of Taiwan, with Dutch military deployments marked on it.

In March 1661, Zheng asked his son Zheng Jing to garrison Xiamen while he led 25,000 troops to sail from Jinmen on hundreds of warships across the Taiwan Straits to attack Taiwan. At the time, some of his troops heard of the power of Dutch cannons and were frightened. Zheng arranged his warship at the front row of offensive formation and encouraged his troops, "Don't fear the Dutch cannons. Just follow my ship."

The Dutch invaders concentrated their troops in two fortresses at Taiwan (today's Dongping in Taiwan) and Chikan (today's Tainan) and sank many old ships in the port to prevent the landing of Zheng's navy. Zheng asked He Tingbin to pilot the fleet into Lu'ermen (today's Dongping, Taiwan) during high tide. After the troops landed on the beach, the people welcomed them with tea. The Dutch commander in the fortress dispatched 100 soldiers, but they were encircled by Zheng's troops. The head was killed and the rest fled in panic.

The Dutch then sent their largest warship, the *Hector*, to prevent Zheng's troops from landing. A well-composed Zheng directed his 60 ships to encircle the *Hector*. Then he ordered all 60 ships to fire, which set the *Hector* ablaze before it sunk. Three Dutch ships fled. After the defeat, the Dutch holed up in two fortresses. They sent envoys to ask for peace with Zheng while secretly asking for reinforcements from Batavia (today's Java). The Dutch said that they were willing to pay 100,000 taels of silver if Zheng left Taiwan.

Zheng replied, "Taiwan is Chinese territory, so we will take it back. If you do not go, then we will drive you out!" After repelling the Dutch envoys, Zheng ordered his troops to attack Chikan, but met with strong resistance. A local resident told Zheng that the water supply for Chikan came from a highland outside, suggesting that if the water supply were blocked, the Dutch would be doomed. Zheng accepted this idea and the Dutch in Chikan surrendered within three days.

Zheng decided to lay siege the fortress to force the Dutch invaders to surrender. After eight months, Zheng ordered a violent offensive. The Dutch surrendered, raising white flags. In early 1662, the head of the Dutch came to the headquarters of Zheng to sign the note of surrender. Taiwan returned to China after 38 years of occupation.

After recovering Taiwan, Zheng changed the name of Chikan to Chengtian, which administered two counties: Tianxing and Wannian counties. He named Taiwan "The East Capital." He abolished the Dutch colonial system and began reforms. He fostered trade, established schools, and encouraged the people to migrate from the Chinese mainland to Taiwan to cultivate virgin land, which marked a new chapter in the history of the island. Five months after the recovery of Taiwan, Zheng Chenggong died at the age of 39.

A Day of Universal Grief
Since You Are Spirit of Navy

Deng Shichang (1849–94) came from Panyu County in Guangdong Province. At 14, he was admitted into the Fuzhou Academy of Navy. In 1879, he was transferred to the North Sea Fleet and was appointed a captain of the *Zhiyuan*. Deng was diligent and meticulous in fulfilling his duty. He lived a simple life and was close to his fellows. In 1894, the Sino-Japanese War of 1894–95 broke out. Qing troops suffered a defeat in Asan in northern Korea and Minister Li Hongzhang sent reinforcements there.

On September 17, 1894, the North Sea Fleet led by Admiral Ding Ruchang encountered the Japanese Navy on the Huanghai Sea off the coast of Dadonggou at the estuary of the Yalu River. Ding was severely wounded; his flag was shot down by enemy gunfire, and the whole fleet lost its command. At this critical juncture, Deng volunteered to command the fleet and decided to fight to the last breath. He told the sailors on the ship, "In case of an emergency, we'll sink together with Japanese ships."

During the battle, the signal system of the flagship *Dingyuan* was destroyed and the whole fleet was in disarray. Then, Deng ordered the *Zhiyuan* and its fleet into the enemy formation and inflicted considerable damage on Japan's fleet. However, Japanese ships later regained the upper hand. Deng and the fleet did not retreat; he stood upright at the command tower and shouted to his fellows, "We've made up our mind to sacrifice for the country. We may die, but we must do justice to the motherland by upholding the spirit of our navy."

The *Zhiyuan* was damaged and was doomed to sink. When the Japanese cruiser *Yoshino* moved in front of the *Zhiyuan*, Deng knew that it was the biggest threat to the North Sea Fleet. Sinking it would tip the balance in the battle. Deng then told Lieutenant Chen Jinkui, "*Yoshino* is the key for the enemy. If we sink it, then we can win." Chen agreed. Then Deng moved *Zhiyuan* towards the *Yoshino* firing all the way. In a panic, several Japanese ships fired at the *Zhiyuan*. Unfortunately, the torpedoes carried on the *Zhiyuan* detonated, which exploded and sank within minutes.

After Deng fell into the water, Lieutenant Liu Zhong threw a life ring to him, but Deng refused to take it. When a torpedo boat came to rescue him, he refused to board the ship. His pet dog Solar swam to his side and held his arm, but he pushed it away. When Solar held his plait to keep him afloat, Deng embraced it and sank together with it.

Emperor Guangxu was moved by the heroism of Deng Shichang. He granted him the posthumous title of admiral and gave large grants to his family. He also conferred on him a mourning couplet: "The day was one of universal grief, since you are the spirit of the navy." He eulogised him with a poem: "The massive cannons on the fortress of our wicked adversaries nearly wiped us out, but you with *Zhiyuan* made the greatest achievements."

49

History as a Mirror

"Foreseeing the future by reviewing the past" is an example of Chinese wisdom and a guiding principle in Chinese history.

China's history of five millennia has left it with a splendid cultural heritage that serves as a wellspring of wisdom. It is a history of vivid stories of national elites, breathtaking scenes, mysterious legends and elegant soliloquies. In the gallery of historical figures, stories of sages and heroes are like musical notes that can be played to form a fascinating symphony.

The story of "carrying thorny grass and pleading guilt" that culminated in "the reconciliation of chief minister and general" went down in historical records and became a household story. Lin Xiangru and Lian Po were famed as the chief minister and a general of the Kingdom of Zhao. They cleared their mutual misunderstandings and became staunch allies in serving the kingdom.

Tao Kan (AD 259–334), a well-known general during the Eastern Jin (AD 317–420), developed a habit of moving a hundred bricks from his study to the courtyard in the morning, and then from the courtyard back to his study in the evening, reasoning that he needed to continue to exercise himself diligently. To reduce his expenditures, he even kept scraps from shipbuilding for future use. He was the governor and general of a region, but he remained diligent and thrifty. As a result, his subordinates dared not neglect their duties. His diligence and meticulousness were celebrated by later generations. Even today, he remains a vivid model for civil servants.

When it comes to upright and honest officials, the first and foremost example is the legendary Bao Zheng of the Northern Song Dynasty. Among legends there are The Seven Heroes and Five Gallants, The Five Junior Gallants, A Wild Cat Exchanged for a Crown Prince, Selling Rice at Chenzhou and The Case of Executing Chen Shimei. All the stories relate how Bao Zheng solved cases and convicted criminals in defiance of pressures from above.

During the Qing Dynasty, Ubashi Khan, a prince of Torghut, decided to lead his people away from the oppression of Imperial Russia and back to their ancestral homeland, encountering many obstacles along the way. Their story has long since been a symbol of multi-ethnic solidarity in China.

"I'd rather die than fail" was the oath of Feng Ru, a young scientist who devoted his entire life to the rise of China, specifically in the aviation sector. In his dying moments, he told his assistants to carry forward his wish to develop aviation in China.

These colourful stories constitute the spiritual wealth of the Chinese people, who have renewed their understanding and appreciation of their immortal value. In the face of complex problems, the Chinese tend to seek examples and ideas from history, which serves as a guideline for action and thought.

Broad-Mindedness Brings Reconciliation, Benefits for Country

Lian Po was an outstanding general of the Kingdom of Zhao during the Warring States Period (475–221 BC). In the 16th year of the reign of King Huiwen (298-266 BC), Lian Po led an army to defeat a force from the Kingdom of Qi and captured Yangjin. After that, he was granted the title of a senior noble and acquired a reputation for bravery among the kingdoms. Lin Xiangru was one of the courtiers of a senior eunuch Miao Xian in the Zhao States.

King Huiwen acquired the jade of the He family from the Kingdom of Chu. When King Zhao of Qin heard the news, he sent a message to Huiwen, saying he was willing to exchange 15 castles for the jade. King Huiwen, Lian Po and ministers met to discuss the issue. There was doubt whether King Zhao of Qin would honour his promise of 15 castles, even if they gave him the jade. However, if they refused the deal, the Kingdom of Qin might invade Zhao. Facing this dilemma, they sought a person who could be dispatched to the Kingdom of Qin as an envoy. Miao Xian recommended his courtier, Lin Xiangru. King Huiwen sent Lin Xiangru as the envoy carrying the jade to the Kingdom of Qin. Remarkably, Lin Xiangru was able to persuade the King of Qin to withdraw his request and allow Lin to return with the jade to King Huiwen, who was so impressed that he appointed Lin chief minister.

King Zhaoxiang of Qin had an abiding ambition to subjugate the Kingdom of Zhao, so he continually launched invasions. In 279 BC, he invited King Huiwen of Zhao to meet him at Mianchi in Qin territory. King Huiwen was fearful of being detained by the Qin. However, both General Lian Po and Chief Minister Lin Xiangru encouraged the king to take the risk. Finally, the king decided to go.

At the banquet of the summit, King Zhaoxiang of Qin, said to King Huiwen of Zhao, "I heard that you are good at playing zither. Would you like to play for us?" King Huiwen had no choice but to play a tune. A historian of the Kingdom of Qin immediately recorded the event, as "On the day of the Mianchi Summit, the King of Qin ordered the King of Zhao to play zither." This enraged King Huiwen. At this moment, Lin Xiangru took a bowl, knelt down in front of King Zhaoxiang and said, "The King of Zhao heard that your majesty is good at playing instruments of the Qin. So please play it as entertainment." King Zhaoxiang turned very angry. Lin Xiangru also turned furious and said, "Your majesty, how can you be so aggressive? I know the King of Qin is powerful, but I can now make a sacrifice in front of you, since I'm only five steps away from you." Seeing that Lin Xiangru was so aggressive, King Zhaoxiang had no choice but to strike the bowl several times. Lin Xiangru then asked a historian of Zhao to record the event, which read: "At the Mianchi Summit, the King of Qin struck a bowl for the King of Zhao." A Qin minister stood up and said to the King of Zhao, "Your majesty, please give 15 castles to the King of Qin for his longevity." Lin Xiangru also stood up and said to the King of Qin, "Your majesty, please give Xianyang to the King of Zhao for his longevity." Seeing a heated atmosphere and knowing of the deployment of Zhao's troops, King Zhaoxiang told his ministers to relax and said, "Today is a day for fun." In the end, the summit proceeded peacefully.

Lin Xiangru's great contributions came during the two missions that helped safeguard the Kingdom of Zhao's interests and won him the trust of King Huiwen. However, his promotion to chief minister placed him above Lian Po in ranking. Lian Po was very jealous and told his courtiers, "I'm the general of Zhao and I have made many contributions. What on earth has Lin Xiangru done for the country? I'll let him know my character when I meet him." When Lin caught wind of this, he feigned illness and kept away from government meetings. When Lian's carriage was going down the street, Lin's carriage turned and backed out of the street to let Lian Po pass. When Lin's chief courtier demanded to know why he was behaving in such a manner, Lin Xiangru asked those present, "Which one is more powerful, General Lian Po or the King of Qin?" His courtiers answered, "The King of Qin is certainly more powerful." Lin said, "Right, all kings and dukes are afraid of the King of Qin. However, I reprimanded him openly at his palace. The powerful Kingdom of Qin dares not to invade the Kingdom of Zhao, because I am in charge of the nation's government and General Lian Po the nation's security. If we two fall out, the King of Qin would take the opportunity to invade the Kingdom of Zhao. I cannot let our personal feud ruin the security of the kingdom, so I would rather be humble in front of General Lian Po."

When Lian Po heard of this, all his hatred turned to shame. Deciding to apologise to Lin, he strapped brambles to his bared back and walked from his house to that of Lin Xiangru's, begging for his forgiveness.

Lin Xiangru forgave him. The two became good friends and from then on worked together for the good of the kingdom.

Sawdust, Bamboo Bits Kept for Later Use

Tao Kan (AD 259–334), a diligent official, led an austere life, which won him an outstanding reputation.

After his father died while he was still very young, his family fell into abject poverty. His mother, Zhan, was a lady of strong character. She was determined her son would be somebody. Under her influence, Tao Kan studied diligently and was later was appointed a chief secretary of a county.

After the Eastern Jin Dynasty's capable General Zu Ti died, the reign experienced a lot of internal upheaval. Emperor Yuan (AD 317–420) of the Jin Dynasty intended to undermine the influence of the Wang family, so Wang Dun led troops to Jiankang and killed the ministers who opposed him. After Emperor Ming (AD 322–325) succeeded his father, Wang Dun launched another attack on Jiankang but failed. Later, he fell ill and died. During the reign of Emperor Cheng (AD 325–342 the son of Emperor Ming), Su Jun, the garrison general at Liyang (today's He County in Anhui Province), rebelled and took Jiankang by force. With ministers at their wits end in facing the seizure, Tao Kan, by then the governor of Jingzhou, led a force that crushed the rebellion within two years.

When Wang Dun was still influential, Tao Kan was his subordinate. He was then promoted to be governor of Jingzhou on the basis of his military contributions. People who were jealous of him framed charges against him, so Wang Dun shifted him to Guangzhou, a remote region, as a demotion. Once in Guangzhou, Tao Kan did not lose heart. He formed the habit of moving 100 bricks from his study out to the courtyard in the morning and moving them back into his study in the evening. People thought it very strange and asked him why he did so. Tao Kan said solemnly, "I'm now in the south, but my mind is full of the recovery of Central China. So I must exercise physically in order to take on responsibilities when called upon by the country."

After the demise of Wang Dun, Tao Kan was promoted to Zhengxi General and was reinstated as governor of Jingzhou. The people of Jingzhou, on hearing Tao Kan would come back, held celebrations to welcome him. Though he was back in favour, Tao Kan remained prudent. He was diligent in carrying out official duties and meticulous about details of government. He often told his subordinates, "Dayu was a sage, but he still cherished every moment of his life. We are far inferior to Dayu in terms of wisdom and ability, so we should make the best use of our lifetimes to serve the country and leave a good reputation."

Some of his subordinates liked drinking and gambling and were careless in carrying out their official duties. Tao Kan was very angry with them and confiscated their wine jars and gambling devices, which he threw into the river. He punished them by flogging, which served as a good deterrence to any future would-be offenders.

One day, Tao Kan saw a man carelessly picking a handful of rice grains from a field. Tao Kan asked the man why he did so. He answered, "I just picked them for fun." Tao Kan was infuriated and said, "You destroy farmers' crops for fun. How dare you!" Then he punished the man by flogging. This story inspired the local farmers to put even more effort into growing crops. As a result, Jingzhou gradually became a wealthy region.

As Jingzhou is located along the Yangtze River, there was a lot of sawdust and scraps of bamboo from shipbuilding yards. Tao Kan asked people to collect them and store them in warehouses. People were rather confused as to why but no one dared to challenge the instruction. Then during one Chinese New Year, Jingzhou officials came to visit Tao Kan at his residence. The ground outside the gate of the hall was very slippery because of melting snow, so Tao Kan asked people to take out the sawdust and spread it on the snow. On another occasion, the Jin navy needed bamboo nails to build warships. Tao Kan handed over the bamboo bits he had collected and his far-sightedness suddenly became clear, winning him even greater respect.

Tao Kan was a governor and general for 41 years and won great respect for his strictness, justness and care. It is said people enjoyed peace and prosperity under his administration.

Integrity, Honesty in Administration

Bao Zheng (AD 999–1062) came from Hefei in Luzhou (toady's Hefei in Anhui Province). As a child, Bao Zheng acquired a reputation for his filial piety and integrity. In 1027, he passed the national examination at the age of 28, and was then first appointed as an assistant in the Ministry of Justice. Later he was appointed governor of Jianchang County (today's Yongxiu in Jiangxi Province). Since his parents were old and did not want to move with him to his new post, Bao Zheng resigned and returned home to look after his parents. He won widespread applause from officials for his choice.

While Bao Zheng was the governor of Tianchang County (today's Tianchang in Anhui Province), there was a case in the county. A farmer tied his cow in his cowshed in the evening. The next morning, he found the cow lying on the ground and bleeding in the mouth. Prying its mouth open, he found that the tongue had been cut. Angry and sad, the farmer went to Bao Zheng to request an investigation. Bao Zheng, after thinking for a while, told the farmer, "Don't tell your neighbours about the incident. Go home and slaughter the cow." The farmer did as Bao Cheng told him. The next day, a person came to the government to file a charge against the farmer for illegal slaughtering. Bao Zheng took on a grave expression and shouted, "How dare you! You cut out the tongue of the cow, and now you try to frame the owner for the act." The man was frightened and knelt down. He pleaded guilty. Since then, Bao Zheng acquired a reputation for his detective work in cases.

Bao Zheng worked as a local governor in several places. Once he arrived at a new place, he would abolish a number of taxes and rectify unjust cases. Later, he was appointed as a consultant in the capital and made a lot of good proposals. In Kaifeng, the capital, embezzlement and bribery were rampant among senior officials. Emperor Ren wanted to enforce order in Kaifeng, so he appointed Bao Zheng as the mayor of the capital. After being appointed, Bao Zheng became determined to eliminate corruption.

According to Song Dynasty practise, a plaintiff had to ask a lawyer to write an indictment, which was then passed on to the mayor through a junior official. That enabled some lawyers and junior officials to blackmail plaintiffs. Bao Zheng abolished the rule, so people with grievances could go straight to the government and strike drums, opening the gate of the government for trials.

One year, Kaifeng was flooded and the Huimin River silted up. After an investigation, Bao Zheng discovered that a riverbank had been used by eunuchs and nobles to build gardens and pavilions. He immediately ordered their demolition. When a noble refused to do so, Bao Zheng sent officials to investigate; they discovered the land deed was counterfeit. Bao Zheng was furious; he ordered the noble to demolish the building and reported the case to the emperor. The noble was frightened and had to demolish his garden.

Hearing about Bao Zheng's strictness, nobles dared not violate the law. A senior official planned to send bribes to Bao Zheng, only to be told that Bao Zheng was famous for his integrity and honesty. The official was the former governor of

Duanzhou (today's Zhaoqing in Guangdong Province). Since the place was famous for ink stones, the governor was to send a number of ink stones to the palace. Usually, the governor of the city would commit embezzlement through the process. Normally, for every ink stone sent to the palace, there would be dozens of ink stones embezzled by the governor and then he would bribe his superiors with these ink stones. When Bao Zheng came to Duanzhou, he levied only the amount of ink stones sent to the palace, leaving no room of embezzlement for the governor. Later, Bao Zheng acquired a reputation as an official of integrity and uprightness.

Bao Zheng was very strict even with his family and relatives. Bao Zheng was extremely strict with his children. His eldest son was appointed an official at a local government. He was upright but died young. His youngest son was only five when Bao Zheng died. His instructions for his descendents was that anyone from the Bao family who had committed bribery or embezzlement at official positions was driven out of the family and not allowed to be buried in the ancestral graveyard after death. It is said that all his descendents abided by the instructions.

Bao Zheng was highly appreciated by Emperor Ren, who promoted him to be deputy privy councillor. As Bao Zheng remained an official of integrity, he was regarded as a model of good officials after his death. He was glorified as "Judge Bao." There were many stories about his law enforcement activities, which were written into plays and novels. Although some of the stories were legendary only, they expressed people's respect for upright officials.

Great Deeds Surpassed Ancient Leaders

The migration of the Torghut back to their homeland is a splendid chapter in the history of China during the grand peace of the reign of Emperors Kangxi and Qianlong.

After the Amursana Rebellion was suppressed in 1758, large numbers of Oirut nomads emigrated to avoid the wars. According to Prince Zhaolian's *Xiaoting Zalu (Records of Xiaoting)*, about 30 percent of the nomads fled to Russia and Kazakhstan. The nomads who had fled to Kazakhstan returned to China after peace was restored. Those Oirut who had fled to Russia went to join the Torghut since they originally belonged to the same group. Those new migrants were called New Torghut. However, the lower section of Volga River, where Torghut lived, was by no means a peaceful place. During the early 18th century, Torghut was gradually subjugated by Imperial Russia, and the Torghut people were constantly conscripted for the wars with Sweden and Turkey. Tens of thousands of Torghut died in those wars, which caused great resentment among the people. When he learned from the new Oirut immigrants that Dzungar nobles who suppressed the nomads had been eliminated by the Qing government and Xinjiang had been restored to peace, Ubashi Khan, the leader of the Torghut, thought about returning to the homeland. Those new Oirut immigrants, who saw the miseries of Torghut under the rule of Russia, missed their homeland and tried to persuade Ubashi Khan to return to Yili. After many meetings, Ubashi decided that, since the Torghut were Mongolian, they should return to China. They planned to depart in winter when the Volga River was frozen so that nomads living on both sides of the river could gather for departure. However, the winter that year was very warm, and the Volga did not freeze.

In October 1770, Ubashi Khan held a meeting of senior leaders. He put forward the reasons for a return migration: escaping from the oppression by Russians and the proximity to Tibet, which was convenient for Buddhist practises. Senior leaders made suggestions for the journey and brought the news back to their people. On January 15, 1771, Ubashi Khan gathered his people at the Rein Desert and announced his decision to migrate and his reasons: "The Russian Empress asked us to send the sons of our leaders to Saint Petersburg and ordered to conscript 10,000 young men. Within just a year, 80,000 men from our khanate have died as cannon fodder. To unshackle us from Russian oppression, we must return to our homeland. Then we can live with our compatriots and practise our religion." Tired of Russian oppression, the Torghut people strengthened their determination by shouting, "We don't want our descendents to be slaves. We shall return to our homeland."

Ubashi led the nomads living south of Volga River to begin the journey back to the homeland. The group totalled over 169,000 people in about 33,000 households. The migrants encountered numerous obstacles on their journey. To avoid Russian obstructions, Ubashi Khan told his people to discard all living utensils and to travel light. Within eight days, they crossed the grassland between the Volga and Urals and entered the snow-covered Kazakh grassland. After their departure, the Russian Government dispatched large numbers of Cossacks in pursuit. Torghut nomads defeated them and turned southwards into Kazakhstan towards Lake Balkhash. During the journey, the Torghut were robbed of their livestock and other belongings several times, so Ubashi Khan had to lead them cross a desert that stretches thousands of miles. They had to feed on the blood of cattle and horses, and disease halved the population of both people and livestock.

In June 1771, the Torghut arrived at the border pass at Ili after eight months. Emperor Qianlong thought highly of the return of the Torghut and believed that he should help them resettle. He said, "They returned from faraway places, which showed their confidence in the Chinese Government, so we have to plan for their permanent settlement." After days of planning, Emperor Qianlong set aside two million liang of silver from the coffers of Shaanxi Province to purchase materials in Gansu for the immigrants. In September 1771, Ubashi led Torghut leaders to pay a visit to the emperor, who awarded them generously.

Talent for Aviation
Road to National Rejuvenation

Feng Ru was born to a farming household in Xingpu Village in Enping County of Guangdong Province on January 12, 1883. As a child, he was clever and excelled at making kites and model vehicles and vessels out of mud and wood. As his family was poor, he dropped out of school and helped his father on the farm.

At the age of 12, he went to San Francisco with his uncle, a pedlar. After seeing the advanced manufacturing of the United States, he believed that technology was the only road to the rise of China. At the age of 18, he went to New York to study mechanics. Five years later, he became a mechanical engineer.

As Feng Ru was conducting research in mechanics, the Wright Brothers flew the first manned aircraft in the world in a test flight in Kitty Hawk, North Carolina, on December 17, 1903. The event was a sensation and inspired Feng Ru to develop aircraft. Feng Ru, then an accomplished engineer at the age of 22, saw the miseries of his compatriots. Since then, his ambition of "aviation for the rise of China" had drawn widespread support from overseas Chinese. A factory was established in Auckland, east of San Francisco in 1907. The first aircraft, named *Feng Ru I* was manufactured in 1909. Feng Ru himself was the test pilot but the aircraft crashed shortly after taking off. Fortunately, Feng Ru survived.

On January 18, 1911, Feng Ru piloted the *Feng Ru II* on a test flight. It took off and ascended to a height of 12 metres. It then circled a square for 1,600 metres before flying to the Bay of San Francisco. Four minutes later, the plane landed on the square where it took off. The flight covered a distance of 2,640 feet, 1,788 feet longer than the record set by the Wright Brothers. The performance of the plane was the most-advanced of the time, so a report, "China Surpasses the West in Aviation Technology," was published by a local newspaper noting the event.

In February 1911, Feng Ru turned down several invitations in the United States and returned to China with his assistants, research materials and two aircraft. After the 1911 Revolution, the Guangdong Revolutionary Military Government appointed him captain of the Air Force. Soon after, he established the Guangdong Aircraft Corporation at Yantang of Guangdong Province and became the chief engineer, the first aircraft factory in China. In March 1912, an aircraft similar to the *Feng Ru II* was manufactured, the first in China. Feng Ru is one of China's aviation pioneers.

To build support for aviation in China, Feng Ru made a number of demonstration flights. In April 1912, he made a flight in Taishan County, Guangdong Province, in which he made some minor modifications in accordance with the environment. On August 25 of the same year, another flight was made at Yantang in Guangdong. As it was bright on the day, there were many spectators. Before taking off, Feng Ru told the spectators about the manufacturing, usage and piloting of aircraft, which was applauded. Then, Feng Ru piloted the plane and it took off to a height of 120 feet before flying southeast for five miles. As the plane flew delicately, the spectators kept applauding enthusiastically. Feng Ru intended to fly higher, so he pulled at the joystick. As he pulled too hard, he lost control of the plane and crashed to the ground. Feng Ru was injured seriously on the head, chest and hip. While he was dying, he told his assistants the reason of the crash. With his last breath, he told his colleagues not to lose heart because of the accident. He died at the age of 29, sacrificing for Chinese aviation and leaving a shining chapter in the history of revolution in China.

Feng Ru devoted his life to aviation, which stimulated widespread support for the sector. During the three years from 1913 to 1915, a number of aviators, namely, Chen Guipan, Tan Gen, Tan Ming and Lin Fuyuan, came back from the United States, bringing their aircraft back to China. When Sun Yat-sen established the Guangdong Revolutionary Aviation Academy in 1924, the story of Feng Ru was used for patriotic education.

To honour Feng Ru and lament his death, Sun Yat-sen, China's interim president, issued an order to commend Feng Ru for his great contribution as a pioneer of Chinese aviation on November 16, 1912. His achievements were exhibited at the Museum of National History. One thousand yuan was allocated from state coffers as compensation for Feng's bereaved family. In accordance with Feng Ru's will, his children and assistants buried him at Huanghuagang. During the Cultural Revolution (1966–76), Feng Ru's tomb was destroyed and his remains were moved to a hill near Sanbaoxu in the eastern suburbs of Guangzhou. In 1980, Feng Ru's tomb was rebuilt at Huanghuagang and was declared as a key cultural heritage site of Guangzhou Municipality.

55

Chinese classical literature has a long history and is closely associated with China's history and culture; it represents and reflects our unique national character, inheritance and the characteristics of the times. It consists mainly of literature by the Han nationality, but it is also compatible with the literature of other ethnicities.

Preface

Chinese characters existed long before Chinese literary classics were created, although no one knows exactly when the first Chinese character was created.

The Chinese written language first emerged as our ancestors began to record daily events in their lives, and it has continued to evolve over several thousand years, up to today.

Chinese characters are used to record what people say and think. There are many stories about the origin of Chinese characters, from tying knots to keep track of events, and the eight trigrams, to the *Hetu* and *Luoshu* (two ancient Chinese diagrams that interpret the plan of stars and rivers) and to Cang Jie, the creator of Chinese characters and finally to the use of pictographs. From these unproven stories to the discovery a century ago of tortoise shells and animal bones of the Shang Dynasty (circa 16th–11th centuries BC) that bear inscriptions believed to be an early form of written language, Chinese scholars have never ceased studying the origin of Chinese characters. The use of written languages led human beings from their primitive stage to becoming creators of civilisations. If the earlier inscribed symbols are considered the beginning of our written language, then the primitive symbols found by archaeologists in the ruins of Jiahu, Wuyang County, in Henan Province are proof that the use of a written language in China dates to about 8,000 years ago. Chinese characters provide all Chinese people a cultural home. Chinese is a language full of cultural connotations and aesthetic beauty. With 1.6 billion people using Chinese today, it is the most widely used language in the world.

The total number of Chinese characters that exist or have existed remains a mystery. The history of Chinese dictionaries alone is a long one. The *Kangxi Dictionary*, a 42-volume Chinese dictionary compiled during the reign of Kangxi (1661–1722) of the Qing Dynasty (1644–1911), has 47,000 characters; the *Chinese Language Dictionary* (*Zhonghua da zidian*), compiled by Ouyang Bocun and others in 1915, has 48,000; the *Chinese–Japanese Dictionary*, compiled by Tetsuji Morohashi of Japan in 1959, has 49,964; the *Chinese Language Dictionary* (*Zhongwen da cidian*), compiled by Zhang Qiyun in 1971, has 49,888; and the *Chinese Dictionary* (*Hanyu da zidian*) has 60,370. The *Zhonghua Dictionary* (*Zhonghua zihai*), compiled by the Zhonghua Book Company Limited and the China Friendship Publishing House, has 85,568 characters, reputedly the most characters in any Chinese dictionary. Given such large numbers, it is almost impossible for anyone to know every Chinese character, much less use them fluently.

How many treasures are hidden in this "deep sea" of Chinese characters? How many of them are "shining stars" that people of the modern age still haven't had a chance to know or understand? Voluminous works were created by people who relied on clever combinations of Chinese characters throughout Chinese history. These works are like an old well that never runs dry, creating a vast and profound basis for studies of the ancient Chinese civilisation.

Chinese civilisation began with the emergence of the first Chinese characters; both have continued to evolve over 5,000 years. Innumerable people have devoted their lives to studying this civilisation, yet intense studies yield only a glimpse of this vast treasure. All descendants of the Chinese nation are filled with a sense of pride and awe when the meet with this unique heritage. The *Yongle da dian*, or *Great Encyclopaedia of Yongle*, which was completed in 1408 during the Ming Dynasty (1368–1644), has 11,095 volumes that contain 370 million characters. Its table of contents alone fills 60 volumes. It is a huge collection of 7,000–8,000 works written throughout the dynasties. The *Encyclopaedia Britannica* regards it as the biggest encyclopaedia ever created. *Siku quanshu*, or the *Complete Library in the Four Branches of Literature* was compiled under the aegis of Emperor Qianlong (reign: 1735–96) from 1772 to 1782. Its 3,503 classical works are contained in 36,000 volumes. The *Great Encyclopaedia of Yongle* and the *Complete Library in the Four Branches of Literature* are but two representatives of this large trove of ancient Chinese documentation. Other forms of creation that represent the essence of Chinese civilisation, such as architecture, music, dance, poetry and paintings, are too numerous to count. It would be impossible for even the best and most earnest scholars to examine China's entire cultural and historical heritage.

Studies of Chinese ancient civilisation are like quaint pagodas; generation after generation of writers, artists, musicians and architects have added poise and charm to this pagoda. People do not hesitate to pay homage to it.

Let's begin our exciting exploration of the Chinese culture via Chinese characters.

Writings Convey Truth

The term "classical" is used to refer to the most representative works within a civilisation. During the European Renaissance, literary theorists used excellent Greek and Roman works as examplars. In China, certain valuable literary works including original songs and myths handed down from ancient times, until the time of the May Fourth Movement (1919), are known as classical literature.

Chinese classical literature has a long history and is closely associated with the overall history and culture of China; it represents and reflects our unique national character, inheritance and the characteristics of the times. It consists mainly of literature by the Han nationality, but it is also compatible with the literature of other ethnicities. Whether Chinese ancient poetry, prose, drama or novels, they all have traceable histories and they are enriched, developed and perfected in both theory and creation.

The emergence of primitive dance is intimately related to early people's communal lives. In ancient times, people in villages made sacrifices to gods or ancestors as they began their spring planting to pray for good harvests. Primitive dances served as re-enactments of their daily living conditions, their celebrations and sacrificial activities. The ancients created new songs and dances every day, while never forgetting the ones they admired and respected. These songs became a fount for Chinese literature. Primitive myths, legends and songs were handed down from generation to generation in oral form; in time, these became part of the written record, and these ancient songs and myths became part of the Chinese literary saga.

During the pre-Qin literary period (before 221 BC), the main body of literary creation experienced an evolution from a creation of groups to creations of individuals. The poems in the *Shijing* (*Book of Songs*) were mostly group creations. It took hundreds of years for the first poet, Qu Yuan (340–278 BC) to emerge. After Qu Yuan, Song Yu (298–222 BC), Tang Le (290–223 BC), Jing Chai (290–223 BC), and other poets transformed the *Chu Ci (Songs of Chu)*, a style of poetry created by Qu Yuan, into *fu*, a music-free literary genre. The rich and colourful pre-Qin literature is a cornerstone of Chinese literature; it established poetry, prose, *fu* and various other literary styles, but it also became a starting point for the literary development of Chinese realism and romanticism.

Han Dynasty (206 BC–AD 220) literature inherited the *Book of Songs*, *Chu Ci* and the pre-Qin prose tradition, and vividly reflected the historical characteristics and demands of the times of the unified feudal empire. A unique contribution to Han Dynasty literature was the development of new forms of literature, such as *cifu*, a literary prose form similar to *fu* that was interspersed with verse; historical biography; and *Yuefushi* poetry, folk-style poetry and ballads popular during that era.

Between the Wei (AD 220–265) and Jin (AD 265–420) dynasties, individuals with literary reputations were considered literary and artistic celebrities. Their works reflected true feelings, "as natural as a lotus flower growing out of water," with no vulgar aesthetics that favoured the exaggeration of colours. The *Youjun* style of Wang Youjun (AD 321–379), also known as Wang Xizhi, sparkles with the clarity and elegance of dignified clerical script. The poems of Tao Yuanmin were also refined and elegant, carefree and leisurely, yet natural. The atmosphere of the Wei and Jin dynasties reflects the beginning of cultural consciousness and the origin of ideological emancipation.

The Tang Dynasty's (AD 618–907) open atmosphere created many eclectic poets with distinct personalities; the fame and reputation of each figure was powerful enough to shake the whole nation. In addition to Wang Bo (date of birth and death uncertain), Yang Jiong (AD 650–693), Lu Zhaolin (AD 637–689), Luo Binwang (AD 640–684), considered the "four great poets of the early Tang Dynasty," Li Bai (AD 701–762), Du Fu (AD 712–770), Li Shangyin (AD 813–858), Du Mu (AD 803–852), there were other famous Tang Dynasty poets such as He Zhizhang (AD 659–744), Li He (AD 790–861), Wang Zhihuan (AD 688–742), Meng Haoran (AD 689–740), Wang Wei (AD 699–761), Wang Changling (AD 698–756), Gao Shi (AD 700–765), Han Yu (AD 768–824), Liu Zongyuan (AD 773–819), Liu Yuxi (AD 772–842) and Bai Juyi (AD 772–846). Among these, Bai Juyi is one of the three great poets of the Tang Dynasty. He was the main advocate for the new musical conservatory movement and was sometimes referred to as "Yuan-Bai" along with Yuan Zhen (AD 779–831). Liu Zongyuan and Han Yu were the leaders of the Classical Chinese Literature Movement of the Tang Dynasty. They were called "Han-Liu" and were regarded as the "Eight Prose Masters of the Tang and Song Dynasties."

In Chinese classical literary history, *ci*, a new style and genre of classical Chinese poetry, took its place alongside the poetry of ancient China in the literary tradition. Song Dynasty *ci*, which began during the Liang Dynasty (AD 502–557), continued to develop through the Tang Dynasty, but it prospered during the Song Dynasty (AD 960–1229), producing many outstanding poets. Famous masterpieces emerged in an endless stream of expressions, styles and genres. The existing *Poems of the Song Dynasty* and the *Supplemental Poems of the Song Dynasty* contained more than 20,000 works by at least 1,430 authors: evidence of poetic achievement during the Song Dynasty.

Yuan Dynasty (1271–1368) verse came into its poetic form from popular folk slang, bringing distinctive colloquial features, temperaments and topics with it, reflecting an unrestrained and simple nature. Greats included Guan Hanqing (1220–1300), Ma Zhiyuan (1250–1321), Wang Shifu (1260–1336) and Bai Pu (AD 1226–1306). Guan Hanqing's poetic drama, which is about the state of the world, tactfully expresses subtleties and observes that writing styles are continuously transforming; the *xiaoling* (short lyric) style is lively, deep, glittering, translucent, mild, indirect and beautiful. The cycle of songs is bold and unconstrained with great eloquence. The creation themes of Ma Zhiyuan are broad and employ lofty moods, vivid images, beautiful language and phonological harmony; he is known as "the first master of Yuan lyrics" and a "progenitor of tender moments." Mid-Yuan creations begin a transition to creations by cultural and professional people; non-dramatic songs became the main genre of poetic circles. Chinese *sanqu* (lyric verse) poetry writers at the end of Yuan Dynasty made a profession of creating *sanqu* poetry; they paid attention to classical rhetoric, the art of advocating epigrams with a style that was mild and indirect, elegant and beautiful.

Chinese classical novels have unique cultural connotations and historical significance. Between the Song Dynasty and the Qing Dynasty (1644–1911), more than 300 novels and tens of thousands of short novels were produced. These works reflected on all aspects of social life at that time in an unprecedented breadth and depth and became the main literary style for people to understand social and cultural life.

The vernacular novel depicts characters dynamically, with vivid and fluent language and a unique style; the creative method of large numbers of intellectuals and the masses blended together in a rare example of world literature. Luo Guanzhong (1330–1400) created *Sanguo Yanyi (Romance of the Three Kingdoms)* on the basis of Chen Shou's (AD 233–297) *Sanguo Zhi (The History of the Three Kingdoms)*. This book describes the complex history of the end of the Eastern Han Dynasty and the separation of the three countries. At last, the Sima's unified the world and successfully portrayed many characters' images. *Shui Hu Zhuan (All Men Are Brothers)* written by Shi Nai'an (1293–1371) was the first novel written in popular language in ancient China; it has a very high value in literary history and the history of Chinese language. Wu Chengen (1510–1582) wrote *Xiyou Ji (Journey to the West)* on the basis of folklore and the ancient play. He created two lovely images of Sun Wukong who has great magical power and a timid and selfish pig who shouted out anti-feudal slogans like "take turns to be the emperor, next year is my turn." Sun Wukong hoped the ideals of the people would conquer the forces of evil. It is an excellent work that sparked the development of a school of its own in the genre of vernacular novels.

These vernacular novels had a great effect on modern Chinese literature, drama and film, but also continue to have a great influence on the literary creations of Japan, Korea and other countries. Some of the outstanding works have been translated into dozens of languages, contributing to cultural exchanges worldwide.

Precedent of Classical Literature

Myths and legends rank among China's most ancient and precious cultural heritage forms, mainly conveyed in an oral literary tradition that was collectively created by the ancients. Myths handed down include creation myth of Pangu, who created heaven and earth; the myth of how Nüwa created man; hero myths of the "archer and the suns"; how "King Yu tamed the flood"; and the "clan myth of the Yellow Emperor against Chi You." Later writers turned to these ancient Chinese literary sources for their are rich content, imaginative and profound imagery. Classical Chinese literature began with great splendour.

Origin of Pre-Qin literature

Poetry in the initial stage of its development is a kind of oral creation. The *Book of Songs* was the earliest known poetry collection in ancient China. From the early years of the Western Zhou Dynasty (11th century–771 BC) to the mid-Spring and Autumn Period (770–476 BC) about 500 years of poetry were collected: 305 works in all. The *Book of Songs* has very high artistic value, but it also has a very high value in terms of historical data, which is important for the study of ancient customs.

The *Book of Songs* is divided into three parts: "custom," "elegant" and "odes." "Custom" is local music from various regions, mostly folk songs created based on farmers' lives; it is realistic. "Elegant" and "odes" are basically the creation of noblemen and mainly represent a flattering description of aristocratic life. National customs serves as the "essence" of the *Book of Songs*; it reflects social realities and is a source of realistic literature. The early stages of poetic creation involved "mouth-to-mouth" transmission. Working people played a pivotal role in spreading poetry through the local tradition. Working people were the main body of the early stages of poetic creation.

The *Songs of Chu* represent regional characteristics of new poetry peculiar to southern China. Qu Yuan was the main writer of the *Songs of Chu* and the originator of romantic literature. His *"Li Sao" ("Encountering Sorrow")* is representative of *Chu Ci* songs; so later generations also call the songs of Chu *"Sao."* According to modern scholars, Qu Yuan's works include *"Li Sao,"* "The Nine Elegies," "Nine Songs," "Asking Heaven," "Requiem" and 23 articles. These works are notable in the history of Chinese poetry for their profound thoughts and artistic qualities.

Qu Yuan was the first great patriotic poet in Chinese literary history. He was born into a royal family of the Chu state (Chuguo, 740–223 BC), "Good at knowing how to suppress riots and well versed in speeches," he had high literary achievements. He held an officer's rank as high as *zuotu*. He was an important figure both in domestic and foreign affairs in the King Huai of Chu period (329–228 BC), who ended up being slandered by his opponents. Once he had been disgraced, he was sent into exile. Still, he wouldn't change his mind and remained concerned about national affairs and people's livelihoods, taking responsibility for the world. Twenty-one years into the reign of King Qingxiang (298–263 BC), Qin entered the capital of Chu. The King of Chu died in Qin and the Chu state fell into decline. Qu Yuan committed suicide by drowning himself in the Miluo River in grief, indignation and in despair. The Dragon Boat Festival is the traditional festival used to commemorate Qu Yuan; his patriotic feelings left a good name forever.

After Qu Yuan, Song Yu is one of the most famous representatives of Chu poets. According to legend, he was a student of Qu Yuan. His representative works are "Custom Ode" and "Ode of Gaotang."

Litterateur of the Western Han Dynasty, Liu Xiang (77–6 BC), often makes mention of Qu Yuan, Song Yu, Jia Yi (200–168 BC) and others. Liu Xiang's own works consist of *Nine Signs*, a total of 16 articles, and an essay on the *Songs of Chu*. *Songs of Chu* was the first romantic poetry collection in literary history and had a far-reaching influence on ancient Chinese literature.

Maturity of *Dafu*

Pre-Qin literary achievements were significant, had a far-reaching influence and communicated ancient myths and legends. They inspired the growth and development of Han Dynasty poetry, a kind of rhyming prose that emerged during the dynasty, mainly through several stages of development from the *"Li Sao"* and *dafu* to a form of lyrical prose that combined prose and verse in a specialised elaboration.

The epitome of *dafu* during its mature period was Sima Xiangru (179–118 BC). Representative works are *"Zixu Fu"* (a proper name), *"Shanglin Fu"* (Shanglin was a place where emperors hunted), *"Changmen Fu"* (chamber of a concubine), *"Meiren Fu"* ("Beauty Fu") and Daren Fu (refers to an emperor). His style is flowery and complex with a grand structure; it is mainly rendering gorgeous palaces and cities and descriptions of the emperor's hunts, great in strength and impetus; singing praise of the ruler while a satirical meaning can be detected in the undertone; this created the basic theme of *dafu* in the Han Dynasty.

The King of Liang was urged to invite Sima Xiangru (179–118 BC) to compose odes. Xiangru wrote "Jade Ode" as a gift. The ode's rhetoric was magnificent and artistically extraordinary. The King of Liang was so happy that he gave Xiangru a *lüqi*, a kind of *guqin* (zither) from his own collection as a gift in return, with an inscription that read: "essence of paulownia and catalpa combined together." When Xiangru got the *guqin*, he considered it a treasure and made *guqin* music with it with an excellent *lüqi* tone. The *lüqi* became so famous that *lüqi* later became an alternative name for a *guqin*.

Later generations called Sima Xiangru the "Saint of Odes" and a "Master of Poetry" to recognise his outstanding Han Dynasty poetic achievements. Lu Xun (1881–1936), a beloved modern Chinese writer, thinker and revolutionist mentioned in the same breath with Sima Qian in the outline of *The History of Chinese Literature*, said: "Literati during Emperor Wu of Han [141–87 BC]…odes no better than Sima Xiangru; articles no better Sima Qian."

After Sima Xiangru, a different master of poetry emerged in Sichuan Province. Yang Xiong (AD 542–612), considered the most famous poet of the Han Dynasty after Sima Xiangru, was good at rhymes, perhaps because of his stuttering. He used silent and simple language but appeared thoughtful. His early works imitate Sima Xiangru, so later generations called them "Yang-Ma." In his later years, he changed his views on poetry, leaning towards satire, while continuing to offer advice. He also proposed that "poetry is flowery: somewhat suitable for satire, but songs are too flowery to be able to offer advice." His work had some influence on the later development of odes and comments on odes, but also influenced the later prose writer Liu Xie (AD 465–520), Han Yu (AD 768–824) and others. Zhang Heng (AD 78–139) is a representative writer of lyrical prose, the creator of "Returning to the Farm Land," a new kind of ode. He was a pioneer of pastoral literature, a forerunner of rhythmical prose characterised by parallelism and ornateness.

Rise of Jian'an style

Towards the end of the Han Dynasty, great turmoil and partisan discord erupted. Under these circumstances, a number of unique literary styles spearheaded by strong personalities emerged. Cao Cao (AD 155–220), Cao Pi (AD 187–226) and Cao Zhi (AD 192–232) were called "three Caos"; Kong Rong (AD 153–208), Chen Lin (AD 156–217), Wang Can (AD 177–217), Xu Gan (AD 170–217), Ruan Yu (about 165–212), Ying Yang (AD 177–217), Liu Zhen (186–217) are called the "Jian'an Seven." Jian'an poets and their vanguard focused on unrest. They were concerned about the suffering of the people, but they also expressed their desire to realise their ideals and achieve their aspirations in troubled times. The poetic style of this period is sad and dreary; the language is bold and concise. It has peculiar thought and artistic characteristics; later generations call this the characteristic "Jian'an Style."

Cao Cao was good at poetry: in "Walk in the Artemisia" and "In View of the Sea" and other works, he expressed his own political ambitions and reflected the suffering life of people towards the end of the Han Dynasty with a magnificent spirit, generous language and empathy.

According to the records of *A New Account of the Tales of World Literature*, when Cao Pi (Cao Cao's son) became emperor, he always held a grudge for Cao Zhi, his witty younger brother. On one occasion, he ordered Cao Zhi to compose a poem within seven steps, and told him that if he couldn't he would be sentenced by law. Cao Zhi did not wait for the order to end; he answered with a poem of six lines:

Beans are cooked with beanstalks while percolating for juice.
Beanstalks burn under the kettle while the beans weep in the kettle.
Born of the same root, why are you fratricidal?

This poetry won universal praise. Since it was composed within the limit of seven steps, later generations called it the "Seven Steps Poem." It's said that after Cao Pi heard the poem, he felt ashamed, not only because of the extraordinary talent of Cao Zhi that was reflected in the poem, but also because of his outstanding eloquence, which made the emperor feel inferior. In the poem, he used a simple and vivid analogy to explain that brothers are like hand and foot; they should not be suspicious or hate each other. Being confronted with such righteousness made Emperor Wen feel ashamed.

The Jian'an style had a very deep influence on later generations, especially the masters of he Tang Dynasty who loudly advocated the "Style of Han and Wei Dynasties" especially during the early Tang Dynasty by the famous poet Chen Zi'ang (661–702). Li Bai also highly raised the "literary forms of Penglai [a place, but also a reference to Han Dynasty literature] and the spirit of Jian'an *fenggu* [a reference to the Jian'an Seven's literary style]." The Jian'an style also had far-reaching influence on Li Bai's poetic style; the strong personality of Li Bai's poems, the heroic spirit of leaving home, realising ambitions with a sword and the strong will are closely associated with the moral principles of the Jian'an period.

Wei-Jin Style Celebrity

The style of the Wei and Jin dynasties is a true scholar-celebrity style. From initial talents, He Yan (AD 193–249) and Wang Bi (AD 226–249) to the Bamboo Grove scholar-celebrities Ji Kang (AD 223–263) and Ruan Ji (AD 201–263) to Mid-Wei-Jin talented literati such as Wang Yan (AD 256–311) and Yue Guang (?–304) and to the leaders south of Yangtze River, such as Wang Dao (AD 276–339) and Xie An (AD 320–385), all were elegant and unconventional. They epitomised the "stream and steam" and "romantic self-appreciation" style almost as a divine gesture. They were respected and admired by later generations.

Zong Baihua (1897–1986, a Chinese master of aesthetics) wrote in the *Walk in Aesthetics*: "Jin people discovered nature outside and found their affections inside their hearts. Their landscapes were virtually spiritualised and also the environment they lived in. Is it because Tao Yuanming (AD 365–427) and Xie Lingyun's (AD 385–433) found the intoxicating and mysterious tastes of nature that their landscape poems are so good?"

'While picking asters neath eastern fence,
My gaze upon southern mountains rests...'

The extreme of the Wei and Jin style is the idea of the "peach garden" that was put forward by Tao Yuanming. Intellectuals were the most devout believers in social groups of the time, even while the political regime forced them to keep a low tone. They remained concerned about the nation and the people. Tao Yuanming's work "I'm Going Home" was full of political enthusiasm with a peach garden influence.

Tao Yuanming was a low ranking official for several years before he resigned and became reclusive. Because he clung to his moral principles, he lived a "farming and self-financing" life. His wife shared his contentment with poverty. "The husband plowing in front and the wife hoeing after," working together to sustain life. They became increasingly close and related to the working people. Tao Yuanming loved chrysanthemums and planted chrysanthemums around his house. 'While picking asters neath the eastern fence, my gaze upon the southern mountain rests…' still wins universal praise. He loved drinking, and got drunk every time he was drinking. When friends came to visit, he drank with them no matter how gentle or simple as long as there was wine in the home. He got drunk first and then he said to the guests: 'I am drunk and need to go to bed; you can go freely'."

His main works were "Drinking," "Returning to My Farm," "Peach Blossom Spring," "I'm Going Home" and "The Biography of Mr. Willow." The main content of his work is the idyllic life. Tao Yuanming's poems are plain and natural, clear and easy to understand. A fertile inspiration was conveyed in a simple and plain style. The lyrics, depictions of scenery and comments combined together, blending feeling and scenery, had an important influence on later pastoral poetry.

Tao Yuanming was the most accomplished poet of the Wei, Jin and Southern and Northern Dynasties (AD 420–589). Li Bai, Du Fu, Bai Juyi (AD 772–846), Lu You (1125–1210) and other poets highly praised Tao's poems.

Recalling of Zhuangzi, Laozi during enjoyment of wines

In considering literary rhetoric and essays, many feel that metaphysical topics, calligraphy and salons should also be considered. In such a way we can accommodate ourselves to the Wei-Jin style: that is, engage in completely informal drinking; do as one pleases; talk about metaphysical topics in an easy and comfortable world; take leisurely walks among the groves; write to record one's ambitions; and get together to write something.

The Wei-Jin style reflects a personality, using idle talk to consolidate an ambition. Real Wei-Jin scholars were not actually involved with the world. Their concern was the nation. Still, as times were bad, and they were not able to use their own talents, most of them sought escape from the world. Idle talk emerged because of a dark society on one hand and an attempt to maintain moral integrity on the other.

Politics is not merciful; the scholar-celebrities talked of the philosophies of Laozi and Zhuangzi and did not concern themselves with current affairs. Their goals were high and pure. He Yan and Wang Bi also started questioning the universe because of its naturalistic nihilism and explored ontology. Xie An, a talented strategist, consistently resisted the idea that "idle talk endangered the country"; the essence of idle talk celebrities was more pragmatic.

The Wei-Jin style is a kind of performance of personality, an approach to official ideology that became an aesthetic ideal. The more you understand, the more natural you are. Unconventional and unconstrained, not serving influential officials or when joining into officialdom, it is with the mind of getting away from the world. This was known as "body in the officialdom and mind is getting away." The true scholar celebrities in this period, whose personalities were true and feelings pure, engaged in leisurely behaviour and often improper gestures. Later generations often criticised them. However, a real scholar-celebrity has no exaggerated comportment; instead he shows wilful behaviour to achieve a natural realm of life.

Romantic scholar celebrities advocated natural living and freedom from worldly affairs. Truth, engaging romance and self-appreciation were held in high esteem. During the Jin Dynasty, they repeatedly invited Wang Youjun to be the head of the ministry of government personnel, but he refused. In the spirit of "hold cup to drink, chant *Zhuangzi* and *Laozi* in idle talk" and "do idle talk as daily affairs," "love drinking and do not serve public affairs," the philosophy of the recluse created the legendary "Preface of the Orchid Pavilion." This era's scholars created the literati calligraphy that influenced later generations.

Wander, live in bamboo grove:
Seven sages gather

The *Book of Songs* reads: "The sound of woodcutting and chirping birds. Sound from the dark valley, move into a new house/ A bird sings out to draw a friend's response/ Look at the bird as it is still seeking the voice of its companion/ We are human beings, why not seek to have friends?"

The birds were singing in the trees looking for friends. Birds are still acting so, and how can human beings have more affection and faith without friends? In the Wei-Jin and Northern and Southern Dynasties, there is such a group of people, like birds seeking friends; they wandered and lived in bamboo groves, met friends with poems and wine and lived happily in the bamboo grove; they were known as the "Seven Sages of the Bamboo Grove."

Ji Kang is one of the main representatives of Wei-Jin metaphysics. He was extraordinary in appearance! At seven-feet, eight-inches tall, people who saw him sighed and said, "elegant and unconventional, elegant and just." He is good at melody and advocating nature and knows the way of keeping good health and Confucian nature. He had very good relations with Shan Tao in his earlier years. Shan Tao said, "Uncle Ji is a man of striking appearance, he is tall and straight like a lonely pine; when drunk, he is like the falling mountain Yu."

Shan Tao was an orphan and poor when he was young; he enjoyed the philosophies of Laozi and Zhuangzi, after which he entered the realm of politics. Regarding Shan Tao, there is a lot of criticism; he was even called a "traitor" by some, but this was not a fair evaluation. He did not persecute any righteous people when he was an official; he placed talented people in important positions and played a positive role in correcting the social order during a dark period.

When Shan Tao left his post, he wanted Ji Kang to replace him. Ji Kang did not want to get involved in politics and wrote a letter to sever relations; this is the famous "Letter of Severing Relations with Shan Tao." In fact, Ji Kang wrote a letter severing relations to protect his good friend; with this letter; Shan Tao would not be affected by Ji Kang's actions.

Zhong Hui, a general who served under Wei Dynasty General Sima Zhao, persecuted Ji Kang for insolence, among other things. When approaching his end, Ji Kang entrusted his children to Shan Tao and told the children, "As long as Juyuan (aka Shan Tao) is here, you are not alone." Soon, Ji Kang was killed, and Shan Tao adopted his children. Shan Tao recommended Ji Kang's son for service as an official in the imperial court.

Ruan Ji relied on the philosophical outlooks of Laozi and Zhuangzi; he sought ideal harmony in his music. Eighty-two of his most famous poems are found in "Poems from My Heart." *The Book of Jin: Biography of Ruan Ji* characterised him as "sometimes wilful drive alone without purpose, when the road ends, he is often wailing and returns." He often drove and wandered randomly without purpose until the end of the road; then he cried out. When he was an official, he drank and ate meat all day with Liu Ling (a fellow in the Bamboo Garden); he never published any political opinions. The Jin emperor wanted to marry his daughter to him, upon which he went crazy and stayed drunk for 60 days. The envoy of the Jin Emperor was not able to get him to even discuss the possibility of marriage and eventually gave up.

Ruan Ji could roll his eyes to show either the green or white of his eyes; he often rolled his eyes to white to express disdain. When Ji Kang heard about this, he took wine and a *guqin* and went to visit him. Ruan Ji exulted and showed the green of his eyes. Rolling one's eyes to show green to mean favour comes from these two friends to express appreciation and love for others.

With his son, Ruan Xian, the pair was called "Junior and Senior Ruan." He was good at playing the *pipa* and became famous for his musical achievements.

Xiang Xiu was once farming with Lü An (?–AD 262), son of General Lü Zhao in Shanyang. Ji Kang's home was in Shanyang, and these three people were very close. After Ji Kang and Lu An were killed, Xiang Xu passed by the former residence of Ji Kang and sighed when he heard his neighbours playing *guqin*. He wrote the famous "Missing Old Friends." Though the ode is short, it became a representative work of mourning dead friends, which lives on to this day.

Liu Ling was good at drinking and tasting wine; he was completely informal, uninhibited and unruly and he only got along with Ruan Ji. Ji Kang is known to the world as "the drunkard."

Wang Rong, the youngest of seven sages, was close with Ji Kang and Ruan Ji. Since he was born into a family with power and influence, his political ideology was unlike that of the other six. Despite ups and downs in his official life, he died holding his official post.

The Seven Sages of the Bamboo Grove were later oppressed and fell apart as a result of the dark politics, but the image of friendship they embodied and their fearlessness in the face of the secular and absurd and their sense of freedom in history survived them to become powerful cultural symbols. The common people often use "bamboo grove tour" or "wander and live in bamboo grove" to describe an intimate friendship.

Very rare, unrestrained and broad-minded lives can be found in Chinese cultural history. Without the activities of the Wei and Jin dynasties, Confucianism, Buddhism, Taoism and their influence, the Chinese literati would never have engaged in metaphysical talk or speculations or have sought the Wei-Jin-style easy and comfortable life. Without the way the Wei-Jin administered affairs and made political corrections to keep things on track, there would have been no "fragrance of chrysanthemum of Taoqian, no trend toward righteousness and reason, no new rules for poetic expression, no Chinese scholar celebrities daring to sing and drink, no hair-pulling poets on a mountain, no rolling of eyes to white to influence officials. All this harks back to Ji Kang playing *"Guanglingsan"* a thousand years ago. The Seven Sages of the Bamboo Grove represent eternal ethereality.

Recalling Great Tang Dynasty

The Tang Dynasty was a unified empire unprecedented in Chinese history. During the Tang, China was rich in material wealth and had a vibrant, prosperous culture. It was the golden age of Chinese poetry and a period in history of high maturity. Tang poetry is a bright pearl in the history of ancient Chinese literature and occupies a unique position in the history of Chinese classical literature.

According to the *Complete Tang Poems*, there were at least 2,300 poets with their names recorded and nearly 50,000 poems written during the 289-year Tang Dynasty. Among the more than 2,000 prestigious poets, 50–60 famous poets stand out because of their unique styles, such as the poets Li Bai, Du Fu, Bai Juyi and Wang Wei.

Wang, Yang, Lu and Luo represent Tang poetic styles and genres
Superficial commentator's ridicule will never end

During the early Tang Dynasty a circle of four great poets emerged: Wang Bo, Yang Jiong, Lu Zhaolin, Luo Bingwang, collectively referred to as Wang-Yang-Lu-Luo. Du Fu gave a high evaluation of their historical contributions: "Wang, Yang, Lu and Luo expanded the style and genre of poetry of that time; superficial commentator's ridicule would not end. When you guys turn to ashes, there is no influence to eternal streams."

The "Tengwangge Foreword" composed by Wang Bo is a famous masterpiece in Chinese classical literature and was widely read for a long time. It is said that he prepared his pen, ink, paper and ink stone before writing and then drank and slept with a quilt. When he woke up, he wrote with his pen and immediately finished and did not change a single word: "a draft in his mind." The birth and death of Wang Bo is still a matter of controversy, but it is certain that he lived for only 27 years. A poet full of wit dying at such a young age is regrettable. Yang Jiong was born in Hongnong Huayin; he was known for frontier war poems, including "Joining the Army," "On the Frontier" and "Combating South of the City." Lu Zhaolin are good at seven-word long songs such as "The Memory of Chang'an," a masterpiece of ancient and famous Tang Dynasty poetry that still wins universal praise. Luo Binwang was known for drafting "An Official Call to the World on Behalf of Li Jingye." Li Jingye was defeated and killed, and Luo Binwang later disappeared. Some of his famous works handed down are "Yu Yishui Sees Somebody Off" and "Chant Cicada in Prison."

Four great poets of the early Tang Dynasty laid a foundation for the five-character octave, and pushed the seven-character octave to a mature stage, creating high quality works in great quantities that later influenced Shen Quanqi and Song Zhiwen.

Wind, rain were shocked
Poetic compositions moved gods

Poetic genius Li Bai (AD 701–762) was a literary miracle in the prosperous period of the Tang Dynasty; he influenced people at home and abroad.

Li Bai was born in Jinzhou of Jiannandao (there is also one saying that he was born in Suiyecheng of the Western Region), Shanxi Province, and he was ancient China's greatest romantic poet. He created the peak of ancient positive romanticism and opened the doors for the development and prosperity of Tang poetry. Li Bai's life was full of rich, legendary and magical colour. It is said he received his name because his mother dreamed of the god Venus and then became pregnant. When Li Bai was 25, he left Sichuan by himself to "serve the country with the sword, bid farewell to his relatives and to travel around." His footprints are all over the country, on well-known mountains and rivers; he travelled more widely in ancient times than more than a few people can do today. Referring to Li Bai, the ancients said that in, "Travelling tens of thousands of miles and reading tens of thousands of books," Li Bai became a poet who lived life to its fullest.

Li Bai was uninhibited and despised dignitaries. It is said that he tried to make the imperial eunuch Gao Lishi remove his muddy boots in front of the emperor [unsuccessfully] and made "the imperial consort Yang [Guifei] hold an ink stone." Later, Gao squeezed him out and Li Bai was given gold and other items to leave. "How can I bow and scrape to serve influential officials to make my heart not rejoice" is the most carefree catharsis. At the same time, Li Bai also dealt with contradictions of Chinese ancient literati; the universal tenet: with "get away from worldly affairs" and conversely "enter into worldly affairs" he felt great contempt for powerful nobles; yet, he longed to become a general or prime minister to serve the motherland and build a career. When Li Bai was 42 he got a chance to meet the emperor, based on someone else's recommendation; he received a grand reception by Emperor Xuanzong (reign: AD 712–756), but the emperor did not give him an actual official position, allowing him to become a literary attendant of honour with the academy only. Li Bai, tired of the empty flattery and a lack of respect, departed on a "wine saint" tour with He Zhizhang (AD 659–744), one of the Eight Immortals of the Wine Cup.

In AD 755, the An Lushan Rebellion (aka An-Shi Rebellion or *An Shi Zhi Luan*) broke out. Li Bai was invited to serve as an aide of King Yong Lilin (721–757) with the mission of securing the state and comforting the people. King Yong was defeated and committed suicide. Later, Li Bai was arrested, imprisoned and threatened with death until he was rescued by Gen. Song Ruosi. [Some accounts say it was Gen. Guo Ziyi]. He became Song's aide but was exiled to Yelang for his role in the An Lushan Rebellion." But when Tang Suzong (reign: AD 756–762) ascended the throne, a drought struck China. To appease furious gods, the emperor's court proclaimed a general amnesty that included Li Bai. His freedom restored, Li Bai wrote "Early Departure from Baidi Town" to express his feelings. Later Li Bai distanced himself from officialdom and travelled to relieve his inner yearnings. He spent his time visiting mythical landscapes and seeking truth for many years.

Li Bai's poetry, Pei Min's art of fencing and Cursive Script are called the "three combined unique techniques of the Tang Dynasty." Li Bai was also respected as a calligrapher and for his attainments in Taoism.

Li Bai's *yuefu* and *jueju* poetry song styles created during the Han Dynasty are high achievements. Poets of the prosperous Tang Dynasty, Wang Wei and Meng Haoran were good at five-character, four lines poems; Wang Changling was good at seven-character, four lines poems; but only Li Bai was good at both. Li Bai's poetic style was magnificent and elegant, colourful, bright and vivid, with artistic conceptions of magic and a strong romantic temperament.

Poems of Li Bai, Du Fu
Far-reaching influence on later generations

In AD 734, Li Bai travelled to Yanzhou in Shandong where he met Du Fu for the first time. These two souls met in the "the greatest planetary communication and collision out of the most gorgeous light in poetic circles." At that time Li Bai and Du Fu were China's best-known poets. The two people felt like old friends, brothers even; they drank and travelled together spawning endless anecdotes.

Du Fu called himself an "aged rustic of Shaoling"; he was the greatest realist poet of the Tang Dynasty. Four words could be used to describe Du Fu's poetry: profound, depressed, rhythmic and strong. Du Fu was born during the Tang's decline; he experienced the Great Tang Empire from its peak to its valleys, its ups and downs, and most of his works were written during this time. His process was called "poetry to record history," and he was respectfully called a "sage of poetry" even by common people.

Du Fu's poetry is filled with the human sentiment of concern for the fate of the country and people from the beginning to its end. He experienced the An Lushan Rebellion and the turmoil of the late Tang Dynasty. He saw and experienced the sufferings the war brought to the people, when many became destitute and homeless. He also saw people swallow humiliation and bear heavy loads. They often joined the army to serve the country. He was filled with a thousand regrets when he wrote the immortal "Three officials": "Xin'an Official," "Shihao Official," "Tongguan Official"; the "three separations": "Newly Married Separation," "Aged People Separation" and "Homeless Separation." Du Fu was depressed and frustrated in his life, wandering about without a fixed abode. After several incidents he went to Chengdu and with the help of friends built a cottage near the bank of Huanhua Brook: "Du Fu Thatched Cottage." Even when he was frustrated and distressed and suffering adversity, he did not forget the common people living in dire straits; he kept their suffering in mind, raised his voice and called for "… tens of thousands of mansions to shelter the poor in the world and make them happy." Later poets praised Li Bai and Du Fu's historical achievements, saying, the "Poems of Li Bai and Du Fu had a far reaching influence on later generations."

If Li Bai and Du Fu are seen as an unreachable peaks in Tang literary history, later poets such as Li Shangyin and Du Mu are considered the most beautiful and the most energetic poets in the history of poets describing social decline. Later generations called Li Bai and Du Fu "Senior Li-Du and Li Shangyin and Du Mu "Junior Li-Du" to distinguish them.

No wonder I long for simple life
Sigh with emotion and chant '*Shiwei*'

The most famous poet of landscape and pastoral poetry was Wang Wei. Wang Wei enjoyed the rank of a minister; customarily he was called Wang Youcheng. He was influenced by Buddhism and loathed the bureaucratic life; so he sought long-term seclusion in his home, Wangchuan Garden, pursuing other interests; he loved nature and was familiar with the countryside. His poems were quiet and easy with a static beauty, such as "House on the Wei River":

In the slant of the sun on the countryside, cattle and sheep trail home along the lane
And a rugged old man keeps thinking about a herder boy using crutches, leaning on a thatched door and
thinking of his grandson.
There are whirring pheasants, while the wheat is in the ear…silk-worms asleep, and mulberry-leaves sparse.
Farmers finish hoeing and talk about a good harvest.
No wonder I long for the simple life and sigh with emotion and chant 'Shiwei.'

By quoting 'Shiwei,' a poem in the *Book of Songs*, Wang Wei expressed his interest in pastoral seclusion. He was adept in music, painting and calligraphy.

Su Dongpo praised Wang Wei's works as "painting-in-poetry, poetry in painting," drawing an idyllic picture.

Meng Haoran, a poet, was as famous as Wang Wei; his ancestral home was in Xiangyang (now in Hubei Province). He was often called Meng Xiangyang. He is said to have met Emperor Xuanzong by chance in Zhang Jiuling's government office. Emperor Xuanzong knew of his poems and ordered him to recite some. He chanted "Old Age and Returning to South Mountain," in which there was a verse that confusingly said, "unwise emperor abandon me," which did not please the emperor at all. The emperor said: "You are not seeking officialdom; and how could you be? How can you blame me?" He then ordered Meng into seclusion, condemning him to roaming that resulted in Meng becoming known as a landscape poet. His poem, "Visiting an Old Friend Village," is still popular today.

Old friend prepared chicken and rice, invited me to his farm home.
Green trees circle the village and green mountains extend to far away.
We open the window facing the yard, drink and talk about growing mulberries and hemp.
Wait till the double ninth day, I am coming again to see the chrysanthemums.

Drinking wine and eating delicious foods with friends in such a natural picture, enjoying laughing; this is how happiness and comfort feel. After drinking, the friends were still reluctant to part, and agreed to meet again on the Double Ninth to drink wine and enjoy chrysanthemums.

As long as Li Guang is in Dragon City
He definitely will not let barbarians cross Yin Mountains

Many scholars who got involved in wars against foreign forces during the Tang Dynasty had personal experiences on the frontier and with military life; they joined the army while writing poems depicting desolate frontier fortress scenery, singing the praises of the soldiers' chivalrous spirit or cursing the disasters of war; therein lies the origin of the frontier fortress poetic style.

War was cruel. In AD 714, the Tang Dynasty army battled a Tibetan force near the Great Wall in Lintao (in present day Dingxi, Gansu Province), leaving tens of thousands of soldiers dead on the battlefield. Wang Changling's "Under a Border-Fortress" wrote about this war:

Water the horse while we cross the autumn water
The stream is cold and the wind like a sword.
Only can see the sandy plain while even not sunset
Lintao is far away.
Old battles happened on the Great Wall
Thinking of this, the soldiers were proud and high in spirit.
Yellow dust full of this place since old times
Bones of the dead are in the chaotic weeds.

Though many years had passed since the war, the battlefield remained bleak and desolate and was covered with yellow dust and sand; amid the rambling wormwood, bones of the dead could still be found, as no one ever retrieved them. Neither victory nor defeat mattered anymore. For the dead solders' families, there was nothing left but a miserable memory.

Wang Changling's "To the Frontier" reveals the misery of the war and expresses a hope for a good general to defend the homeland.

Great heroes

Han Yu was a master of prose and poetry. He admired Li Bai and Du Fu most, but he did not imitate them; he explored a unique style of his own. Han Yu's poetry is considered unique and elegant; he and his friend Meng Jiao were known as the founders of the "Han-Meng School" of poetry.

Han Yu's poetry influenced Li He's, but their styles were different. Li He's were full of imagination, with grotesque themes and grandiose expressions. In his ghost stories, you could feel horror and darkness; that's why he was nicknamed "grotesque talent." He was said to ride a donkey when travelling for inspiration. He wrote down all the lyrics that came to mind. He edited them at home. One of his poems, "South Park" expresses his resentment as a poet:

The waning moon hung in the sky
It looked like a jade bow hanging on a curtain
I am meditating on passages and phrases.
The Liao-Hai War is ongoing; as a writer
I could do nothing but express my sorrows!

Lu Xun said: "Since the end of the Tang Dynasty, there have been no great poems, thus it's necessary to try to write until you are gifted enough to make a difference.

Of course, this does not mean there were no good poems. In fact, when people today try to write poems, it is indispensable to refer to the Tang Dynasty poems. Tang poetry is considered to be the most classical representation of Chinese poetry; it is an important literary heritage of China and the world and a cornerstone in the development of world civilisation.

67

Song Lyrics

The importance of Song Dynasty lyrics is comparable to that of the Tang poetry in Chinese literature; it is the most representative achievement of Song literature. Lyric writers could be generally divided into two categories: strong and tender. Both schools co-existed in the literary circle of the Song, and together they created numerous great works that resonate even today.

Song lyrics originated in folk traditions; the earliest works were written during the Southern Dynasties (AD 420–589) and were closely related to the spread of folklore style music during the Southern and Northern dynasties and the Sui and Tang dynasties. At the same time, the music of the western minorities were gradually integrated into the main stream Chinese music and gave birth to the unique *yanyue* or festive music for banquets. The music should feature uneven lengths, cadences and graceful lyrics; thus, various lyrics made for the tunes were created. Gradually, the rules for writing these lyrics were preserved and developed into a new poetic form independent of music.

People of the Ming Dynasty were the first to divide the lyrics into strong and tender categories. "Tender styles emphasise the implications of gentle and graceful feelings; the strong style pursues grandiose expressions." Tender school writers such as Liu Yong and Li Qingzhao tended to write about lovers and sorrowful separations, while strong writers such as Su Shi and Xin Qiji were more concerned with heroic and grandiose topics.

Ancient China's versatile talent

Su Shi and his brother Su Zhe, along with their father Su Xun, were collectively referred to as the "Three Sus"; but Su Shi was also associated with Ouyang Xiu and Huang Tingjian as 'Ou-Su' and 'Su-Huang.' His works included poetry, prose, calligraphy and painting, religion as well as other artistic and literary topics; he was a versatile ancient Chinese talent.

Su Shi secured a foundation for the lyrical tradition. Chen Shidao said Su Shi incorporated poetic characters into his lyrics; this comment represented elements of Su Shi's work. In general, the promotion of lyrics into literature was a process of the assimilation of lyrics into poems and the transcendence of emotion and ambition.

Su Shi deliberately pursued a strong style in his works and integrated his ambitions into the lyrics to invoke a feeling of grandeur and glory through the description of people and nature. The "Nian Nujiao: Meditate on the Past" and "Jiangcheng Zi: Hunting in Mi State" are the most representative of his works. The grandiose lyric style best represents Su Shi's personality and his ideal of a life in hermitage and his hopes for peace. In the "Prelude to Water Melody," the lines reveal "people with grief at separation and joy in union / the moon waxes and wanes / this sorrow of separation found no cure in ancient times. May we all long live / and share the same moon though being apart" remained popular for generations; the work is a good example of the expression of personal feelings through the description of the moon. The tender school inherited and developed the traditional tender style, and it was endowed with lofty, pure and sincere feelings. The "Jiangcheng Zi: On a Dream of the 20th January of the Year Li Mao" and "Butterflies over Flowers" are immortal works. "Jiangcheng Zi" was a lament written by Su Shi in memory of his first wife, Wang Fu, to express his endless yearning and sorrow for his wife; its sincere and sorrowful lyrics were so touching that readers could feel the tears and cries of the author and the work became the most classical example of laments in China.

Patriotism of dragon of lyric writers

Xin Qiji is the most recognised writer of the strong school of the Southern Song Dynasty; he was gifted both in writing and fighting and was associated with Su Shi and Li Qingzhao as "Su-Xin" and "the two reputed writers of Jinan." More than 600 of Xin Qiji's lyrics were recorded. He was a patriot, a military strategist and statesman.

Born into a general's family in a war torn era, Xin Qiji expressed great concern for the country and the people. His representative works include "Pozhengzi: Composing an Agitating Poem for Chen Tongfu Fu as a Gift," and "Yongyule: Meditate on the Past at North Pavilion in Jingkou" and "Qingyu An."

Xin Qiji built his reputation with moral integrity and military achievements; he advocated resistance against aggression. His "Ten Comments of Meiqin" and "Nine Proposals," showed his gifts in military strategy and patriotic passion. He maintained a firm friendship with Chen Liang, a man famous for his integrity, and Zhu Xi, a noted Neo-Confucian theorist; they shared the same moral principles and helped with each other in learning. The recovery of the lost land from the Jin regime was the main theme of all his literary creations, many of which also expressed resentment for being unable to realise his political and military visions.

In general, Xin Qiji's verses were endowed with a strong patriotic feeling and martial spirit. His concern for the northern lands lost to Jin regime was a constant theme in his writings. He criticism of the Southern Song Dynasty's cowardice in their struggle to survive was clearly revealed in terms such as "reduced territories of a nation" and "the setting sun over desolate willows made me sad" in the lyrics to "Congratulations to a Bridegroom" and "Catching Fish." Xin enriched the themes of Song lyrics, and relying on Su Shi, he could use the lyrics to record all events and express all feelings. Lyric writing reached its peak under Xin Qiji.

Wither their respective features, the lyric writers of both the strong tender schools were equally important in Song literary circles.

Where there are people, lyrics of Liu can be heard

Liu Yong was the first professional lyricist; he enriched lyrics but also explored their themes. In addition, he created a large number of slow lyrics, developed narration techniques and promoted the use of the vernacular and the popularisation of lyrics. Liu Yong's unique style featured sorrow, tenderness and vividness, exercising a great influence on the history of poetry.

Liu Yong, born in a family that had contributed lots of governmental officials to the country for generations, expected to sustain his family's pride by hard studies. However, he failed again and again in the academic examinations for official recruitments, so he wrote a lyric "A Crane Fledging into the Sky," with the line "I'd rather have a little sip of the wine," to pass the examinations and win a vanity academic title. During the early years of Song Emperor Renzong's reign (1022–63), Liu Yong was awarded the title of *jinshi* (a successful candidate in the imperial academic examination). However, when the emperor heard about "A Crane Fledging into the Sky," he ordered the deprivation of Liu Yong's title and remarked: "If you are so fond of the taste of the wine, does this title of vanity matter to you?" A multitude of misfortunes drew Liu Yong into depression, but he dared not to show his resentment; he named himself sarcastically "The imperial lyric writer Liu Sanbian" and the "white gown minister." Afterwards, he frequented parlours inspiration and devoted himself to writing lyrics. His most representative works were: "The Ringing of the Rain," "Tide Watching," "Phoenix on Parasol" and "Eight Rhythms of Ganzhou."

Liu Yong spent all his life with marginalised people, especially prostitutes, to whom most of his works were addressed; his works were popular and widely read.

Most talented woman in history

Li Qingzhao was another important figure of the tender school; her "Shuyu Lyrics" remain popular today. Li Qingzhao, who called herself the "Yi'an hermit," was born into a family of scholars in Zhangqiu, Jinan, Shandong Province. Because of her privileged family environment, she was able to receive a good education, which, together with her diligence and talent, ensured her good mastery of writing (especially prose), music, calligraphy and painting.

She and her husband Zhao Mingcheng had a happy marriage; they often shared their own writings and played music together. Zhao Mingcheng was fond of stone inscriptions, on which he spent much time even as he continued his classical studies.

In 1127, the Northern Jin regime broke into Bianjing and captured the abdicated Emperor Huizong and Emperor Qinzong. Newly recognised Emperor Gaozong, the ninth son of Huizong, fled to the south. Li Qingzhao and her husband travelled to Jiangnan. One year later, during the 29th year of their marriage, Zhao Mingcheng died on his office as prefect of Jiankang. His death was a blow to Li Qingzhao, and the miserable situation after the loss of the northern lands and the migration to the south of the Song people depressed her even more. She travelled with her and her husband's calligraphy and paintings, stones, monument carvings and other antiques everywhere she went, eventually settling in Hangzhou. After several years of efforts, Li Qingzhao attentively proofread her husband's writings, stone inscriptions and wrote supplements, creating the *Record of Stone Inscriptions*.

The establishment of the Southern Song Dynasty (1127–1229) was a dividing line in Li's life and literary creations. Her early works mainly reflected her maidenly and married lives and sentiments; the themes focused on natural scenery and feelings of separation and longing. After the death of Zhao Mingcheng, Li Qingzhao remarried and divorced. Suffering physically and mentally, her grief was deepened by the numerous migrations she endured because of uncertainties arising from the country's decline since the fall of the Northern Song regime (AD 960–1127) and her writing style began to embody a more sorrowful feelings, which expressed nostalgia for her lost husband, her hometown and her miserable solitude. The lyrics "Wuling Spring," "Bodhisattva Pretty" and *"Sheng Sheng Man"* were the best examples.

Prosperity of Yuan Verses

Yuan Dynasty verses are exotic treasures of the Chinese culture, because of their charm and unique content, both great achievements in artistic expression. Yuan verses share similar influence with Tang poems and Song lyrics; they combine to form the three milestones of Chinese literary development.

The development of verses reached its peak during the Yuan Dynasty, which enjoyed a vast territory and a prosperous economy depending on the cities of a vast empire. Grand theatres, popular storytelling houses as well as loyal audiences created a foundation for the rise of Yuan verses, which was furthered by communication and exchanges among various ethnic cultures.

Leading singer and alternation of sings and plain speaking

In general, Yuan verses refer to *zaju*, verses for operas and *sanqu*, non-theatrical tunes; both of them were sung in the northern style. The verses for non-dramatic tunes were a literary form of the Yuan Dynasty; however, the influence and achievement of Yuan opera greatly surpassed the non-theatrical tunes. Thus, some people think that the Yuan verses refer to those for the opera.

The Yuan opera was developed on the basis of Jin drama, which became a mature theatrical form under the influence of popular southern dramas. The structure of four main acts with one introduction was a particular feature of Yuan opera, which also featured only one lead singer. Singing and plain speaking were used alternatively during a performance. The opera also incorporated many other features, such as a focus on the stage, the categorisation of characters and the use of creative make-up. Inner sentiments implied by playwrights were expressed through stereotypical and symbolic approaches, while abstract feelings were combined with the reality of life. Yuan opera was endowed with all the characters needed for theatrical arts. It concluded the development of dramas and formed an integrated, unified and unique theatrical form.

Under the direct influence of Jin dramas and the *zhugongdiao* (a style of oral performance, as in medleys, in China) the Yuan opera absorbed a variety of performing arts to form an integrated art. Based on lyrics, story-telling and story-chanting literatures of the Tang and Song dynasties, Yuan operas were mature plays, a breakthrough compared to the farces (once very popular in the army) and the dramas of the Song. As a mature theatrical form, Yuan operas enriched folklore, but they also faithfully reflected existing social realities and were thus popular with the people.

Sublimation of folk song

According to scholastic research, non-theatrical verses originated from folk songs created during the transition from the Jin to the Yuan dynasties. Jin lyrics had shown some characteristics of verses, tending to be vernacular, frank, humorous, plain and simple. Jin lyrics featured large quantities of folk songs and the vernacular tunes of North China. Many Jin-lyric forms were applicable to writing verse and many lyrics were very close to Yuan verses.

As the access to government positions via academic examinations was closed at the end of Jin and the beginning of the Yuan dynasties and the social trends at the time were the segregated from political affairs, the intellectuals' pursuit of the enjoyment and temporal happiness prompted them to spend much of their time in parlours. At the same time, lots of prostitutes began to compose tunes and perform. They modified folk music to suit their performance needs. Due to their close relations with the intellectuals, the folk tunes began to be associated with literary creations. During the Song and Jin period, with the invasions of people from the north, northern music came to be integrated with the original music forms of the Han people and a new musical form—non-theatrical tunes—came about.

People of the Yuan Dynasty called the non-theatrical tunes *yuefu* or *jinyuefu*. The *Chengzhai Yuefu*, a collection of non-theatrical tunes written by Zhu Youdun during the Ming Dynasty, was the first literature to mention the term "non-theatrical tunes," which was used to refer specifically to *xiaoling* (little tunes) but not *taoshu* (serial tunes). Ever since the mid-Ming, *taoshu* had been included in non-theatrical tunes. Scholars in the 20th century had taken both *xiaoling* and *taoshu* as non-theatrical tunes in their essays. Thus, the verses for non-theatrical tunes were confirmed as a literary form.

The non-theatrical tunes consisted of *xiaoling* and *santao*. *Xiaoling* is also called *yer*, and is usually a short and independent piece of music. *Santao* consists of a number of tunes with a single rhythm. There were various *qupai* (a form of verses for tunes), such as *"Shanpo Yang"* (Sheep on Hillside) and *"Hong Xiu Xie"* (Red Embroidered Shoes); these names were plain and vernacular, showing their relation with folk music.

Literature of prosperity

Yuan verse is featured in Chinese literary history because of its profound revelation of social realities, its extensive content, the plainness of its languages, the vividness of its forms, the freshness of its styles, the vivacity of its descriptions and the diversity of its approaches. Yuan verse has its own unique charms as a prosperous literary form after the Tang poems and Song lyrics and inherited its artistic tastes from the latter. The tyranny of the government and the darkness of the society combined with the decline in the intellectuals' social status endowed Yuan verse with a sentiment of fighting, revealing their resentments. The authors of the verses criticised society sharply and directly mocked a society in which "the illiterate were well acclaimed, while educations became meaningless" and "Mammonism flourished." Still, Yuan verse was more open and bold in the description of love themes. All these ensured its literary importance.

Yuan verses emerged during three periods of development. Under the influence of early social unrest, it was concerned with the reflection of life and fate; in the second period, it focused on love, immortality and human deeds, and expressed the unique pursuits of playwrights; in the third period it began to become propaganda for feudal ethics. The plots became grotesque, and theatrical production declined. The content and style of plays became conservative, and the playwrights moved south.

The rise of Yuan verse represented the highest achievements of this period's literature, mainly because of its fully developed verse forms of which there were more than 220 known writers. They left a legacy of more than 4,500 works, among which there are more than 3,800 *xiaoling*, 470 *taoshu* and 160 operas. In general, as literature representing an entire dynasty, the Yuan verses were a great contribution to Chinese literature because of the genre's diverse themes, creative vision, vivid reflections of society, rich character development and simple lingual expressions.

Great writers in the north

Among other writers, Yuan Haowen made a pioneering contribution to Yuan verses. He was born to a family that had produced scholars and officials for generations. He eventually became a shining star in poetic circles of the Jin and Yuan dynasty. His works were clear and beautiful, and he led and standardised the development of Yuan verses.

Yuan Haowen was good at poetry and prose and had built a good reputation by the end of the Jin Dynasty and the beginning of the Yuan. His poems were grandiose but carefully planned, vivid but without extravagance. He formed the Hefen poetic school and was known as the most successful of writers and historians, the leader of a literary circle at the end of the Jin and at the beginning of the Yuan Dynasty. He was the main representative of Northern Literature during the confrontation between Song and Jin, and a "bridge" for the transformation of Jin to Yuan literature. He was respected as the "great leader of the north."

His poems, essays, lyrics and verses had their own features, while the poems were considered his highest achievements. As many as 1,361 of his poems have been preserved, some of which vividly reflect the social unrest and people's suffering of the time, such as "The Sun of Qi," which was acclaimed as "history in the form of poetry" because of its exact description of gloomy and desolate scenes and the imitation of Du Fu's styles. His lyrics were comparable to the great lyric writers of the Song, and he was praised as the champion of lyrics of the Jin Dynasty. Although only night verses written by Yuan Haowen were well preserved, they exercised great influence over the period and led to innovations to transform the vulgar and old tunes into an elegant and new literary form.

Yuan Haowen's essays reflected the influence of Tang and Song dynasty masters and their tradition. They were fresh and vigorous, free in length, varied in styles. He was a giant as a literary critic. The "Thirty *Jueju* Commenting on Poems" was an imitation of Du Fu's "Drama is Six Quatrains"; it had a great influence on the history of literary criticism. In artistic styles, he took Su Shi and Xin Qiji as his models and integrated both strong and tender styles. All this made him the foremost essayist during the Jin Dynasty.

Four masters of verse of Yuan Dynasty

The development of theatrical art reached its peak during the Yuan Dynasty; the opera was the most prominent theatrical form and a number of distinguished playwrights appeared, such as Guan Hanqing, Bai Pu, Ma Zhiyuan, Zheng Guangzu and Wang Shifu. The first four men were called "four masters of Yuan verses."

The verse writers were relatively close to the marginalised population during the Yuan; many of them were closely associated with actors and were familiar with various elements of drama, properties and even performed onstage. Guan Hanqing once performed his own play in person. Jia Zhongming called him "leader of the operatic circle, the chief play writer and chief actor," which reflected his importance in Yuan Dynasty theatrical arts. Guan Hanqing once wrote *"Nanlü: Yizhihua"* (*Nanlü* is a flower; *nalü* is a pattern for writing a play) for an actress named Zhu Lianxiu: proof of his close relation with actors. According to various sources, Guan Hanqing wrote 67 poetic dramas; 18 have survived.

Ma Zhiyuan, nicknamed "Qianli," called himself "Dongli" in his later years to express his allegiance to Tao Yuanming's ideals. His works mostly took the theme of socially distant, secluded rural lives; he relied on both strong and tender styles. *Dongli Yuefu* was a collection of his verses, in which the "Fall of the Han Palace" was taken as the most representative work of Yuan verses.

Baipu was equally famous as a poet and lyricist and as a writer of non-theatrical and opera verses. He was born to a family of Jin Dynasty officials. When Baipu was born, the Jin dynasty was in jeopardy, threatened with attacks from the Southern Song Dynasty and the Mongols. He suffered bitterly from uncertainties as a child and had to move from one place to another. The poet Yuan Haowen adopted him near the end of the Jin Dynasty, a chaotic time. He repeatedly declined offers of Yuan Dynasty official posts and led a cynical and idle life, travelling around China for 15 years. At age 55, he finally settled in Jinling. Baipu was born to a family with a literary tradition, learning poetry and prose writing from the famous poet Yuan Haowen during his youth. His works were full of sadness and often endowed with nostalgia for a fallen dynasty, the sorrow for the loss of youth and the miserable memory of his life tragedy. He was a famous Yuan writer and playwright with masterpieces such as *Indus Rain* and *Ideal Setting for A Couple in Love.*

Zheng Guangzu was another famous verse writer for both non-theatrical tunes and operas whose name "shocked the nation and who enjoyed great popularity among the women." He was known to be the author of at least 18 plays, among which 8 have survived. Zheng Guangzu also wrote verses for non-theatrical tunes; six xiaoqu and two *taoshu* that are still preserved today.

Wang Shifu's *Romance of the West Chamber* was also famous; its call for "all people to marry for love," an ideal considered immoral at the time, expressed the wish of people to pursue genuine desires.

Four great tragedies

The influence of Confucianism on drama was extensive and profound in China. The ethics embodied by the era's Confucianism and its related "culture of historical officialisation," which emphasised reality over imagination, led to a close relationship developing between drama and history. History and legend became important sources for playwrights. The Confucian ideal of "following one's heart's desires but not beyond rules," which advocated harmony by preserving social rules and orders was given an aesthetic form by the theatrical arts. The intellectuals, greatly influenced by Confucianism but depressed by social realities, actively participated in theatrical creations. With their efforts, the theatrical arts never went beyond the artistic form of the feudal society but still differed, generally, from mainstream art.

Tragedy is one of the earliest forms of drama, as in ancient Greece. Guan Hanqing's *Injustice to Dou E*, Ma Zhiyuan's *Fall in the Han Palace*, Bai Pu's *Indus Rain* and Ji Junxiang's *Chinese Orphan* were collectively known as the four Yuan great tragedies.

The four works shared the same cultural character, which challenged traditional literature as all of them revealed the spirit of the time, promoted individual personalities, exposed the darkness of society and praised humanity, showing a new literary style and great vitality. These works broke the tradition of "euphemism," boldly criticised the social with a sarcastic, wild and cynical style with exotic features that remind us of the frankness and directness of the nomadic culture from the north.

Injustice to Dou E originated from the folk tale of "The Filial Women of the Eastern Sea" of the Han Dynasty. Guan Hanqing discreetly incorporated his own experiences and understanding when writing the play. Dou E was from a poor family and was sold to the Cai family as a child bride, but her husband died at young age. Afterwards, she struggled to live with her mother-in-law. Donkey Zhang, a despicable man, forced Dou E and her mother-in-law to marry him and his father. Dou E refused, so Donkey Zhang wanted to poison her mother-in law, but he accidentally poisoned his father. Then he claimed that it was Dou E who killed the old man. The governor of Taowu forced Dou E to confess and then sentenced her to death. The criminals were not punished, while the just were sentenced to death by "law." The play directly questioned feudal society. Dou E's appeal to heaven represented a call for justice by Guan Hanqin and the spirit to challenge social injustice. The Yuan operas were full of resentment and sadness, a natural reaction to the darkness the authors experienced in person under a regime established by Mongols. But what Guan implied in Dou E was an objection to and a negation of the entire society, which enhanced its significance.

The *Chinese Orphan* story comes from the *History of Zuo* and *The History: Zhao's Family*, which the author modified, revised and adapted. In the Jin state during the Spring and Autumn period, Gen. Tu Angu plotted to murder Zhao Dun, a just man, and managed to kill more than 300 members of the Zhao family. Zhao Dun's grandson was the only one rescued, by Cheng Ying, a family servant. When Tu found the baby was still alive; he ordered the killing of all babies aged 1 to 6 months. To save the orphan and the other babies, he used his own son to replace the orphan. His close friend Gongsun Chujiu lost his life for convincing Tu that the orphan of Zhao was found. Twenty years later, after the orphan matured, he killed Tu Angu for revenge. This was a great tragedy; the characters were vivid; the conflicts were fierce, and the atmosphere was exciting. Cruelty and despicable acts were criticised and justice was promoted. Despite its elements of feudal morals, the play was wonderful.

The reason why *Chinese Orphan* became a great tragedy lies not only in its use of a tragic historical story of revenge, but also rests on the promotion of the people's historic sacrifices for justice, which was the theme of the play. The script highlighted the contradictions between loyalty and treachery, justice and evil, arousing long-lasting excitement among its audiences. Meng Chengyu of the Ming Dynasty, noted, "This is the best story in history and it deserved the best written comment."

The *Chinese Orphan* greatly influenced the development of drama; there have been many adaptations and performances of this work. During the 18th and 19th centuries, the play was translated in English and French, was adapted and performed in Europe and gained an international reputation.

May all marry for love

A lot of dramatic love stories have been created in China throughout history. "Marrying for love" is a traditional Chinese ideal and a major theme for theatrical creations. With their devotion to life and art, Yuan playwrights tried realise their wishes for love and reunions onstage and presented the "marry for love" ideal in a variety of ways.

Yuan operas dedicated to the theme of love promoted the triumph of love over traditional ethics and humanity over the "heavenly" rules. Wang Shifu's *Romance of the West Chamber*, Guan Hanqing's *The Pavilion for Worshipping the Moon*, Baipu's *Ideal Setting for A Couple in Love*, Zheng Guangzu's *A Charming Ghost* are called collectively the four great love dramas. In addition, Li Haogu's *Zhangxian Boils the Sea*, Shang Zhongxian's *The Princess's Messenger* and Qiaoji's *Two Worlds' Marriage* were also good examples of the genre.

These love plays were endowed with realistic colours, but their romantic sentiment was overwhelming. These works promoted a love and marriage standard that was different from the old tradition and created lots of female characters of strong and rebellious personalities. Despite their different family backgrounds, these females shared a strong sense of equality and the courage needed to rebel against tradition. General plot conceptions involved a girl of noble origin pursuing her own love interest and happiness despite social obstacles; this fully demonstrated the progress of Chinese women in the pursuit of love and their struggles for their freedom of love and marriage.

Yuan verses contributed to and greatly influenced the development of Chinese poetry and its cultural prosperity. As with other literary achievements, the Yuan verses were not only an instrument for intellectuals to express their ambitions and feelings, but also a new artistic form used to reflect social condition of the Yuan Dynasty and to entertain the public.

Classical Novels

Influenced by ancient mythologies and China's literary tradition, classical Chinese novels underwent a long and tortuous course of development. From the perspective of descriptions of rich social lives, the achievements in artistic creation and the implication of an author's political ideals, the novels of the Ming and Qing dynasties reached the peak of Chinese classical literature.

Primitive forms of novels

"Novel is gossip talk" is a definition of novels found in the pre-Qin Dynasty work the *Zhuangzi*. Classical novels originated in ancient myths and legends, which could be found in the *Shanhaijing (Classic of Mountains and Seas)*, a pre-Qin-era work. These myths and legends were the creations of our ancestors and were used to appeal for blessings and the explanation of phenomena beyond their knowledge, but they were equally the source of novels.

Under the influence of the cultural atmosphere and the social factors during the Wei, Jin and Southern dynasties, stories of people and ghosts served as prototypes for novels. "The recording of supernatural forces and the ghost" was not for suggesting social reality (as novels did) but were considered by their authors as faithful records of their true experiences, as the belief in ghosts was universal at the time. However, because of social and cultural situations at the time, these "faithful" recorders unconsciously created novels.

Among them, *In Search of the Supernatural*, a novel by Ganbao, was the most representative; the content was mainly grotesque stories about divination, monsters, ghosts and fairies. The *New Account of the Tales of the World* by Liu Yiqing was a masterpiece about the people's thoughts and feelings. It was divided into 36 categories, such as virtue, language, politics, literature, integrity, generosity: recording the words and anecdotes of ruling class. These accounts were short and simple and were considered by their authors to be faithful records; they were generally termed "antique accounts," a primitive form of novel. These accounts laid a foundation for the development and classification of novels for following generations.

Foundation laid by Tang legends: Storytelling scripts of Song and Yuan dynasties

During the Tang Dynasty, novels underwent a radical change. The unconscious accounts of the Six Dynasties evolved into a conscious creation; ghost and grotesque themes overlaid the social lives of people. The relatively simple language that had been used to record became rich rhetorical expressions. This represented great progress, a breakthrough in Chinese culture and literature. Most works were legends, which were represented by Li Zhaowei's *The Princess's Messenger*, Yuan Zhen's *Biography of Yingying*, Bai Xingjian's *Biography of Li Wa*, Du Guangting's *Biography of Qiu Ranke*, Li Gongzuo's *Nanke's Dream*.

During the Song Dynasty the development of classical novels stagnated; most works were simply repetitions of the forms of records and Tang legends without significant progress. However, certain preparatory and promotional efforts had been undertaken for the development of classical Chinese novels afterwards. In the beginning of the Northern Song Dynasty, the imperial court organised the compilation of *Records of the Peaceful Period* consisting of 500 volumes and incorporating unofficial historical references, novels and biographies of earlier dynasties. This helped the spread of the accounts of grotesqueries of the Six Dynasties and Tang legends, providing rich resources for novel creation during the Ming and Qing dynasties. Still, storytelling became a popular source of entertainment among the lower classes, and scripts during the Song and Yuan dynasties referred to those used by storytellers or popular stories imitating the languages of the storytellers; the works were written in simple and easy vernacular languages, while the characters were mostly the people of the lower classes. The stories were generally those with happy endings, such as getting rewarded for good deeds or living a good life after suffering. The *Sixty Stories, Popular Novels of the Capital* and *Popular Stories of the Three Kingdoms* were the most representative works of this kind.

The novels began to progress and mature during the transitional period between the Song and Yuan dynasties. During this period, vernacular replaced the classical language in novels; the readers of novels increased; their expressions were enriched and their social functions were promoted. A good foundation was laid for the creation of vernacular stories both long and short, which ensured the prosperity of novels during the Ming and Qing dynasties.

Traditional Chinese novels with captioned chapters prevailed

During the late-Yuan and early Ming era, two masterpieces, the *Romance of the Three Kingdoms (Sanguo Yanyi)* and *All Men Are Brothers (Shui Hu Zhuan)*, were published, marking the beginning of a brand new development phase for Chinese novels. The river novels with captioned chapters were taken as the fixed form for novel creation, which was featured its by the division of a long stories with chapters; each chapter dealt with one or two central plots, which were clearly presented. The chapters should be of equal length and ensure the logical connection of the plots. The vernacular expressions such as "as we've mentioned" and "wait for the next time" were used at the beginning and at the ends of each chapter. Prose, lyrics and poems were incorporated in the chapters, while the end was often deliberately designed to attract readers. The novels with captioned chapters became popular.

Representative works of traditional Chinese novels with captions for each chapter of the Ming Dynasty novels are the *Romance of the Three Kingdoms, All Men Are Brothers, Journey to the West, The Golden Lotus* are collectively referred to as "the four masterpieces." Luo Guanzhong's historical novel the *Romance of the Three Kingdoms* tells the story of historically based political and military struggle between Wei, Shu, Wu, the *Three Kingdoms*; it was China's first historical novel; Shi Naian's heroic legend *All Men Are Brothers* describes heroic legendary story of the darkness and corruption of an imperial court and the civilians flight to join rebels. Wu Chengen's *Journey to the West*, based on the prototype of *Pilgrimage to the West*, invented a surrealistic novel of the four masters and apprentices experiencing 81 difficulties. Lanling Xiaoxiaosheng's novel, *The Golden Lotus*, was the first novel about ordinary life and the first successful novel written by a lone literati, creating a new type of writing in the process.

The four masterpieces influenced future plots and forms of development; their environments influenced the people's spiritual condition.

Peak of classical novels

During the Ming and Qing dynasties, the development of classical novels reached its peak; the richness of the themes, the quantity of publications and their achievements were unprecedented.

The novels of the Ming and Qing dynasties covered a great variety of themes and topics. They could be divided into historical novels (such as the *Romance of Three Kingdoms*), legendary novels such as *All Men Are Brothers*, mythological and fabulous novels such as the *Journey to the West* and the *Investiture of the Gods*), novels of social lives such as *The Golden Lotus* and sarcastic novels such as *The Scholars*.

There were four main schools of novelists during the period; the Antique School proposed the imitation of the records of grotesqueries of the Six Dynasties and the Tang legends. The most representative works of this school were the *Strange Tales of Liaozhai* by Pu Songling and the *Records of Ji Yun* by Ji Yun. The *Strange Tales of Liaozhai* included stories on fairies, goblins and monsters, most of which were of human personalities and emotions. The *Records of Ji Yun* was an imitation of the records of grotesqueries of the Six Dynasties; the writing was compact and classical, while most of the stories were made up by the author to express his resentment against social injustices. The novels of the Sarcastic School, represented by Wu Jinzhi's *The Scholars*, were full of satire and irony. The four critical novels, namely Li Baojia's *Scandals of the Mandar*, Wu Woyao's *Observations of the Strange Society over Twenty Years*, Zeng Pu's *Flower of the Ocean of Sins* and Liu E's *Travelogue of Laocan*, were also considered to be of the Sarcastic School. Cao Xueqin's great masterpiece *A Dream in Red Mansions* was the best example of the works of the Emotional School, which was more concerned with family relations and love affaires. The last school was called the Heroic School, referring to stories of heroic figures, such as *The Stories of Eight Chivalrous Men, Sweeping the Outlaws* and *Detective Stories of Lord Bao*.

Wu Jingzi, Chu Renhuo, Li Baichuan, Qian Cai and Xi Zhousheng were the best-known novelists of the Qing Dynasty. Their works, *The Scholars, The Fall of Sui* and *The Rise of Tang*, were important for the study of the history of Chinese classical novels.

Touching story of red mansions
Ghost tales of 'Liaozhai'

From the beginning of the Qing Dynasty to the period of Emperor Qianlong's reign, novels entered an age of prosperity. During the reign of Qianlong, classical and vernacular novels achieved perfection in *A Dream in Red Mansions* by Cao Xueqin and the *Strange Tales of Liaozhai*.

As a great realist writer, Cao Xueqin kept keen eyes on society and observed the people objectively. A "stout" man "with a big head and dark skin," Cao was proud and cynical; he was talented and fond of drinking and talking. Born in a traditional and privileged family favoured by the emperor that expected to maintain their prosperity forever, Cao grew up in luxury. However, he felt the cruelty of society and injustice with the decline of his family. Afterwards, he devoted himself to writing.

Based on the rise and fall of the Cao family, Cao Xueqin wrote the famous touching story contained in *A Dream in Red Mansions*. As in his own life, Cao's book was full of sorrow and suffering. In the 27th year of Qianlong's reign, the premature death of Cao's son made him extremely sad and sick; he finally died of disease and in poverty. Although neglected, the literary star managed to leave to the world a tremendous work. *A Dream in Red Mansions* is the best novel ever produced in the history of old Chinese novels.

A Dream in Red Mansions was originally named the *Story of the Stone*, only the first 80 chapters were preserved due to the social situation at the time. The present version contains 40 chapters that were written by Gao E to complete the story. In the first chapter, Cao Xueqin introduces the theme of the story: "The words seem to be ridiculous, but they are my tears; don't ridicule the author, for no one's really aware of his sufferings." The book took the rise and decline of four great families the Jia, Wang, Shi and Xue families and the tragic love story between Jia Baoyu and Lin Daiyu as its main plots. It describes a series of female characters with unique personalities and tragic fates, among whom the talented but unfortunate Lin Daiyu was the most representative. The tragic ending made it stand out among the novels of its time.

The publication of the *A Dream in Red Mansions* shocked literary circles; its importance in Chinese literature remains incomparable. As the greatest realist novel of ancient China, it promoted the democratic trend during the early Qing period. Numerous scholars have specialised in studying this novel.

Pu Songlin was a writer of strange tales during the Qing Dynasty; he was born in the present Zibo City, Shandong Province, and was generally known as "Mr. Liaozhai." Pu had been fond of folk stories ever since his childhood and extensively collected news and accounts about ghosts and other grotesqueries. Based on his collections, he integrated his own life experiences and produced the *Strange Tales of Liaozhai* collection in classical languages.

The strange tales about the ghosts and fairies reflected social realism and expressed the ideals of the author. It was said Pu was a village teacher at the time. To write the *Strange Tales*, he set up a tea booth on the street (in his hometown of Liuquan) and offered free tea to passersby in return for their stories. He adapted these stories at home and compiled them into the *Strange Tales of Liaozhai*. Guo Moruo said Pu's novels represented "a vivid description of ghosts and a sharp criticism of social injustice." Pu's optimism and perseverance were also appreciable; Lu Xun read the *Strange Tales* for the first time when he was 12; he later commented in *On the Tang Legends* in 1921; "In the *Strange Tales of Liaozhai*, Pu Songlin imitated the Tang legendaries; however, his inspiration came from the records of grotesqueries of the Six Dynasties. There were few ancient books at the time, so the readers found Pu's book quite interesting, and his popularity remains to this day."

The old Chinese novels reflect more than 1,000 years of history. Numerous classical works with rich content and elegant taste were produced during the development of these novels. They were treasures of Chinese culture and represented Chinese civilisation. These old Chinese novels will be passed from one generation to another for people's study and appreciation.

World in Unity

"Understand yourself and discover your own form of beauty; befriend others and appreciate the warmth of different people. If beauty represents itself with diversity and integrity, the world will be blessed with harmony and unity." The sociologist Fei Xiaotong expressed these ideas in his later years. Looking back upon history, Chinese strived to "discover their own beauty," but also learned from each other to "appreciate the radiance of others"; thus, they achieved "beauty with diversity and integrity" and created an enduring and glorious Chinese culture: a harmonious part of world civilisation.

Since ancient times, China's traditional moral philosophies on interpersonal and ethnic relations have incorporated the ideas of "harmony is precious," "love people and treat neighbours with kindness" and "all nations live side by side in perfect harmony." These philosophies were a foundation for external relations, with the goal of achieving "Great Harmony."

As the chapter *"Xu Gua"* ("Orderly Sequences") of the *Zhouyi (I Ching* or *The Book of Changes)* states, "The doctrine of couples cannot be transitory; so it should be interpreted as permanence, which means everlasting," while the *Zhongyong (Doctrine of the Mean)* confirms that "Gentlemen's doctrines start with conjugality." That is to say, human relations originate from conjugality. Of all cultural, religious and philosophical ideas, Confucianism most values doctrines of conjugality and family ethics.

From literary works *Shijng (Book of Songs)*, *Xixiang Ji (Romance of the West Chamber)* and *Honglou Meng (A Dream in Red Mansions)* to musical works such as *"Feng Qiu Huang"* ("Song of Courtship"), *"Liang Zhu"* ("The Butterfly Lovers") and *"Gui Fei Zui Jiu"* (*"The Drunken Concubine"*), literati and musicians throughout the ages have praised love and expressed romantic feelings in a variety of forms. Love has inspired great works of art, literature and drama throughout history, leaving us countless immortal characters.

Though human society has experienced great changes over the centuries, one social principle remains intact: family serves as the basic social unit and human relations start with conjugality. In modern society, men and women should also be equal, and couples should share mutual respect and establish harmonious relations.

The Chinese word for "friend" *(pengyou)* is endowed with deep meaning. As Confucius said, "Men of disparate principles can never act together. They only behave in line with their own ambitions." Only the like-minded can strive together to pursue their ideals with one accord. In the pursuit of truth and justice, true friends stick together and support each other. The purity and loftiness of their ambition can be compared to mountains and running waters.

According to legend, during the Spring and Autumn period (771–476 BC), a musician named Yu Boya was playing the *guqin* (traditional stringed instrument or zither). A woodcutter called Zhong Ziqi caught the spirit in his music and commented, "Your ambition is as high as the mountain and as broad as the flowing water." Yu Boya exclaimed in surprise, "We share the same spirit!" When Zhong Ziqi died, Yu Boya felt he had lost his soulmate. He smashed his *guqin* and never played again.

In the ancient literary world, there are many such examples of like-minded friends. In AD 826 during the Tang Dynasty, Liu Yuxi, a prefectural governor, returned to the capital Luoyang. At the same time, Bai Juyi arrived at Luoyang from Suzhou. Bai Juyi highly praised and respected Liu Yuxi's poems, calling him "Master of Poems." Bai Juyi composed a set of three poems named "Memories of the South," and Liu Yuxi composed two poems in response. In "Prefectural Governor Bai," Liu Yuxi praised Bai Juyi for his outstanding governing achievements, and said that when Bai left, "Countless local residents cried like infants at his departure."

The world in unity embodies the spirit of natural law as well as the Confucian social ideal "Within the world, all men are brothers." Chinese people of different ethnic backgrounds live together like a family, enjoying brotherly love. At the end of the 19th century, the *Datong Shu (Book of Great Harmony)* by Kang Youwei advocated the building of an ideal society under the principles of "everyone shares love with each other, everyone enjoys equality, and all under heaven are equal."

Since ancient times, Han Chinese have enriched their culture by absorbing those of other cultures. Selections from the *"Guofeng"* (folk ballads) and *"Xiaoya"* (odes and epics) chapters in the *Book of Songs* were collected from ballads handed down by various peoples. Later, from folk songs and lyric poetry to Song and Yuan dynasty verses, elements of diverse non-Han ethnic literary works were absorbed into Chinese contents and genres. Even the "Song of Bamboo Fronds," written by Liu Yuxi of the Tang Dynasty, proved to be closely related to ballads of the Tujia people. In Chinese literature, the earliest translated ethnic works are "The Song of Yue People" written in the Spring and Autumn Period, "Chile Ge" ("The Ode to the Chile Prairie") produced during the Northern Dynasties and "The Ode to the White Wolf King" created during the Han Dynasty. Lines such as "On the hill trees, and branches are everywhere; in my heart I am fond of you, but you are not aware" and "The sky ash grey, the plains boundless, cattle and sheep appear on the wind-swept plain" remain popular now.

In historiography, the three greatest Mongolian historical works, the *History of Mongolia* written during the Hongwu era (1368–98) of the Ming Dynasty (1368–1644), the *Erdeni-yin tobchi (Erdenlin Tobchi)* in the Qianlong era (1735–96) of the Qing Dynasty (1644–1368) and the *Golden History of Mongolia* (1627–1634), were translated into Chinese, enriching Chinese historical documentation in some aspects. The *Complete Annals of Ancient Bai People*, and *Xuanfeng Years Annals*, both written in the ancient Bai language from 1271–1368 have been lost now, but these two books were compiled as the *Dian Annals* during the Ming Dynasty, (after "minor abridgments and alterations," by Yang Shen, an eminent writer of the Ming Dynasty. It is a work translated into Chinese from ethnic literature. As for other aspects, there are the *Nongsang Summary of Food and Clothing* (1314), written by Uygur agronomist Lu Mingshan and the "Perpetual Calendar" compiled by Hui astronomer Jamal al-Din during the Yuan Dynasty (1271–1368), the *Shortcut to Partition of Circular Mil* (1774), created by Mongolian Mathematician Mingantu; during Qing Dynasty (1644–1911), Qu Huanzhang of the Yi ethnicity made Yunnan Baiyao, a traditional Chinese medicine, according to medical recipe written in the Yi language. All of these ideas developed in ethnic cultures have been absorbed by Han Chinese. They represent the common wealth of all Chinese people. Only through the integration and complementation of all ethnic groups, can Chinese civilisation be constantly perfected and developed.

Absorbing essential ideas from borderland peoples enabled mainstream Chinese culture to bring forth new things from the old. This combination of the Han and other ethnic cultures continues to enable Chinese civilisation to flourish, endure and thrive with the changes of time.

Sino-foreign cultural exchanges in modern times experienced a completely different road from the ancient times. Since the beginning of the Industrial Revolution (circa 1760–1840), western civilisation has continuously spread worldwide. After nearly a century's seclusion, China was forced to accept the challenges wrought by western culture. Thus, Sino-foreign and Sino-western cultural exchanges in modern times have often been characterised by integration sometimes upset by clashes.

Confronted with western cultures introduced by military force and imposed via unequal diplomatic treaties, well-educated and open-minded Chinese intellectuals inherited ancient China's tradition of opening to the outside world. With the ambition to revitalise the nation and catch up with the western powers, they consciously embarked on the road of integrating Chinese and western culture.

They were the pioneers of making contact with western culture, and they fully expected the awakening of the Chinese people and the revitalisation of China. They initiated the Westernisation Movement (1861–95) and the New Policy Reform (1901–08), acted as the advocates for the "Gongche Shangshu Movement" (1895), and Sun Yat-sen's "Three Principles of the People" (Nationalism, Democracy, the People's Livelihood) of 1905. Two prominent figures, "Chen in the South and Li in the North" (Chen Duxiu and Li Dazhao) became legends in Chinese revolutionary history, with their support for the New Culture Movement and their call to promote national rejuvenation.

The lofty ideals and spirit of liberty, equality and fraternity had been integrated into Chinese traditional ideal of "world in unity." Together they gave full expression to the ultimate goal of the social development of mankind.

Lofty Mountains, Flowing Water

The melody "Lofty Mountains and Flowing Water" has stirred the hearts of people for thousands of years. The story was associated with music, which eternalised the loneliness of separation and the beauty of the lyre, and inspired friendship between soulmates. Few words are powerful enough to describe this noble and uncommon feeling; "Lofty Mountains and Flowing Water" represent the intense and common misty-eyed expectations of the Chinese.

Mencius once said, "Mutual understanding is the highest value of all relations, while knowing each other's heart is the most valuable of all understandings." In your lifetime, you might meet a person as ordinary as a woodman, a hermit or just a passerby. However, with just a little conversation you would be surprised, and you would take him as your sworn friend. Still we can experience the glamour of Chinese literati in their friendship that often involved unexpected encounters and a sharing of ambitions.

No acquaintances around, ideals and regrets of hermits

"Picking Osmund" is a famous painting by Li Tang (1066–1150), of the Song Dynasty (AD 960–1229). It was inspired by the historical story "Refusal to the Food of Zhou Dynasty" (11th century–256 BC). The heroes in the story are Bo Yi and Shu Qi during the last years of Yin Dynasty (11th –14th century BC). It is said that Bo Yi and Shu Qi refused the food of the Zhou Dynasty (1045–221 BC) and fed on osmund plants. The story has been passed down for more than 2,000 years in China, and it still enjoys great popularity.

Bo Yi and Shu Qi were sons of King Guzhu (1600 BC) of the Shang Dynasty (1700–1045 BC). The King's testament required his second son Shu Qi to assume the throne. Shu Qi admired Bo Yi and wanted to pass the crown to him, but Bo Yi firmly declined. Shu Qi did not want to inherit the throne either, so they both fled. During King Wu's (1087–1043 BC) conquest over Shang, they thought it was unfilial for King Wu to start the war before burying his own father, and it was treacherous to offend the superior, so they dissuaded King Wu, but he turned them down. King Wu established the Zhou Dynasty after the collapse of Shang. They thought the new regime did not live up to the moral principle of loyalty, so they felt they would be shamed to eat any food from the Zhou regime. Thus, they fed on osmund, and eventually died of hunger on Mount Shouyang, today Qianan, Hebei Province.

In "Picking Osmund," the painter focused on portraying two people dying for dignity. In the painting, Bo Yi and Shu Qi sit face to face on the slope of a cliff. Bo Yi sits with his hands laced on his knees; his eyes are bright, concentrated and calm. Shu Qi sits with his upper body inclined, showing his willingness to accompany Bo Yi. Bo Yi and Shu Qi both look angular and emaciated; their bodies are in miserable shape because of living in the wild and eating potherbs, but their spirit had never been overwhelmed by hardship.

Friendship between Guan and Bao

Guan Zhong (716–643 BC), prime minister of the Qi state, who assisted Duke Huan (723–645 BC) of Qi to become one of "Five Hegemons of the Spring and Autumn Period (770–476 BC)," once said, "It was my parents that brought me into the world, but it was Bao Shuya who truly understood me." The friendship between Guan Zhong and Bao Shuya was taken as model in later generations.

Guan Zhong and Bao Shuya became acquaintances in their early years. At that time, Bao Shuya was rich, while Guan Zhong was poor. They went into business together. Every time they split their profits, Guan Zhong always took more. However, Bao Shuya never viewed him as a money-grubber, but understood his impoverished condition. Guan Zhong frequently fled from the battlefield during his service in the army; his companions laughed at his cowardice, but Bao Shuya understood that he fled only to attend to his mother. Guan Zhong was dismissed from official posts three times; yet, Bao Shuya believed he was a capable but star-crossed man. Guan Zhong and Bao Shuya assisted Prince Jiu and Prince White. After Prince Jiu's failure to usurp the throne, Guan Zhong was sent to jail, ceding his pride for life. Bao Shuya knew Guan Zhong could not endure an ignoble existence. He understood that Guan Zhong would be ashamed of not receiving honour and fame, and that he would be reluctant to die without achieving his great ambitions. Duke Huan of Qi wanted to nominate Bao Shuya as the prime minister, yet Bao Shuya held that the Qi state could not be a great power unless Guan Zhong held the post. Finally, he persuaded Duke Huan to appoint Guan Zhong as prime minister. With the assistance of Guan Zhong, Duke Huan enriched the country and increased its military force and eventually became one of "Five Hegemons of the Spring and Autumn Period."

People often speak highly of Guan Zhong's talent in governing the country and Bao Shuya's ability to discover talent and the "Friendship between Guan and Bao."

Sworn brotherhood in peach garden

Imperial power has long been venerated in Chinese tradition; however, some people still held: "What truly matters is not the imperial power, but sworn friends." During the Three Kingdoms Period, Liu Bei, Guan Yu and Zhang Fei became "sworn brothers in the peach garden," a best example of the overwhelming power of friendship over royalty.

During the Three Kingdoms Period (AD 220–280), Liu Bei, the founder of Shu Kingdom (AD 221–263) recruited chivalrous men to start a royal career. He successively met Zhang Fei and Guan Yu, who held the similar ambitions. In a peach garden behind Zhang Fei's house, beneath the smoke of incense burning on an altar, they swore oaths of brotherhood and said, "We, Liu Bei, Guan Yu, and Zhang Fei, though from different families, swear brotherhood. We will rescue each other when in difficulty and aid each other in danger. We will serve the state and save the people. Though of different dates of birth, we seek to die together. May heaven and earth be our witnesses! If we turn aside from righteousness or betray our brotherhood, may justice be brought down on us by heaven or people alike!"

Later, with the help of Zhuge Liang, Guan Yu and Zhang Fei, Liu Bei established the Shu Kingdom. Though he became king, he never betrayed his oath. The three brothers always ate and slept together. They fought battles together and were inseparable for decades. Then they passed in succession, which accorded with the oath "Though of different dates of birth, we seek to die together." They fought together and developed a friendship of life and death unlike any other in the world.

My old friend appeared in my dream, for he knew I missed him

The Tang Dynasty (AD 618–907) was an unprecedentedly prosperous period during China's Chinese feudal age. The social climate of Tang inspired many enduring friendships.

The friendship between the poets Li Bai and Du Fu can be described with the line "Long distance separates no bosom friends." Li Bai and Du Fu met in Luoyang in their middle ages. They felt like old friends at first encounter and became sworn friends thereafter. They did not meet each other for a long time. Du Fu wrote a great number of poems in memory of Li Bai, though the chance of seeing him again was remote; his admiration and appreciation for Li Bai was largely expressed in his poems. Li Bai's demotion to an inferior post in Yelang weighed heavily on Du Fu; he wrote two poems entitled "Dream about Li Bai," which have been read through the ages. "My old friend appeared in my dream, for he knew I missed him," through these two masterstroke lines, their friendship has been deeply embedded in the memory of literati of the following generations.

There are many descriptions and definitions of friendship in China. True friendships can endure life and death experiences, difficult financial conditions and disparate social statuses.

During the Tang Dynasty, Han Yu and Meng Jiao's friendship transcended differences in social conditions. Han Yu was the leader of the Eight Prose Masters of the Tang and Song Dynasties, as well as an advocate for the Classical Prose Movement. He was an outstanding writer and a dignitary of the imperial court. Meng Jiao was poor and miserable all his life, but Han Yu came to respect Meng when Meng was studying in the capital. Han Yu presented him a poem upon his departure for an official post in Jiangsu Province. A famous line in the poem, "Injustice provokes outcry…" is remembered even today. When Meng Jiao lost his child, Han Yu wrote poems to comfort him. Later, Meng Jiao passed away; Han Yu wept bitterly and wrote an epitaph for him. Meng Jiao also wrote many poems to Han Yu, expressing gratitude for his appreciation. Their friendship surpassed social statuses, surmounted life and death and shone brightly in literary history.

Bai Juyi once wrote a poem in memory of his friend Liu Yuxi, which reads, "We went through poverty, hardship and demotion together, but were separated by death in our twilight years." Previously, they both held positions in Luoyang. They drunk and sang every day, happy and carefree. Bai Juyi once wrote a poem entitled "To Mengde": "I have three wishes to toast for: First, I wish the world will be peaceful and orderly; second, I wish we will be strong and healthy; third, I wish in our twilight years we can meet frequently." Meeting frequently in the twilight years…what a simple and wonderful wish! It connotes deep friendship and unadorned expectation.

During the Tang Dynasty, many famous and reputable stories about the friendship of poets deserve high praise, such as the friendship between Bai Juyi and Yuan Zhen, Wang Wei and Pei Di as well as Liu Yuxi and Liu Zongyuan.

A monk and a layman, an old man and a youngster

The openness of the Tang Dynasty promoted deep social integration. There was a pair of friends whose friendship surpassed the spiritual domain, Jiao Ran, "The First Monk Poet of the Tang Dynasty" and Lu Yu, the "Saint of Tea."

After the An Lushan Rebellion (aka An-Shi Rebellion, began December AD 755), Lu Yu sought asylum in Huzhou and met Jiao Ran. That was the beginning of a 50-year-long friendship between a monk and a layman. Jiao Ran introduced Lu Yu to some celebrities in Jiangnan (regions south of the Yangtze River in China), such as Liu Changqing and Zhang Zhihe, and assisted him in completing the *Classic of Tea*.

Later, Jiao Ran built Shaoxi Cottage for Lu Yu; he went to Southern Jiangsu Province to invite Lu Yu to return to Huzhou and presented Lu Yu a poem. After Lu Yu changed his residence, Jiao Ran visited him again and left him a poem as a gift. When Lu Yu grew tea in Shangrao, Jiangxi Province, Jiao Ran missed him very much; despite his age, 70, he returned to the mountain to invite Lu Yu back to Huzhou, and Lu Yu returned with him. A short period later, Jiao Ran passed into *parinirvana* (complete nirvana in Buddhism). Then, after Lu Yu died of an illness on Mount Zhu, his tomb faced Jiao Ran's brick pagoda.

A monk and a layman, an old man and a youngster, regardless of his personal interest, Jiao Ran attended Lu Yu in every possible way. Such a pure and lofty friendship has reached beyond all worldly concerns.

Battlefield troop review, poems chanting and wine tasting

Xin Qiji, representative of the Strong Style of the Southern Song Dynasty, developed a close friendship with Chen Liang. They shared patriotic ideals. Xin Qiji and Chen Liang met in the precarious Xiaozong era (1162–89) of the Southern Song Dynasty (1127–1229). They were talented in literature and the martial arts and were advocates for the recovery of lost territories and for resisting Jin encroachments.

Common patriotic ideals cemented the foundation of their friendship. They travelled together on the western lake for dozens of days, tasting the wine and chanting the poems and discussed anti-Jin strategies. Xin Qiji later sent Chen Liang many poems to express his soaring ambitions, among which the most famous one was "Break the Formation":

With drunken eyes, in flickering light, I appreciate the sword.
The horn's call is still lingering from the camps in my dream.
Share the beef with my soldiers, listen to the frontier songs of the northern tribes,
And review the soldiers in the autumn.
Steeds speed like lightening, and bows snap like cracks of thunder.
When the work is done for the king and the country,
One's name shall be at once renowned and set for posterity.
Pity how the white hair has grown!

Filled with loyalty and indignation, Xin Qiji could never forget his lofty and profound patriotism and devotion, whether awake or asleep or drunk. And this ambition was shared with his like-minded friends.

Twin stars in poetry world

Nalan Xingde, top poet of Qing Dynasty, was generous and fond of making friends with celebrities. He had a noble birth, but never showed arrogance and was associated with many people in hard-up days.

In the 15th year of Kangxi (1676), Nalan, 22, met Gu Zhenguan, 40. He felt as if they were old friends at first sight, and composed the popular poem "Gold-Woven Dress: To Liang Fen." The poem precisely expressed his pursuit of lofty sentiments and his permanent devotion for his friends. They both admired each other's talent and moral qualities and shared the same literary ideas. Their "Temperament Theory" was an important literary idea in poetry circles of the early Qing Dynasty. Their works shared similar styles. Nalan's "Water Drinking" and Gu Zhenguan's "A Short Moment" were taken as the twin stars in the poetry world of that age.

Wu Zhaoqian, a good friend of Gu Zhenguan, was exiled to the frontier because of an unjust court sentence during the early Qing Dynasty. Nalan rose to Wu Zhaoqian's defence after learning of the matter. Wu Zhaoqian was ransomed back to Beijing thanks to years of Nalan's efforts. When Nalan died at 31, Gu Zhenguan cried bitterly and wrote a moving funeral oration for him. As the best friend of Nalan, Gu Zhenguan treasured their friendship with all his heart and soul.

As an official, Nalan "lived in the silt but was not imbrued," like a beautiful lotus growing in muddy water. All his life, he protected his friends selflessly. His pure and lofty heart consolidated the intimate friendship with Gu Zhenguan.

"Long distance separates no bosom friends"; in a life full of detours and uncertainties, Chinese scholars selflessly helped each other with genuine hearts and lofty and broad minds. In sharing wine and poems, they established friendships that surpassed worldly desires. A true soulmate is enough for a life long journey.

True Love Values More Than Immortality

"Dead or alive, apart or together, with you I've made an agreement: I grasped your hand, together with you I was to grow old." Love is a lifelong theme for all people. Chinese literature is full of stories of sharing weal and woe between lovers. Let's open the ancient *Book of Songs*, and travel back to the Zhou Dynasty 2,000 years ago, when rituals were still maintained. Let's erase our troubles, enter that remote era and listen to songs of love.

'Beauty of harmony' in *Book of Songs*

"Zhounan: Crying Ospreys," the first chapter of the *Book of Songs* has the following lines, "The ospreys are singing, on the sandbank of the river; there is a beautiful lady that a gentleman would like to pursue." It depicts the harmony between gentlemen and ladies." The lines "Outside is windy and rainy, the rooster crows loudly. Seeing my lover, I'm so happy!" portrayed the subtle inner emotions of a maid. The lines "I have been deeply enchanted by you. Even though I'm too shy to contact you, why don't you contact me?" expressed a girl's longing for her lover…. The beautiful poems in the *Book of Songs* have crossed time to touch the hearts of modern readers.

"Water was overflowing in River Zhen and River Wei. A young man and a lady came with orchids in hand. The lady proposed to have fun along the river. The young man agreed though he had been there before. The area along River Wei was large and lively." These lines described the beauty of love in ancient times. Young men and women dated and enjoyed the freedom of love. On the sixth day in March of the lunar calendar, the weather was warm and the sun shined brightly. Young people would gather together along the bank of River Zhen and Wei to offer sacrifices and to pray for good fortune in marriage. A pair of lovers walked in the crowds with orchids in hand, appreciating the charm of spring and enjoying the sweetness of love. "She gave me a pawpaw; I gave her a jade. It is not a gift in return, but a token of love." (*Book of Songs: "Weifeng: Pawpaw"*) These lines tell a love story. The lady gave her beloved a tasty pawpaw, while the gentleman presented his jade to the lady as a token of love.

"The reeds are green and dense; the dewdrop is as lucid as the frost. My beloved lady is standing by the river." In the morning of late autumn, along the riverbank, the reeds were green and dense and dewdrops as lucid as the frost. A shy lady gracefully walked along a riverbank. The gentleman was deeply charmed by her. Now and then, she appeared along the bank or on the mid-river island; he spared no efforts in looking for her, but failed. He was so depressed and disappointed, eager but helpless; his heart was full of pain. The lover in his heart seemed to be an illusion. He began to miss her: "One day's separation seems to be as long as three days, three months, or even three years." Finally, in a grand musical banquet, the two lovers became a couple.

The beauty of conjugality is an ancient Chinese moral virtue. Zhu Xi, a Song Dynasty Neo-Confucian philosopher, once stated in the *Annotation of Book of Songs*, "The two chapters entitled 'Zhounan' and 'Zhaonan' have been moralised by King Wen of Zhou, from which people could learn righteous temperament. It was once said that these two chapters represented purity and integrity, which could be applied to moralise ladies, townsmen, states and even the world."

Enjoy tranquillity with music chords

"The phoenix returned to his hometown, travelling around to find his mate": Sima Xiangru wrote this famous line under an instantaneous inspiration; he was a noted ode master during the Western Han Dynasty (206 BC–AD 25). In the song, he expressed his admiration for Zhuo Wenjun, the "First Beauty in Bashu." Even today, the lines still give full expression to conjugal bliss and the deep affection between couples.

The story of Sima Xiangru and Zhuo Wenjun is widely known. Sima Xiangru was a noted master of the ode and a musician. Zhuo Wangsun was a wealthy man from Ligong during the Han Dynasty. He invited Sima Xiangru to his house to exhibit his taste for the arts and literature, a fashion of the time. During a banquet, it was a custom to compose verses and play music. Sima Xiangru knew the daughter of Zhuo Wangsun was outstanding in appearance and literary grace, so he made up a song, "A Song of Courtship," to express his admiration.

The phoenix returned to his hometown, travelling around to find his mate.
But I failed and don't know where to go, how could my feelings be understood when I came here today?
There is a beautiful and elegant lady in her boudoir; the boudoir is near but the lady is far away. It really tortures my heart.

How can I win your heart, and soar together in the sky?
I hope you can live with me and be my spouse forever.
We share the same heart; no one will know if you follow me in the midnight.
If you spread wings and soar high, I will be full of sorrow as I miss you so much.

Zhuo Wenjun also admired Sima Xiangru's talent, so she hid behind a curtain and eavesdropped. She understood the lyric's meaning. The song was bold and passionate and proposed a secret tryst at the midnight and an elopement. That night, Zhuo Wenjun left home with some money and joined Sima Xiangru, who had been waiting outside. Together, they accomplished the most glorious thing in their lives.

Zhuo Wenjun was an extraordinary woman. When she arrived at Chengdu (Sichuan Province) with Sima Xiangru, finding herself in poverty, she set up a wine shop. They were content with their poor life, making their living by selling wine in the street. The expressions "Wenjun selling wine" and "Xiangru washing drinking vessels" both originated from this story.

Emperor Wu (156 BC – 87 BC) of the Western Han appreciated Sima Xiangru's literary talent very much. Before long, he issued an imperial edict to offer Sima Xiangru a post in the capital. Xiangru and Wenjun reluctantly bid farewell to each other. Five years passed quickly, and Wenjun longed for a letter from Xiangru day and night. Unexpectedly, she received a letter containing only 13 numbers: "One, two, three, four, five, six, seven, eight, nine, ten, hundred, thousand and ten thousand." She read the letter repeatedly and understood her husband's meaning. These numbers did not include "one hundred million," because in Chinese this number shared the same pronunciation with the word "affection." It indicated that he no longer had any affection for her anymore. She realised Sima Xiangru ceased to be faithful to their love. In great grief and anger, she wrote back with numbers:

"Once we parted, the love sickness was separated in two places. You said you would come back in three or four months, now it has been five and six years. I have no mood to play the harp with seven strings, and there is nowhere to send the brief letter of eight lines...

Even tens of thousands of words cannot express my heart. Out of sheer boredom I would lean against the railing. I would climb the mountain on the ninth day of the ninth lunar month to view the lonely wild geese. On the Mid-Autumn Day, the moon was round, but we never had a reunion. In the middle of July, I burnt the incense and cried to heaven. Under the heat of June, everyone kept fanning, but my heart shivered with coldness. The kite in February lost its line. Eh, My lover, in the life beyond; I wish you were a lady and I a man!"

Sima Xiangru read the poem composed with numbers time and time again, and felt ashamed for betraying his wife, who was so devoted to him. Finally, he went home and took Zhuo Wenjun to Chang'an in a luxurious carriage pulled by four horses.

Sima Xiangru became illustrious and influential afterwards, and wanted to marry a concubine. According to *A Miscellany of the Western Capital*, when Sima Xiangru wanted to marry a lady from Maoling, Zhuo Wenjun wrote the "Love till Old and Grey" to cut herself from Sima Xiangru.

"Love should be as pure as the mountain snow, as bright as the moon in the clouds. I've heard about your disloyalty, so I come to break up with you. This is the last time we will be together, and tomorrow we will part forever. I would walk slowly along the trench, leaving you as the flowing water. Looking back, I did not cry when I married you, because I thought I could catch your heart and we would never separate. The love of a couple should be as long as the bamboo pole and as happy as the fish. A man should value neither money nor power, but genuine affection."

Xiangru felt ashamed after reading the poem. Afterwards, their love increased with each passing day.

When living in Chengdu, the noted Tang poet Du Fu wrote the poem "Lyre Platform" in which "Looking into the distant evening mist and clouds from the lyre platform, I think about the wine shop of Wenjun and Xiangru became famous. Today, "Wenjun Well" and "Lyre Platform" still exist in Qionglai. On the "Lyre Platform" of Wenjun's courtyard, there is a couplet that reads, "Above the well is the mild wind and bamboo with charm; before the platform is the moon and lyre without strings." This couplet records the love story between Sima Xiangru and Zhuo Wenjun.

Blessed couple, concubine in joy of intoxication

Emperor Xuanzong, Li Longji (AD 685–762), was talented in military and politics but also an expert in melody and rhythm. During his reign of more than 20 years, the country enjoyed peace. He thought his reign had surpassed the years of the Zhenguan Period (AD 627–649), so he changed the calendar title into Tianbao. Every day, he indulged himself in concerts and conviviality. One day, during an imperial banquet, he found Yang Yuhuan (Yang Guifei), a dancer of Chinese Classical Dunhuang Dance. She was beautiful but also gifted in art, so he chose her to be a high-ranking imperial concubine.

Yang Yuhuan and the emperor always studied melody and rhythm together. The emperor established an operatic garden and allowed theatrical companies to rehearse there. The actors and actresses performed various dances army and Jiao-Di operas for the emperor and his concubine. Yang Yuhuan came from the imperial music office, and was once an opera actress. She felt lucky to meet her soul mate in the Emperor Xuanzong, and she admired his efforts in establishing the operatic garden and promoting art. Below the pear trees, she led the actors and actresses to bow down before the emperor, worshipping him as the founder of the operatic garden.

There were many women in Emperor Xuanzong's harem, and sometimes he would stay with other concubines. One day, Yang Yuhuan had a date with the emperor to drink in the Flowery Pavilion, but the emperor went to visit Concubine Mei. Yang Yuhuan got drunk alone in the Flowery Pavilion, giving vent to her anguish and dissatisfaction. With the help of Gao Lishi, a eunuch, she cut off a curl of hair, and asked him to take it to the emperor, so that she could express how she felt.

Receiving the hair of Yang Yuhuan, Emperor Xuanzong visited her in person. It was the seventh day of the seventh lunar month, and Yan Yuhuan was praying to the moon in the Palace of Eternal Life. She held a gold basin with both hands to hold the refection of the moon, confiding her love sickness for the emperor, as well as her pursuit for pure and everlasting love. The emperor was deeply moved by Yang Yuhuan's words when he arrived at the palace. Thus, they got back together and made an oath of loyalty under heaven.

Based on this historical anecdote, Du Fu wrote the "Ode of Everlasting Regret." In the poem, he said the emperor's indulgent style spoiled the country, leading to political tragedy, and, in turn, a tragedy involving the emperor and Concubine Yang. In the actual writing, Du Fu complied with the ideas in folk love stories, depicting people's instincts for beauty and desire for affection. In this way, the whole story has been endowed with more profound and connotations.

The story of Emperor Xuanzong and Concubine Yang is also the basis for a much-loved Beijing Opera. In the 1950s, Beijing Opera master Mei Lanfang presented his revised version of *The Drunken Concubine*. The natural figures and rhythms of the work make it one of the most representative pieces of the Mei Lanfang School.

Chinese scholars in the past were typically reserved and restrained, but the subject of love is frequently manifested in ancient literary works. The value of love, as well as the genuineness, kindliness and beauty shed by love remained the eternal theme of life, thus, the accomplishment of a peaceful world begins with a harmonious family life.

Endless Way Ahead

Throughout China's history, countless scholars have embarked on the search for harmony. These devoted cultural ambassadors have travelled the road of cultural exchanges between different ethnic groups, composing paeans to national integrity.

During the pre-Qin period, wars broke out between states, and all thoughts diversified. Diplomatic activities and contentions of various schools promoted cultural transmission and communication among different states and peoples. During the Qin and Han dynasties, the rise of minority groups in western and northern regions played a significant role in the development of the borderlands, but at the same time, posed threats to the stability of China. To achieve harmony with surrounding ethnic regimes, the Chinese monarchs constantly sent cultural ambassadors to these areas. These ambassadors made great contributions to national integrity and economic development, as well as to cultural communication.

From scholar to ambassador: a name shook Western Regions

Zhang Qian was an adventurer, diplomat and explorer during the Han Dynasty. He was dispatched by Emperor Wu of Han to the Western Regions on a mission to seek an alliance with the Yuezhi people against the Xiongnu. In doing so, he opened a Silk Road through the Western Regions, connecting Chinese Han culture to western states. The culture of Central China spread rapidly along the Silk Road, giving Zhang Qian's mission historical significance on the history of cultural exchanges with ethnic groups.

He made a detailed report of what he had seen and heard during his travels, which provided a reliable reference for the historian Sima Qian to compile the *Shiji (The Historical Records)*. The report also became a valuable resource in studying ancient geography and the histories of various states from the Western Regions. Zhang Qian introduced Ferghana horses, walnuts, cloves and grapes from the Western Regions, which contributed greatly to economic exchanges. Zhang Qian can be considered the first cultural ambassador of ancient China.

Ban Chao was a noted militarist and diplomat of the Eastern Han Dynasty. He was also a good model for those who gave up their scholarly studies to take up arms. Ban Chao had lofty ambitions when he was young. Though laughed at by others, Ban Chao said, "Commoners can never know the ambition of a great man!" Emperor Ming of Han later appointed him secretary general of the Imperial Archive.

In AD 73, Ban Chao was sent to Shanshan (a country in southeastern Xinjiang); at that time, the Xiongnu were also seeking an alliance with the King of Shanshan. At first, the king treated Ban Chao with great courtesy, but a few days later, his attitude changed unexpectedly. Ban Chao suspected that the arrival of Xiongnu ambassadors was the cause. Deciding bold action was called for, Ban Chao and his men started a fire in the camp of Xiongnu ambassadors, leading to a chaotic situation. Ban Chao killed three men himself, and his men killed more than 30 Xiongnu. One hundred more were burnt to death. The next day, Ban Chao presented the head of the Xiongnu ambassador to the King of Shanshan. The king quickly agreed to pay allegiance to the Han Dynasty, and Ban Chao's famous words, "Nothing ventured, nothing gained," went down in history.

During the following years, most of the states in the Western Regions paid allegiance to the Han Dynasty. In AD 94, Ban Chao conquered Yanqi, Weixu (northeast of today's Yanqi Hui Autonomous County in Xinjiang) and Yuli (south of Korla in Xinjiang). After this, more than 50 western states paid allegiance to the Han Dynasty. The next year, Ban Chao was appointed Marquis of Dingyuan.

In AD 102, Ban Chao retired to Luoyang after spending 31 years in the Western Region. He was not only talented in conquering by force, but also gifted in allying with remote states through diplomacy.

Zhaojun's marriage to Xiongnu chief
Wenji's captivity and return

During the early Han Dynasty, to avoid conflict with the Xiongnu while the economy was restored, the emperors of Han sought to make peace with the Xiongnu by marriage-alliance. It was expected that the Xiongnu could be gradually assimilated by the Central Plain culture.

"Zhaojun's marriage to Xiongnu" is a popular story about such a marriage.

Wang Zhaojun was one of "the four ancient beauties" of China. There are many stories about her, and many idioms that can be traced back to her, such as "Make the fish sink and wild geese fall; obscure the moon and make flowers blush." According to legend, it was autumn when Wang Zhaojun left her home for her arranged marriage, and the geese were flying south. Zhaojun worried about her destiny and missing her home, played a sad tune on her *pipa* (stringed instrument). When the geese flying overhead heard the sad melody and saw such a beautiful lady, they forgot to flap their wings and fell to the ground.

According to the *Book of the Later Han: Collected Biographies of Southern Xiongnu*, "Zhaojun, courtesy name Qiang, was born in Nanjun. At first, during the reign of Emperor Yuan, she was chosen as maid of the Ye court." Zhaojun was selected to the court during the reign of Emperor Yuan (48–34 BC). According to custom, the painter should paint their appearance and hand the portraits to the emperor, as the palace maids could not meet the emperor unless he summoned them. The painter, Mao Yanshou, was highly skilled, but also greedy. He always asked for money from the palace maids in exchange for a flattering portrait. Zhaojun was confident in her beauty, but she was too proud to pay a bribe, so Mao Yanshou drew a large mole on her face. Consequently, Zhaojun lost the chance to meet the emperor.

When Emperor Yuan of Han sought to make peace with the Xiongnu, he decided to choose a palace maid who could pretend to be a princess whose hand in marriage he would offer to the chief of the Xiongnu. As Zhaojun was unhappy with her lonely court life, she volunteered. When Emperor Yuan summoned her before her departure, her unparalleled beauty stunned him. In fury, he ordered the execution of Mao Yanshou, but he could not break his promise to the Xiongnu chief, so he had to bid Zhaojun farewell. He presented her with silk, gold and fine jade, and then he personally accompanied her as far as five kilometres out of Chang'an.

Zhaojun's marriage to the leader of the Xiongnu chief contributed to the friendly relations between the Xiongnu and Han Dynasty. The two nations flourished and people lived in peace and prosperity. A dozen years later, Zhaojun passed away. She was buried south of Hohhot. Her tomb stands by Daqing Mountain and the Yellow River.

During the last years of the Eastern Han Dynasty, a young woman with extraordinary beauty and talent left her name in this period doomed by the flames of war. Her beauty was comparable to that of Wang Zhaojun, while her talent exceeded her beauty. She also married a Xiongnu chief, and held an irreplaceable position in the history of the Han Dynasty. She was Cai Wenji, the composer of the famous tune "*Hujia Shiba Po.*"

Cai Wenji was the daughter of Cai Yong, the renowned Eastern Han Dynasty writer. She was knowledgeable, good at writing and was also talented in astronomy and mathematics and gifted in poetry; her eloquence and mastery of music were equally distinguished. She could recite 400 volumes of books without one mistake, proof of her talent.

"Wenji's Captivity and Return" is a well-known story. When the Xiongnu invaded the Han territory, Cai Wenji was captured along with many other women. She was married to King Zuoxian of the Xiongnu and suffered bitterly from the pain of losing her country and home as well as living in a strange place. Twelve years later, Cao Cao unified North China. Owing a debt of gratitude to Cai Wenji's father, Cai Yong, he ransomed Cai Wenji with 500 kilograms of gold and a pair of white jade rings. Cai Wenji was 23 years old when she left, but a middle-aged woman on her return.

Cai Wenji's return to Han contributed much to the preservation of ancient Chinese culture. During her 12 years with the Xiongnu, she integrated the tonalities of the Central Plains into the melodies of Xiongnu, and opened a new path for the development of music. She also brought the advanced Han civilisation to the Xiongnu, and made indelible contributions to the development of Xiongnu and to the integration of the two peoples.

Twin snow lotus flowers on icy mountains

During the Sui and Tang dynasties, relaxed ethnic policies greatly promoted exchanges among ethnic groups and their integration. Emperor Taizong of Tang was referred to as "Celestial Khagan" by some minority nationalities, sound evidence of the popularity of the ethnic policies during the Tang Dynasty.

In AD 641, Emperor Taizong of Tang arranged the marriage of Princess Wencheng to Tibetan King Songtsan Gampo and designated Li Daozong as imperial envoy to escort her to Tibet. King Songtsan Gampo led his troops to welcome her. He treated her with respect and built a magnificent palace for her, the famous Potala Palace.

Princess Wencheng brought a rich dowry to Tibet, including classical Buddhist scriptures, medicine, constructional and technical references as well as seeds for a variety of crops. Medical works, Confucian classics and literary works promoted the economic and cultural development of Tibet and helped to enhance friendly relations between the Han and Tibetan peoples. Princess Wencheng loved Tibetans and was deeply respected by them. She participated in designing the Jokhang and Ramoche temples, and introduced advanced spinning, brewing and papermaking technologies to Tibet. Today, the gold statue of Sakyamuni brought by her is still worshipped by Tibetans.

Princess Jincheng was the adopted daughter of Emperor Zhongzong of Tang. In AD 707, King Me Agtsom of Tibet asked for a marriage alliance with the Tang Dynasty. Emperor Zhongzong sent Princess Jincheng to Tibet to marry him in AD 710. During her 30 years in Tibet, Princess Jincheng devoted herself to the alliance between the Tang Dynasty and Tibet. Through her constant efforts, in AD 733, the Tang Dynasty and Tibet defined their borders, set boundary monuments at Chiling, today's Huangyuan, Qinghai Province, and promised peace.

Both Princesses Wencheng and Jincheng made great contributions to the unity of the Tang Dynasty and Tibet. Like two brilliant crystal snow lotuses, the two princesses devoted their youth and lives to the remote icy mountains.

Universally acknowledged charm of Sui and Tang dynasties

The tolerant social atmosphere of China was spread overseas, appealing greatly to Japan and other Asian nations. Sending ambassadors to China four times during the Sui Dynasty, Japan's admiration for China became profound.

In AD 623, Japanese monks Huiqi and Huiri returned to Japan after years of studying in China. They reported to the Emperor of Japan that the Tang Dynasty had the most complete legal system and suggested that ambassadors should be sent to learn from the Tang Dynasty. To learn the advanced systems and culture of the Tang Dynasty more effectively, the Japanese Government decided to organise missions consisting of outstanding talents as ambassadors and to send students and monks to China. In AD 630, Emperor Jomei sent the first mission to the Tang Dynasty. Between AD 630 and AD 895, the Japanese Government of the Nara and Heian Periods sent 16 missions to China.

The aim of the Japanese missions was to learn from China and absorb Chinese culture. The Japanese Government carefully considered the selection of the mission's members. Takamuko no Kuromaro and Kibi Makibi had studied in China for a long period, and Yamanoue Okura was a renowned writer in Japan. As for students in the mission, Abe no Nakamaro developed a close friendship with the poets Li Bai and Wang Wei. When he was unable to return to Japan, he stayed in China and became an official of the Tang Dynasty. Tachibana no Hayanari passed the imperial examination and was awarded the title of *xiucai* (scribe). Chao Heng, a student from Japan, was a good friend of Li Bai. He studied in the Imperial College and introduced cultural and other Tang Dynasty traditions to Japan.

More than 90 Japanese monks came to China with missions or with merchant fleets. They made pilgrimages to famous mountains, consulted masters on Buddhist doctrines, and brought numerous Buddhist scriptures, Buddha statues and Buddhist utensils back to Japan. Saicho and Kukai established the Tiantai and Shingon orders in Japan. They also followed the tradition of the Tang Dynasty in building Buddhist temples in the mountains. Three books written by Saicho, *On the Looking Glasses of the Secret Mansion of Literature* and *Dictionary of Seal and Official Scripts* as well as *Diary of Yuanren, Travel Notes in the Tang Dynasty for Learning Buddhism*, which recorded his ten years of study during the Tang Dynasty, became precious references for the study and criticism of art, literature and history of China and Japan.

Choe Chi-won came to China from Silla (a Korean kingdom) at the age of 12. He was awarded the title of *jinshi* (one who has passed all three imperial examinations) at 18, and returned to Silla at 29. His 20-volume-work in Chinese, *Ploughing the Cassia Grove with a Writing Brush*, preserved a great amount of historical materials of China. The book remains a precious reference for the study of the Tang Dynasty. He devoted himself to the spread of Confucianism and Tang Dynasty culture. His efforts contributed to alchemical and cultural progress in Silla.

Six sea voyages eastward amid terrifying waves:
A ten-thousand-mile pilgrim of stormy sands

In the history of Sino-foreign cultural exchanges, monks should be mentioned. The numerous missions of Buddhist monks within China or abroad played a crucial role in the cultural transmission and exchanges of that era. The eminent monk Faxian of the Eastern Jin Dynasty (AD 265–316) was the first Buddhist master to make a pilgrimage overseas in search of Buddhist scriptures.

During the Tang Dynasty, the monk Jianzhen made remarkable contributions to the cultural exchanges between China and Japan. At the invitation of Japanese monks, Jianzhen attempted to reach Japan by sea six times, finally arriving in Japan in AD 754. His first attempt failed due to an unjust trial and imprisonment caused by a careless joke made by his disciple. Several subsequent attempts failed due to severe storms and terrifying waves. Jianzhen lost his sight due to the long and exhausting journey, before finally reaching Japan.

Jianzhen brought many medical and Buddhist works to Japan. He emphasised the importance of rituals and became a grand master of Japanese Buddhism. He taught Japanese physicians to identify herbs, promoted architectural and carving arts of the Tang Dynasty and designed and presided over the construction of the Toshodai Temple, taken as a classic example of Buddhist architecture. After his death, his disciples made a sitting statue of him. This statue is still worshipped in Toshodai Temple and is considered a national treasure by Japanese.

As Jianzhen spared no efforts to spread Buddhism in the Far East, another monk was struggling in the stormy desert in the west. As a counterpart of Jianzhen, he also vigorously pursued the orthodoxy and promotion of Buddhism. This great pilgrim to the west was Master Xuanzang.

Xuanzang was one of the greatest sutra translators in the history of Chinese Buddhism. Xuanzang, Kumarajiva and Paramartha are viewed as the top three translators of Chinese Buddhism. Xuanzang visited many masters after becoming a monk. Realising there were too many divergences among different orders, he determined to study in India, the cradle of Buddhism. In AD 627, he left Chang'an and headed west via Liangzhou and Yumen Pass. He endured hardships and dangers before finally reaching India. He debated with Indian scholars of Buddhism and won great fame there.

Xuanzang's journey to the west covered 2,500 kilometres and took 17 years. He brought back 520 sets and 657 volumes of sutras written in Sanskrit as well as 150 Buddhist relics. He organised translation work after his return to Chang'an and translated 75 sets of scriptures and treatises into Chinese: 1,335 volumes in total. Xuanzang relied on literal translations; his work *Records of the Western Regions of the Great Tang* was a crucial resource for the study of the history and geography of India and Central Asia.

In AD 664, Xuanzang died in Yuhua Palace of Chang'an and was buried in the White Deer Plain. His relics were taken back and worshipped in Tianxi Temple, Nanjing. His story has been widely told among the people, and he is the prototype of Tangseng in the classic work *Xiyou Ji (Journey to the West)*.

To give, not to take: Zheng He's western expedition

During the reign of Ming Emperor Yongle (1360–1424), Chinese diplomatic policies were based on the principle of "opening-up and peace." In the Yongle years, the government advocated the spirit of "to give, not to take" and adopted a peaceful diplomacy of "promoting moral doctrines and treating distant peoples with tolerance." These policies enabled Chinese civilisation to reach out to the world and to absorb foreign cultures at the same time. Hence, the cultural connection with other nations was enhanced, paving the way for Zheng He's expedition to the west.

Zheng He was a famous navigator during the Ming Dynasty. In 1405, Emperor Yongle ordered Zheng He to lead a large fleet of more than 240 ships and more than 27,400 sailors on an expedition. He visited more than 30 nations and areas in the Western Pacific and Indian Ocean regions. This expedition strengthened friendly relations with the people of East Africa and the South Sea region and was historically known as Zheng He's western expedition.

Zheng He sailed to the west seven times, promoted peaceful diplomacy, stabilised the international order of Southeast Asia, developed foreign trade, opened up the marine industry, determined sea routes between Asia and Africa and laid the foundation for western exploration. Zheng He was the pioneer of the Age of Discovery. His expedition was a century earlier that those of the adventurers from Portugal and Spain, and he arrived in Africa 57 years earlier than Bartolomeu Dias.

These ancient Chinese cultural ambassadors enhanced political, economic and cultural communication between China and western nations against all odds. They have made historical contributions to the opening of the Silk Road and the unity of the multi-ethnic nation. Their efforts have facilitated the promotion of China's rich and diverse culture.

Broad Way for A Nation

Foreigners, introduced western culture to China. Since the 19th century, the trend of the spread of western culture by foreigners evolved into the introduction of western studies by Chinese themselves. With the aim of absorbing western civilisation to improve Chinese culture, the intellectuals of the 19th century eventually found a road of national renaissance in China.

Countless Chinese people have made remarkable contributions to the introduction of western culture. Though different in social status, they bore the same noble ambition and struggled to revive the nation, make the country prosperous and enlighten the people.

Pioneers with a global insight

Wei Yuan referred to Lin Zexu as "the first man with a global insight." He advocated the learning of advanced cultures and technology from the West and insisted on the development of national industry and commerce.

Lin Zexu served as an official of the Qing Dynasty during the Opium Suppression Movement in Guangzhou. To learn more about western countries, he arranged the translation of the British *Encyclopaedia of Geography* into Chinese and re-edited it as *World Geography*. The book was the first comprehensive geographical work in China that introduced geographical, historical and political conditons of more than 30 countries. This book promoted the fashion of foreign studies and influenced the publication of a series of works on western cultures.

Wei Yuan was also one of the pioneers who advocated western learning. He compiled *Records and Maps of the World* based on Lin Zexu's *World Geography*. The book dealt with world geography, history, politics, economy, religion, calendar, culture and products. It promoted national revival, resistance against foreign invasions, the correction of social problems and the prosperity of the nation. He stuck to the principle of "being practical" for academic studies and suggested the idea of "learn from your enemies." He supported the introduction of advanced western technologies, the reform of Chinese troops and China's independence and sovereignty. He appealed for the development of civil industries and criticised the seclusion policy of the Qing Dynasty. Besides, Wei Yuan thought highly of the democratic institution of the western capitalist countries. As for the taxation system, he emphasised the protection of tax sources and condemned harsh impositions. He was a political and economic pioneer of the 19th century.

Appeal of Westernisation Movement, New Political Reform

The Qing government was greatly weakened by the Second Opium War (1850–60) and the Taiping Rebellion (1850–64). With the aim of finding a way out amidst internal and external crisis and safeguarding the rule of the dynasty, the government initiated the Westernisation Movement, which lasted for more than 30 years.

Zeng Guofan is regarded as "the last hero in Chinese ancient history and the first hero in modern history." He advocated and participated in the planning of coastal defences, the building of a modern navy and schools, sending students overseas and the translations of western works.

A contemporary of Zeng Guofan, Li Hongzhang was the founder and leader of the Huai Army and served the Qing government as the governor of Zhili and minister of foreign trade. The former Japanese Prime Minister Ito Hirobumi praised him as the only man of the Qing Dynasty that could compete with world powers.

Li Hongzhang built an army equipped with western weapons. He established a series of modern military industries and "The Third Ammunition Bureau of Shanghai." He initiated the largest civil enterprise in modern China—China Merchants Steamship Navigation Company—and then set up the Jiangnan Manufacturing Bureau. He successively established a series of civil enterprises, covering the fields of mining, railways, textiles and telecommunications. He pushed the development of the Westernisation Movement, originally militarily oriented, toward a civil-industry orientation and thus promoted the birth of the modern Chinese capitalist industry.

Zhang Zhidong, together with Zeng Guofan, Li Hongzhang and Zuo Zongtang were called "Four Famous Officials" in the late Qing Dynasty. He proposed the idea "learning western techniques on the basis of Chinese culture." The most eminent accomplishment of Zhang Zhidong was his promotion of modernising education in China. He prioritised education over all government policies and created modern schools and transformed old-style colleges. He widely promoted standard education, which radically changed ways of instruction in China. He established Sanjiang Normal School (Nanjing University), Wuhan Self-Strengthen School (Wuhan University) and Wuchang Kindergarten in Hubei. These schools formed the basis of the modern educational system and exercised great influence over the entire country.

Education played a leading role in the course of the introduction of western cultures in modern China. With the spread of western thoughts, enlightened intellectuals pushed forward reforms in economic and political systems and lead to the birth of the New Culture Movement.

Menaced by internal and external crises, the Qing government carried out "new political reform." Students studying abroad played a crucial role in the promotion of advanced western culture. After the first Sino-Japanese War, studying in Japan became popular. After 1900, an increasing number of students chose to study in the United States. Around 1912, Li Shizeng and Cai Yuanpei initiated a work-study programme, which enabled many students to study in France. These students came to know about western education directly and spread western learning to China in a more direct way. The modernisation of China could not have been achieved without the efforts of students studying in the West.

First Chinese student abroad

There have been countless talents among the Chinese students who have studied overseas. As the first person ever to study abroad in modern China, Rong Hong, can be said to have marked the beginning of that part of history.

On January 4, 1847, Rong Hong, a young Cantonese man with few belongings, boarded a ship to the United States from the Huangpu Port in Shanghai, arriving in New York on April 12. He was 19.

Rong Hong was the first Chinese to study in the United States and the first Chinese student to attend Yale University. He is respected as the pioneer of overseas students from China.

Rong Hong made contact with the Taiping Rebellion in his youth. Afterwards, he participated in the Self-Improvement Movement (1861–95), the Hundred Days' Reform (1898) and The Charter Movement as well as the Xing Zhong Society Revolution (1894–1905). During the last 60 years of the Qing Dynasty, from the Taping Rebellion to the Eve of the Revolution of 1911, he could be found involved in each and every important nationalist movement.

In Rong Hong's autobiography *The Introduction of the West to the East*, he combined his own experience of more than 60 years and depicted the transformation of thoughts of a democratic revolutionary. The book was acknowledged to be an important work in the history of the introduction of the West to the East, particularly in the history of cultural exchanges between China and the United States. It is a must-read book for every Chinese student studying overseas.

Beating drum of Gongche Shangshu Campaign

In the spring of 1895, scholars who had passed the provincial academic exams from all over the country gathered in Beijing to participate the National Academic Examination. During this time, while they were waiting for the results of the exam, China was forced to sign the *Treaty of Shimonoseki* with Japan, a result of being defeated in the first Sino-Japanese War. According to the treaty, China had to cede Taiwan and the Liaodong Peninsula to Japan and pay Japan 10 million kilograms of silver. The news had an explosive effect in the capital. Officials of all ranks in the capital and provincial candidates were filled with anger.

The provincial scholars wrote many petitions, appealing to the court to reject the treaty. There were two eminent Cantonese among the petitioning intellectuals, Kang Youwei and Liang Qichao. Together they drew up a petition of 18,000 characters. It was said that, on May 2, Kang Youwei united more than 1,300 provincial scholars to sign the petition and sent it to the Court of Censors. This was the "Gongche Shangshu" Campaign.

The movement was viewed as "the second largest movement after the anti-Jin campaign initiated by imperial students of the Song Dynasty in the 12th century." It was also an important turning point in the history of modern China, which represented the transformation of the role of Chinese intellectuals in modern society. The 100 Days Reform led by Kang Youwei and Liang Qichao pushed forward the political, economic, cultural and ideological development of China.

Kang Youwei was the most influential theorist in the late Qing and early Republic period. He led the Enlightenment Movement among Chinese intellectuals, initiated the integration of Chinese and western political systems and made remarkable contributions to the progress of nationalist culture and theories.

Liang Qichao was prominent in the studies of literature and history. He introduced western culture and new literary concepts to Chinese literature theory. He firstly advocated style innovation and created "the new literature style," which still bears great research value today.

Kang Youwei and Liang Qichao advocated upholding civil rights and establishing constitutional monarchy in politics. In economy, they proposed to develop capitalism. In ideology, they learned from western science and set up western style newspaper agencies. They introduced western elements to institutional and social aspects and enlightened the whole society.

Three Principles of People

Sun Yat-sen was the forerunner of the democratic revolution in modern China. After the failure of the 100 Days Reform, in 1905, Sun Yat-sen proposed the *Three Principles of the People*, to save China through through capitalist revolution.

Sun established the first Chinese capitalist revolutionary democratic party in Japan: the Revolutionary League. In 1911, the Wuchang Uprising broke out. Sun Yat-sen returned to China from the United States and led the Revolution of 1911. The revolution brought an end to the more than 2,000-year period of feudalism in China and led to the foundation of the Republic of China. In 1912, Sun Yat-sen was elected temporary president of Republic of China.

Sun Yat-sen died on March 12, 1925. At the public memorial ceremony in the Altar of Land and Grain in Beijing, Fan Zhongxiu, commander-in-chief of the Henan Army, presented a plaque to mourn him. It was decorated with white flowers and the two Chinese characters "Founding Father" were in the centre. As the wife of Sun Yat-sen, Soong Ch'ing-ling also made great contributions to the founding of the Republic of China and had a high reputation. Hence, she was addressed as the "Founding Mother."

Among all the revolutionists, another woman received great attention and respect. She was the feminist Qiu Jin.

At one time, Qiu Jin went to study in Japan at her own expense. During her stay in Japan, she participated in revolutionary activities organised by overseas Chinese students. She set up the Common Love Association with Chen Xiefen and created the *Colloquial Chinese Newspaper* with Liu Dao. In 1901, the periodical *Chinese Women* was published. In it, Qiu Jin wrote an article to promote women's liberation and feminism. In 1907, she served as the supervisor of Datong School. She and Xu Xilin simultaneously started uprisings in Zhejiang and Anhui provinces. Later, she was arrested and subsequently executed for her role in the uprisings at Xuanting in Shaoxing, Zhejiang Province.

Both Sun Yat-sen and Soong Ch'ing-ling spoke highly of Qiu Jin. Sun Yat-sen once presented an elegiac couplet to her, which read, "Your revolutionary heart was embedded in hearts of people in Jiangnan." In 1942, Soong Ch'ing-ling praised Qin Jin as "one of the loftiest revolutionary martyrs" in her article *Chinese Women's Struggles for Freedom*.

'Chen in South and Li in North': Legend in Chinese revolutionary history

During the New Culture Movement, democracy and science were revered. The introduction of western culture had a great influence on ideology, and with the introduction of Marxism, the trend enjoyed a wider scope for development.

In 1915, Chen Duxiu started *Youth* magazine (becomes *New Youth* in 1916) in Shanghai and took the post of chief editor. Li Dazhao was in charge of writing and editing the periodical. This marked the beginning of the New Culture Movement. In 1918, both established the *Weekly Review*, aiming to advocate for a new culture, capitalist democracy and Marxism.

Since the Russian Revolution, Li Dazhao had published a great number of famous essays and speech drafts to promote the Russian Revolution and Marxism in the *New Youth* and *Weekly Review*, such as "Victory of the Masses" and "My View on Marxism." He praised the Russian Revolution in these articles and vigorously promoted and led the May Fourth Movement. During the New Culture Movement, Li Dazhao and Chen Duxiu prepared the foundation of the Communist Party in Beijing and Shanghai. Li Dazhao set up the first Marxism Research Society in China, which gathered a group of Marxist intellectuals.

Chen Duxiu and Li Dazhao fought energetically for the spread and promotion of Marxism in China. They made eminent contributions to the founding of the Chinese Communist Party and the Chinese communist revolution. "Chen in the South and Li in the North" became legends in Chinese revolutionary history.

Appeal of New Culture Movement

Under the influence of Darwinism, Nietzsche's philosophy and Tolstoy's humanitarianism, Lu Xun went to learn medicine in Sendai of Japan at an early age in 1904. Later, he concluded that only through literature could the people of China be saved.

In 1918, under the pseudonym "Lu Xun" for the first time, Zhou Shuren published *A Madman's Diary*, the first novel written in the vernacular language, which laid the basis for the New Culture Movement. Around the May Fourth Movement, as one of the leading figures of the New Cultural Movement, he worked for *New Youth*, and supported young people and provided guidance to young writers.

Ah-Q Zhengzhuan (The Story of Ah Q) is Lu Xun's first novel written in vernacular language. Its publication marked a milestone in the history of the New Culture Movement and exerted profound influence on national and international writers.

Nahan (A Call to Arms), published by Beijing New Tide Press in 1923, is a collection of Lu Xun's short stories written between 1918 and 1922. The stories portray social life from the Revolution of 1911 to the May Fourth Movement and revealed deep-rooted social problems. It analysed and criticised the old regime and corrupt traditions and expressed Lu Xun's longing for social reform.

The abolition of the imperial examination system and the establishment of new schools facilitated the New Culture Movement. Under the influence of western literary trends, overseas students from China explored new styles in writing. Yan Fu and Lin Yu translated many western literary works, introducing a great number of western philosophical, technical, literary and artistic theories, while Wang Guowei applied Schopenhauer's aesthetic theories to *A Dream in Red Mansions*.

The May Fourth Movement in 1919 greatly enriched cultural reform. Appeals were made to oppose the old culture and promote new culture. Against this background, Hu Shi and Liu Bannong put forward the literary revolution. They advocated writing in a vernacular language, criticised feudalistic literature and promoted new literature. These activities contributed to the rise of literary associations such as the Literary Research Association and the Creation Society.

Cai Yuanpei was a noted national democratic revolutionist and educator who adopted the principle of tolerance and diversification. During his tenure as president of Peking University, the university became the most open and active school in China to cultivate many young intellectual thinkers.

The New Culture Movements were marked by Chen Duxiu and Li Dazhao's proposal to promote democracy and science. Then Lu Xun, Hu Shi and Liu Bannong called for reform and creation of a new literature. Later, the proletarian revolutionists represented by Mao Zedong promoted Marxism in China, and under its guidance, the Chinese proletarian revolution succeeded.

Sino-foreign cultural exchanges operate in different aspects and levels. In an open China, Chinese people should not only bear an open heart and a broad vision, but also be able to criticise and question as well as to identify their own problems. To achieve this goal, it is essential to further develop and improve education in China.

Cultural diversity is the basis for all cultural exchanges. The communication between cultures can only be achieved through mutual integration; neither sweeping disapproval nor unreserved acceptance is appropriate. The Chinese culture, which has lasted for thousands of years, has benefitted from its inclusive capacity and constant impetus of renewal.

Splendid World of Arts, Culture

According to Confucius, "I set my heart on the Way, base myself on virtue, rely on benevolence for support and take my recreation in the arts." Classical Chinese art spans a wide range of disciplines that reflect the Chinese people's traditional cultural values and aesthetic tastes.

Chinese calligraphy, an art form unique to China, epitomises Chinese cultural history, developing, as it has, with the evolution of Chinese characters. There are many touching stories about how renowned Chinese calligraphers diligently studied and used calligraphy. Zhang Zhi, a calligrapher of the Eastern Han Dynasty (AD 25–220), practised handwriting beside a pond so fervently that the pond's water turned black. Zhong Yao, a calligrapher of the Three Kingdoms period (AD 220–280), studied calligraphy for ten years on Baodu Hill, where his handwriting was left on every tree and stone. Zhiyong, a monk and calligrapher of the Sui Dynasty (AD 581–618), practised handwriting for 30 years, and the place where he buried his discarded paintbrush tips, which could have filled five baskets, took the shape of a grave mound. Huaisu, a Tang Dynasty (AD 618–907) monk and calligrapher, was born into a poor family that could not afford to buy paper. So he planted thousands of broad-leafed plantains and used their leaves to write. He even named his hut, which was covered by plantain leaves, "green sky." Tang Emperor Taizong (reign: AD 626–649) practised handwriting while travelling on horseback, and copied the "Preface to the Collection of Orchid Pavilion," a well-known calligraphic work by Wang Xizhi, at night by candlelight. Mi Fu, a Northern Song Dynasty (AD 960–1127) calligrapher and painter, was so absorbed in learning the authentic calligraphic works of the Jin (AD 265–420) and Tang dynasties that not a day passed without his copying these works. Chinese have long considered calligraphy an essential means of mental cultivation. That's why so many people have been so engrossed in practising it.

The graceful forms of the Wei (AD 220–265) and Jin dynasties, the established forms of the Tang Dynasty, the unrestrained styles of the Song Dynasty (AD 960–1229), and the variety of Chinese characters in Ming Dynasty (1368–1644) works, reflect the distinctive characteristics of Chinese calligraphy of various historical periods. Chinese calligraphy's 3,000-years of development clearly shows it has evolved in synch with the development of Chinese society and noticeably reflects the spirit of each historical period.

Chinese calligraphy and painting share the same roots and have nourished each other in their development. Calligraphers in ancient China were often also painters. Traditional Chinese painting is a general term used by people today to differentiate western from Chinese paintings. Traditional Chinese painting emphasises "taking nature as one's teacher and the heart as a source of inspiration," "using form to express spirit," "conceiving a composition before starting to paint and making the artist's sentiments felt in the finished work." It is in these respects that traditional Chinese paintings differ from western paintings.

If a single painting on silk that dates to the Warring States period (475–221 BC) is regarded as the starting point of the art of Chinese painting, then it has a history of more than 2,000 years. But, if primitive rock paintings found in the Inner Mongolia Autonomous Region, in Gansu and Shandong provinces, in the Xinjiang Uyghur Autonomous Region and in Northeast China, and if the primitive ground paintings found at Dadiwan, in Qin'an county, Gansu Province, are regarded as the starting point, then Chinese painting has a history of more than 5,000 years. Traditional Chinese paintings, with their distinctive ethnic styles and various forms of expression and created by artists and artisans of various ethnic groups, have been enriched with the constant introduction of foreign paintings since the Ming and Qing (1644–1911) dynasties, particularly after the collapse of feudalism following the 1919 Revolution.

Unprecedented changes later took place in the creation of Chinese paintings, a result of increasingly frequent contact between artists of China and those of other countries. By learning from foreign art works and absorbing their merits, Chinese artists gradually created their own oil paintings, watercolour paintings, cartoons and publicity works, allowing Chinese paintings to take on a new look.

China is also a country of rites and music, with a long and well-established musical tradition. The joys and sorrows of the Chinese nation are reflected in its thousands of years of musical development. The hunting and sacrificial activities of the ancients gave birth to the earliest folk songs and prefaced the development of Chinese music.

During the Zhou Dynasty (1045–221 BC), the government established a musical organisation that was under the direction of a "musician-in-chief." A period of robust music development appeared during the Spring and Autumn Period (770–476 BC), when various schools of thought contended for influence. In contrast, turmoil spread throughout Europe.

In the history of Chinese metrical literature, along with the emergence of poems of the Tang Dynasty, *ci* poetry of the Song Dynasty and dramas of the Yuan Dynasty (1271–1368), there appeared many renowned writers, music composers and famous works. During the Ming and Qing dynasties, instrumental ensemble music won popular acclaim. For example, there was the wind music of the Zhihua Temple in Beijing, the whistling songs in Hebei Province, the music played with stringed and wood-wind instruments in the lower reaches of the Yangtze River, and the music played by a band of 10 traditional percussion instruments. Famous instrumental pieces include "The Wild Goose over the Clam Sands" from the Ming Dynasty and "Flowing Water" from the Qing Dynasty, while songs accompanied by musical instruments, such as "Parting in Yangguan" and the "*Hujia Shiba Po*" ("Eighteen Songs of a Nomad Flute") were quite popular. The *pipa*, a stringed instrument plucked with fingers sliding along a fretted fingerboard, was used in musical compositions as early as the end of the Yuan Dynasty and the early Ming Dynasty, when some well-known pieces of music were composed, including "Hai Qing Hunting the Swan" and "Ambush from Ten Sides." *Hua Qiuping Edited Tunes of Pipa*, was the earliest collection of tunes accompanied by *pipa*, during the Qing Dynasty.

In its thousands of years of history, Chinese music has been receptive to musical influences from other countries and regions. It is with such an embrace towards the outside world that Chinese music has become what it is today.

Both architectural art and science developed to a high degree in ancient China, producing a unique system epitomised by Han Dynasty wooden structures and with contributions from various ethnic groups. Ancient Chinese architecture has a long history, the widest area of distribution and most distinctive styles in the world.

The discovery of square- and round-shaped shallow-pit-type primitive houses at the Banpo Site in Xi'an, Shaanxi Province, reveal that China's architectural history spans about 6,000 to 7,000 years. The *Chang Cheng* (the Great Wall), winding thousands of kilometres along towering mountains and high ridges, is one of the architectural miracles of human history. The world-renowned terracotta warriors and horses at the tomb of the legendary Qin Shihuang (reign as emperor of China: 247–221 BC) in Xi'an, Shaanxi Province, enjoy fame as "the eighth wonder of the world." The Zhaozhou Bridge built during the Sui Dynasty perfectly incorporates engineering technology and the architectural arts. The Sakyamuni Pagoda of Fogong Temple in Ying County, Shanxi Province, stands 67.1 metres high and is the highest existing wooden building in the world. *Gugong* (the Forbidden City/Palace Museum complex), the elegant residence of Ming and Qing dynasty emperors, is the best-preserved and largest wooden palatial complex in the world. And the country's classical gardens are regarded as a pearl in the Chinese cultural legacy with their unique artistic layouts.

Philosophical concepts find their expression in the arts. The arts embody China's 5,000-year cultural tradition and incorporate the spiritual aesthetics of Confucianism, Buddhism and Taoism, all of which reflect the philosophical ideas and aesthetic tastes emphasised in traditional Chinese culture. The appreciation of art refers to feeling or experiencing beauty at deep levels. It reveals the true cultural temperament and aesthetic tastes of a person, and can help inform a person's knowledge and culture.

Charm of Chinese Calligraphy

Calligraphy occupies a special place in Chinese art. It absorbs the essence of nature and embraces the manner of all objects on the earth to inspire everlasting creativity. Stroke by stroke, a calligraphic artwork takes shape. In Chinese calligraphy, less means more; finitude is used to express a world of infinitude. Chinese calligraphy follows a philosophy of going beyond an object itself to acquire its essence. Over 3,000 years, Chinese calligraphers have created miracles with their brushes and ink. Hence, Chinese calligraphy stands among the world's arts with pride. Shen Yinmo, a well-respected modern calligrapher, said, "Chinese calligraphy has been widely recognised as the highest form of art, because it presents amazing miracles. It is black and white but draws brilliant pictures. It is silent but plays harmonious music. Its charm appeals to people and comforts their souls."

Golden era for calligraphic styles, calligraphers

There are many theories concerning the origin of Chinese characters. Generally speaking, there are three versions: Cang Jie's Invention, Tying Knots and Evolution from the Character "One." Because Chinese characters have evolved and developed over time, academia divides Chinese characters into ancient and modern characters. Oracle Bone Script, Bronze Inscriptions, Inscriptions on Drum-Shaped Stones and Qin Small Seal Script are all styles of ancient characters. Chinese characters used since the beginning of Han Clerical Script (*lishu*) are considered modern characters. The emergence of Clerical Script symbolises the end of ancient characters and the beginning of modern characters and is therefore the most significant revolutionary moment in the history of Chinese characters. The evolution of character fonts has placed the foundation for the development and prosperity of calligraphic art in the Han Dynasty, though its origins are much older. It has also provided a wider stage on which Chinese calligraphic art and its aesthetic sensibility have been improved.

According to historical records, the famous calligraphers of the Qing Dynasty were Li Si, Zhao Gao, Hu Wujing and Cheng Miao, among others. Li Si was the writer of *Cang Jie Pian*, a primer for students of characters. Learning from the advantages of Large Seal Script, he created Small Seal Script, which had a great effect on the development of Seal Script in later generations. His calligraphic style is charming, smooth and exquisite. It is said that Li Si wrote the characters on steles commemorating Emperor Qinshihuangdi's visits to various regions. In addition, both Zhao Gao's *Yuan Li Pian* and Hu Wujing's *Bo Xue Pian* made contributions to the creation of Small Seal Script. Cheng Miao also made efforts to formulate standards for Clerical Script. During the Han Dynasty, many calligraphers may have not been well known, but their work can often be seen on steles. For instance, Guo Xiangcha wrote "Stele of Huashan Mountain"; Qiu Jing wrote "Ode to Xixia"; Qiu Bi wrote "Ode to the Pavilion"; and Ji Boyun wrote "Stele of Wu Ban."

The Six Dynasties period (circa AD 220– or AD 222–589) provided a good environment for innovative and creative calligraphy. Various calligraphic styles were created, and many talented calligraphers emerged. A variety of calligraphic artworks written with diverse styles arose and calligraphy became a more important form of art. Chinese calligraphy reached its second peak in this period.

Zhong Yao, Wang Xizhi: teachers for all calligraphers

During the Six Dynasties period, golden times for calligraphy, two great calligraphy innovators, Zhong Yao and Wang Xizhi, emerged, writing a new chapter in the history of Chinese calligraphy. Thereafter, no calligraphy student in China, or even Japan, learned calligraphy without practising Zhong Yao's and Wang Xizhi's styles.

Zhong Yao was born in Yingchuan (presently Xuchang City, Henan Province) in the State of Wei during the Three Kingdoms period. He learned his skills from Cao Xi, Cai Yong and Liu Desheng's handwriting and became good at various calligraphic styles, especially Clerical Script. An unadorned and precise structure and a natural style were the features of his calligraphic style. He created Regular Script from Clerical Script. Zhong's original calligraphic works have long been lost. Since the Song Dynasty, small Regular Script works, including "Memorial to the Throne" about Sun Quan and "Memorial to the Throne to Recommend Ji Zhi," carved in calligraphic models, are all copies made by people who lived during the Jin and Tang dynasties.

Wang Xizhi was born into a well-known family during the Two Jins period (AD 265–420) and served as a general in the Youjun army. Therefore, people in later generations called him "Wang Youjun." He acquired a general understanding of calligraphy beginning at age 12, guided by his father. As an adult, he visited many famous mountains in northern China to study the features of various calligraphic styles before creating his own.

Widely recognised during the Southern Dynasties (AD 420–589), Wang Xizhi's Regular Script works, "Yue Yi Theory," "Huangting Classics" and "Praise for Dongfang Shuo's Painting" had a great influence on later generations. Wang Xizhi, an innovator, was then named the "Sage of Calligraphy." Being expert in the Combined Script of Semi-Cursive Script and Cursive Script, he was also known as the "Sage of Cursive Script."

There is a tale relating to the *Huangting Classics:* A Taoist priest in Shanyin was trying to acquire calligraphic works from Wang Xizhi. Knowing Wang loved geese, he prepared a cage of big white geese as a gift. Seeing the geese, Wang Xizhi spent half a day writing *Huangting Classics* for the priest. Then he returned home happily with the geese. Therefore, *Huangting Classics* is also called *Geese Exchange Book. Huangting Classics* is not signed. At the end of the book, it says, "May, 12th year of Yonghe Era [AD 356]." However, only rubbings of it have been passed down.

"Preface for the Collection of Orchid Pavilion" was a preface manuscript Wang Xizhi wrote for scholars' poems at a banquet on March 3 during the ninth year of Yonghe Era of the Eastern Jin Dynasty (AD 353). The work contained 28 rows, amounting to 324 characters. This was Wang Xizhi's favourite work at the age of 33, featuring perfect composition, structure and calligraphic style. According to later critiques, "Youjun's handwriting was innovative, powerful, classic and natural. Hence, people in the past and at present all consider his handwriting a calligraphic model." All calligraphers of later generations consider "Preface for the Collection of Orchid Pavilion" the best model for Semi-Cursive Script.

Flourishing calligraphy of early Tang Dynasty

Chinese culture during the Tang Dynasty was extensive, profound and glorious. Chinese calligraphy also reached its peak. More calligraphic works from the Tang Dynasty have been passed down through the generations than from any previous dynasty.

During the early Tang Dynasty, famous calligraphers included Yu Shinan, Ouyang Xun, Chu Suiliang, Xue Ji and Lu Jianzhi. Later, some creative calligraphers emerged, including Zhang Xu, Yan Zhenqing, Liu Gongquan and Shi Huaisu. Regular Script, Semi-Cursive Script and Cursive Script entered a new era during this period, establishing the outstanding characteristics of this dynasty. Compared with those of previous dynasties, these styles of calligraphy had a greater influence over later generations.

Ouyang Xun was born in Linxiang, Tanzhou (modern day Changsha in Hunan Province). He was an expert in Clerical Script. "Stele of Fang Yanqian, the Governor of Xuzhou" was a Clerical Script work he created in the fifth year of Tang Emperor Taizong's Zhenguan Era (AD 627–649). His brushwork was smooth, powerful, aggressive and handsome. His calligraphic works, "Inscription of Dagola of Huadu Temple," "Stele of Duke Yugong Wen Yanbo" and "Stele of Huangpu Danare" are considered the best Regular Script works of the Tang Dynasty. The brushwork and structure of his Semi-Cursive Regular Script followed strict patterns. Therefore, his Semi-Cursive Regular Script works are the best models for beginners. The "36 Principles of Ouyang's Calligraphic Structure," handed down through later generations, are regular structural patterns summarised from Ouyang Xun's Regular Script. In his Semi-Cursive Regular Script work, "Rubbing of Zhang Han's Seclusion," the characters are elongated with excellent handwriting. Fortunately, this precious work has been preserved.

Ouyang Tong, Ouyang Xun's son, inherited his father's talent for calligraphy. Respected by all calligraphers, Ouyang Xun and his son are called "Ouyang Senior and Ouyang Junior." Ouyang Junior's "Stele of Master Daoyin" presents more features of Clerical Script. His father's handwriting is considered more subtle and regarded highly.

Yu Shinan was born in Yuyao, Yuezhou (today a region in Zhejiang Province) and died at age 81. As a child, Yu Shinan learned calligraphy from the seventh generation of Wang Xizhi. He was also a student of Seng Zhiyong, a well-known calligrapher. Hence, he acquired calligraphic techniques from the "Two Wangs" (Wang Xizhi and his son Wang Xianzhi) and Seng Zhiyong. A quiet person of strong character, Yu Shinan won favour from Emperor Taizong because of his direct and righteous remarks. His calligraphic style was smooth and powerful. Its strong characteristics are hidden beneath its gentle appearance. Like a skirt belt that flies with the wind but restrains the clothes, Yu Shinan's calligraphy is gentle but inviolable.

Chu Suiliang was a native of Qiantang (Hangzhou, Zhejiang Province). His calligraphy follows the calligraphic style of Wang Xizhi and Yu Shinan. "Preface to Sacred Religion at Goose Pagoda" is a fine example of his calligraphic style. On this stele, he combined the calligraphic styles of Yu Shinan and Ouyang Xun, and reflected the charm of Wang Yishao's calligraphy, but the brushwork, structure and the smooth, thin and powerful features were his own style.

Best Tang Dynasty formal script calligrapher
Second best Semi-Cursive Script calligrapher in World

Zhang Xu was a native of Wujun. His courtesy name was Bogao, but people usually called him Zhang Changshi. His calligraphy references the "Two Wangs" but had its own innovations. His Regular Script is upright and precise. Huang Shangu called his calligraphy "the best formal calligraphy in the Tang Dynasty." If people think there are more inherited features than innovations in his Regular Script, his Cursive Script is definitely an innovation in calligraphy. As Han Yu said, "Zhang Xu was an expert in Cursive Script. The variations in his Cursive Script are as unpredictable as gods and ghosts." The original of Zhang Xu's representative work, "Four Rubbings of Ancient Poems," is now displayed in Liaoning Provincial Museum.

Yan Zhenqing's family was originally from Langya (today's Linyi, Shandong Province). He served as a teacher to the crown prince and was known as the Duke of Yan Lu or Yan Pingyuan. He was born in Dunhua Fang in Chang'an County, Jingzhao (today's Xi'an, Shaanxi Province) in the third year of the Jinglong Era (AD 709) during Emperor Zhongzong's reign (AD 684 and AD 750–710) during the Tang Dynasty. He was the fourth generation of the Yan Family to live in Chang'an. The Yan Family had been well respected for its virtue, literary compositions, articles, wisdom and for producing many famous people.

"Draft to Memorialise a Nephew" is the best example of Yan Zhenqing's works. It was written in Combined Script of Semi-Cursive Script and Cursive Script. Composed of 25 lines, it is 28.2 centimetres long and 72.3 centimetres wide. The original work is now displayed in the National Palace Museum of Taiwan. This work was originally written as a draft, not as a calligraphic work. However, the casualness of the calligrapher contributed to the vivid and handsome handwriting on this draft. As Zhang Yan commented, "Notices are inferior to letters. Letters are inferior to drafts. Notices are official, so the handwriting is upright but restrained. Letters are written when the calligrapher wants to, so the handwriting is casual. However, drafts are written unintentionally. Therefore, the handwriting is unrestrained. This is where fine calligraphy lays." Xian Yushu of the Yuan Dynasty praised this calligraphic work as "the second best Semi-Cursive Script Work in the world." In the original work, all details can be clearly observed. People are able to see the process of writing and variations of the tip of the brush. This calligraphic work is a perfect model for those learning of Combined Script of Semi-Cursive Script and Cursive Script.

Four masters of Song Dynasty
Calligrapher, painter, emperor

During the decline of the Northern Zhou Dynasty (AD 557–581), Zhao Kuangyin, who later became Emperor Taizu (reign: AD 960–976), crowned himself and established the Song Dynasty, which put an end to the half-century of chaos the Five Dynasties and Ten Kingdoms period (AD 907–979), and achieved national reunification. For the more than 300 years from AD 960 to 1279, however, the development of calligraphy fell into stagnation.

Zhao Kuangyin, a calligraphy lover, purchased calligraphy works former emperors had collected and had Wang Zhu, a *shishu* (imperial calligraphy teacher), inscribed and rubbed them into a 10-volume collection named the *Rubbings of Chunhua Mansion*; it was followed by *Rubbings of Jiang* and *Rubbings of Tan*, most of which were re-rubbed from the Wang volumes.

The most remembered Song calligraphers are the Four Masters: Su Shi, Huang Tingjian, Mi Fu and Cai Xiang, while Zhao Ji, or Emperor Huizong (1082–1135), was also renowned for his unique style.

Cai Xiang was a native of Xianyou, Xinghua. He was an honest, righteous and learned man. His characters were upright, powerful and classical, with both good appearance and refined temperament. According to records, "outstanding in handwriting, Cai Xiang was hailed as the top calligrapher of the time, and thus favoured by Emperor Renzong [reign: 1023 – 1063]." Among the Four Masters, Su Shi, Huang Tingjian and Mi Fu were all good at running-cursive and running-formal scripts, yet Cai Xiang was the only one working on formal script. With a powerful, upright, majestic and beautiful style, his calligraphy saluted Wang Xizhi, Yan Zhenqing and Liu Gongquan. As Su Shi commented, "Jun Mo (Cai Xiang) is talented and learned. His heart and his hands can create various changes. That is why he is the best calligrapher."

Su Shi learned mainly from the Two Wangs, absorbed styles from Yan Zhenqing, Liu Gongquan, Chu Suiliang and others, and he tried to be creative while respecting and inheriting tradition. With a thorough understanding of calligraphy, he was creative with traditional techniques and enriched traditional techniques through his creativity, instead of simply simulating the tradition. He adopted an abnormal method of holding the brush and stressed the importance of writing instruments.

"Scroll of Poem during the Cold Food Festival in Huangzhou" is representative of his running script. This poem is a time killer, where he expressed his thoughts on life during the Cold Food Festival in the third year after he was demoted and sent to Huangzhou. Dismal and thoughtful, it illustrated his depression and loneliness. The characters match his mood perfectly. The entire calligraphic work is full of ups and downs, radiant, unrestrained yet without any single perfunctory stroke. As Huang Tingjian commented in its postscript, "In this work we see Yan Zhenqing, Yang Ningshi and Li Xitai. Probably another one as good could never be created, even by Su Shi himself."

Huang Tingjian, a self-styled *shangudaoren* (valley Taoist), was a native of Xiushui, Jiangxi Province. He was called Huang Shangu by later ages. As recorded in history, "Tiangjian is both an excellent scholar and an outstanding writer. He was born talented. According to Chen Shidao, his poems carried the essence of Du Fu, and, while good at Running Script, he made a style of his own out of Formal Script. Together with Zhang Lei, Chao Buzhi and Qin Guan, he is a student of Su Dongpo, and they are called The Four Students of Su Shi."

Huang said of himself: "For more than 30 years I've been working on Running Script. I started by learning Zhou Yue, because of which I failed to remove worldliness from my characters within the initial 20 years. It was not until in my old days, when I saw Su Shunyuan and Su Shunqin's characters, that I acquired the ancients' style. Later, I learned writing techniques when I referred to Zhang Xu, Huaisu and Gao Xian."

As Feng Ban commented, he "writes each character almost in a painterly way. Each left-to-right stroke begins with first a feign right-to-left movement and a second with a pause of artifice and then goes rightwards like a floating cloud, blown back by a gust of wind." His bamboo-painting writing technique carried a sense of calmness and boldness. In terms of his Cursive Script, Zhao Mengfu commented, "Huang Tingjian acquired the essence of Zhang Xu." His *"Huaqishi"* ("Ode to Flower Fragrance") is characterised by a powerful style and deliberate clumsiness with varied and dynamic strokes and is nothing less than a combination of Formal-and-Running Script. His "Rubbing of Buddhist Proverbs" is even more precious, with an ethereal style and lively strokes.

Mi Fu's father lived in Taiyuan, but the family settled in Zhenjiang, Jiangsu Province. He was granted the title of Calligraphy and Painting Master, so people called him Mi Nangong (as officials like him were collectively called Nangong Officials). His strange behaviour brought him another name, Mi Dian (癫 reads *dian*, which means pervert). He studied the Two Wangs thoroughly and gained much of their essence. Skilled in various scripts, he was especially good at Running-and-Cursive Script. He called his style "brush writing," because he wrote fast with much strength as if he was brushing, which fully represented his emotions. His calligraphy, whether large or small, were all continuous and imposing, alien and variable, powerful and refreshing, like dancing swords. His best examples included "Scroll of Poems on Shusu Brocade," "Scroll of Poems on Violet Gold Inklab" and "Scroll of Poems on Books."

A political failure, Zhao Ji, or Emperor Huizong, was an artistic genius and a very talented calligrapher and painter. Initially, he was influenced by Xue Ji and Huang Tingjian and to a lesser degree by Chu Suiliang and other calligraphers, but then he altered their styles to form his own style, which was characterised by a slender and upright shape, horizontal strokes ending with hooks, vertical strokes ending with points, left-falling strokes like daggers, right falling ones like hacking knives and vertical hooked ones that were long and thin. Some of his characters with connections between strokes looked just like Running Script. His strokes resembled those of Chu Suiliang and Xue Ji but were more slender and powerful, and his structure resembled Huang Tingjian's big Formal Script and looked stretched and perky. His best examples included "Rounded Fan with Cursive Script" and "Album of Peony Poems." Emperor Huizong was an ardent organiser and advocate of artistic activities. He kept a rich collection of folk relics, especially ancient bronze ware, stone inscriptions, paintings and calligraphy. He also had the *Xuanhe Book Review* and *Xuanhe Painting Review* compiled.

Days of Nostalgia, Rubbing

The early days of the Yuan Dynasty saw little economic development, and nostalgia was the fashion of calligraphy in which the Jin and Tang styles were copied; innovation was rare. Calligraphy did not break free from the rule of the Formal, Running and Cursive scripts until the Qing Dynasty. During the Yuan Dynasty, rubbing was as popular as during the Song Dynasty and calligraphers learned from the Tang and the Song Dynasties, but no one stood out with a unique style.

During the Emperor Wenzong Tianli Era (1328–1329), the Royal Mansion of Literature was built to collect treasures and relics and to appraise calligraphy and paintings, and this caused calligraphy to boom. Calligraphers who best represented this time were Zhao Mengfu, Kangli Naonao, Xianyu Shu and Yelu Chucai. They advocated calligraphy and painting be done the same way and laid stress on the structure and posture of characters.

Zhao Mengfu was a descendent of Lord Defang, son of Zhao Kuangyin (Emperor Taizu of the Song Dynasty). During the Yuan Dynasty, he served in the posts of *Hanlin Xueshi Chengzhi* and *Ronglu Daifu* and was given the title Duke of Wei, with the honorary name Wenmin after he passed away. One historical record claims, "Zhao Mengfu was the best calligrapher of all scripts ever in history, so he became known for his excellent writing skill." His amazing accomplishment in calligraphy was inseparable from his ability to learn from the mistakes of others.

According to Song Lian, a litterateur of the Ming Dynasty, Zhao learned from Zhao Gou (Emperor Gaozong [reign:1127–1162] of the Song Dynasty) when young; Zhong Yao, Wang Xizhi and Wang Xianzhi when middle aged; and Li Yong in his old age. Moreover, he imitated at one time the "Stele of Cauldron," which was built during the Northern Wei Dynasty (AD 386–534), and such calligraphers as Yu Shinan and Chu Suiliang from the Tang Dynasty and armed himself with the strengths of former calligraphers. As Wenjia (1501–1583, a master of art of Ming Dynasty) said, "He learned from and imitated all previous excellent calligraphers." His best works included "Manuscript of Inscription on Qiu E's Tombstone," "Thirteen Afterwords to Preface for the Collection of Orchid Pavilion Poems," "Ode to the Goddess of Luo River" and "Record of Miaoyan Temple in Huzhou."

The Ming Dynasty was another golden period for rubbings. Specimens of calligraphy were often rubbed. Renowned rubbings included Dong Qichang's "Rubbing of Xihongtang," Wen Zhengming's "Rubbing of Tingyunguan," Hua Dongsha's "Rubbing of Zhenshangzhai" and Chen Meigong's "Rubbing of Wanxiangtang." "Rubbing of Tingyunguan" included characters of known calligraphers from the Jin to the Ming dynasties and was a great achievement in rubbing.

Like the Tang Dynasty, the Qing Dynasty was another golden period for calligraphy. The development of calligraphy during the Qing Dynasty fell chronologically into three parts. The early part (the periods of Shunzhi [reign: 1638–1661], Kangxi [1662–1722], and Yongzheng [1723–1735]), a rubbing era, was an extension of the Ming Dynasty's style; the middle part (the periods of Qianlong [1736–1795], Jiaqing [1796–1820] and Daoguang [1821–1850]) was an age when rubbing declined and stele calligraphy increased, and the last part (the periods of Xianfeng [1851–1861], Tongzhi [1862–1874], Guangxu [1875–1908] and Xuantong [1909–1911]) was a boom time for steles.

Wang Duo, a Qing calligrapher, made great contributions in Running Script. He usually wrote on big paper and started in heavy ink; his strokes were powerful. His characters were arranged in an unrestrained and strange way. It's hard to believe that such passionate and grand Cursive Script works were created under such control. It's obvious that, compared with the cursive works of calligraphers of the Ming Dynasty such as Xu Wei and Zhu Zhishan, Wang Duo's cursive works were superior as they were created in a unrestrained yet controllable way. More importantly, he replaced the upright form of characters that had dominated calligraphy since the Yuan and Ming dynasties with a slanted style, which reflected his artistic consciousness.

Chinese calligraphy is a common way for conveying Asian aesthetics and cultures, as has peerless artistic value and enjoys profound popularity among the masses. Today, the calligraphy scene has become diversified, and the development of calligraphy has been sublimated to the level of ideological reform, more diverse a big step forward. The modernity of calligraphy is not determined simply by its external appearance but by its modernisation and the values of modern society that it suggests and conveys.

Brush Dance in Chinese Painting

Traditional Chinese painting expresses ideas and sparkles with wit in its unique ways of combining Chinese brushes, ink, poetry, calligraphy and seals in one work, on which is crystallised the mentality and temperament character of the Chinese people. This distinguishing feature and style gives it a special position in the global gallery of art.

To create a Chinese painting, an artist dips a Chinese brush into water, ink or watercolour paint then applies it to silken cloth or *xuan* (rice) paper. Chinese paintings usually portray figures, landscapes, flowers and birds in realistic ways, using fine brushwork or a liberal style of freehand ink, and the essence of this art is how the brush and ink are used. A master's work never tries to curry favour with people or "seek a resemblance to the real" or "expects feedback from the world," but always expresses the painter's own perspective. The literati saw painting as a way to show their elegance and leisurely moods. They advocated a creative spirit of "imitating nature" and "following the heart" and emphasised the unification of the painter's personality and artistic quality. Chinese painting has a long history, featuring many painting schools, prominent artists, and countless masterpieces.

Figure painting

Figure painting is a main branch of Chinese painting, emerging even earlier than landscape and bird-and-flower painting. As the name suggests, its subject is always people, whether a monk, a beautiful woman, a portrait, a genre or an historical event. The painter always strives to make the figure vivid and expressive by integrating it into the surroundings, atmosphere, and stories.

Its long history dates back to early times. It was written that people of the Shang (1700–1045 BC) and Zhou dynasties had begun to paint figures. During the Eastern Jin Dynasty (AD 317–420), Gu Kaizhi, a famous painter keen on figures, first raised the proposition of "conveying spirit through the image." His work, "Goddess Luo" is highly spoken of by later generations. Painters of the Tang Dynasty, such as Yan Liben, a figure master, Wu Daozi and Han Wo, contributed to the development of figure painting. After the Tang, many famous figure painters created outstanding works: "The Banquet in Han Xizai's Mansion," by Gu Hongzhong of the Southern Tang Dynasty; "Portrait of Vimalakirti," by Li Gonglin of the Northern Song Dynasty; "Picking Osmund," by Li Tang and "Li Bai," by Liang Kai of the Southern Song Dynasty; "Yang Zhuxi," by Wang Yi of the Yuan Dynasty; "Play Drums and the Arhat," by Zhang Hong of the Ming Dynasty; "Gao Huzhi," by Ren Bonian of the Qing Dynasty; "Tagore," by contemporary Chinese painter Xu Beihong, and many others. In modern times, "imitating nature" has become more popular among artists, some of whom have also absorbed western styles of modelling and use colour.

Landscape painting

From early times, Chinese worshipped images of the gods of mountains and waters and, to make the image more expressive, they drew landscapes as backgrounds. Later, some figure paintings were added to the landscapes, which may have been the direct origin of landscape painting.

During the Warring States period, "In Chu State, the temple wall of the deceased emperors and the ancestral hall of the aristocrats were full of magnificent landscapes." The Han Dynasty portrait, "Lotus Picking," which can still be seen today, is a typical landscape painting with a special aesthetic value.

According to historical sources, the typical works of the Wei and Jin Period, the budding time of landscape painting, were "Mount Lu," by Gu Kaizhi; "Xishan Town," by Dai Kui, and "Famous Mountains" by Dai Bo, which were called "terrific landscapes" by Zhang Yanyuan, a Tang painter and art theorist.

During the Southern and Northern Dynasties, Liu Wangzhen's "Sailing Boat in Wu Zhong" and Mao Huixiu's "Village Market of Yan Zhong" are so near to perfect that "one could see a million miles away though viewing it from a very close distance and could feel the grandness of the mountain even on such relatively small paper." Zong Bing and Wang Wei thoroughly explained the profound theories and techniques of landscape painting in their respective works, which established the theoretical foundation for Chinese landscape painting.

The development of landscape painting during the Sui Dynasty can be seen by viewing "Spring Outing," by Zhan Ziqian, a Sui painter praised as the "originator of the Tang Painting." Zhan meticulously drew green mountains surrounded by clouds, a secluded valley full of splendid forests and a bluish river with ripples, ending the Chinese landscape painting tradition that "the figure is always bigger than the mountain and the water never flows."

Tang Dynasty Landscape painting

Tang theorist Zhang Yanyuan wrote that Chinese landscape painting "originated from Wu Daozi, and came of age in the works of Li Sixun and Li Zhaodao," because Sui painters laid an indispensible foundation for the development of Chinese landscape painting, on which Tang artists built. The biggest accomplishment of the change was the heavy-colour paintings of Li Sixun and his son Li Zhaodao. Today, this style can be seen in the surviving Tang frescoes, though very few Tang landscape scroll paintings remain.

Li Sixun might be considered more professional in landscape painting than Wu Daozi, who was gifted in many ways. He began by imitating Zhan Ziqian's work, and soon developed the use of heavy blue and green ink as well as the exquisite and neat composition and a school of painting. Both his contemporaries and future viewers valued his landscape work. Su Dongpo (Song Dynasty) once expressed his praise for Li Sixun's painting, "Lonely Island in Yangtze River." Later, as Li's son, Zhaodao, made further fine changes in style, and the Li School of landscape painting was established. During the Tang Dynasty, the Li School had many successors, including Wang Xiong, Chang Gong, Li Pingjun and Zheng Yu.

Ink painting

Wang Wei is another Tang landscape painting master. His work "Wang River" brought a fresh approach to landscape painting. As a painter and poet, he included poems on his paintings, which started the tradition of "inscriptions on landscape painting." In addition, he integrated Li Sixun's heavy-colour technique and Wu Daozi's style of painting trees and stones, becoming a master who epitomised many predecessors' techniques. He inspired the ink painting style of Dong Yuan (the Five Dynasties) and was the originator of the Nanzong School.

During the Tang Dynasty, artists began to paint landscapes only with ink and water. Though it was a new style, many painters of this time, such as Zhang Zao, Zheng Qian, Xiang Rong and Wang Mo, built up reputations and brought the painting of their century to higher prominence.

Zhang Zao preferred ink and "did not value colourful paint." He liked using the ink-breaking technique to depict "beautiful high mountains, flowing water, quiet surroundings, the falling stones, and the roaring spring." His maxim of "imitating nature and following your heart" became established wisdom. Following him was Wang Mo and Zheng Qian, who mastered poetry, calligraphy and painting, and by Xiang Rong whose "use of ink was inspired by Taoism." They created a new way of ink-breaking in which they "wielded the brushes, sprinkled the ink, made light or thick ink shapes, then, mountains, stones, clouds and waters came to life swiftly on the paper, as if they were created by nature."

Jing Hao, Guan Tong

Jing Hao was the first landscape painter of the Five Dynasties to set up a new standard that valued not only the use of ink but also the brush. He contributed not just paintings but painting theory with his writings on brushwork.

Jing Hao and his successor, Guan Tong, who established the Guan School of landscape painting with the thought that "little strokes can build greater momentum and simpler scenery can bring more profound content," constituted the Jing and Guan landscape painting system.

Following them was Dong Yuan, a representative of the Beiyuan Style, who absorbed Wang Wei's way of using ink and Li Sixun's way of colouring. His works influenced the development of landscape painting in the Northern Song Dynasty and secured his status as a painter of the famous Nanzong School.

Zhe School

Proceding to the Ming, the development of landscape painting was great. The number of painters grew and many painting schools were established, including the Academy School, Zhe School, Wu School, and Huating School. The Academy and Zhe schools were closely related, while the painting styles of the Wu and Huating schools were similar.

Former Academy School painter Day Jin became the main painter of Zhe School. Building on the painting techniques of Li Tang (Southern Song) and Ma Yuan (Southern Song), he made more pauses and transitions with the brush and drew distances meticulously. His works combine the styles of both the Zhe and Academy schools.

Zhe School painters included Ni Duan, Wang E, Zhu Duan, who were all court painters and followed the example of Ma Yuan and Xia Gui (Southern Song). Lan Ying was regarded as the last painter of the Zhe School. He also took the Song and Yuan painters as models. He was talented at portraying autumnal scenery as his paintings were full of vigour.

Wu School

During the mid-Ming Dynasty, with a booming economy, the Wu School was established at Wu Men, a place where talented people had gathered since ancient times. It included many famous painters, such as Shen Zhou, Tang Yin, Qiu Ying, among whom Shen Zhou was the most representative. His refined and beautiful works clearly showed the typical Wu style.

Shen Zhou mainly studied Dong Yuan, Ju Ran, Li Cheng and Fan Kuan, but sometimes also modelled Wang Meng and Wu Zhen and eventually developed his own style. His work "Mount Lu" depicted the mountains, the waterfall, the shade of the pine trees, and the brook using a technique called *cun* (cracking), which was invented by Wang Meng, and embodied the essence of the landscape. His style changed in his later years to be freer and more unrestrained, yet the works were still profound and vigorous. Shen enjoyed a high reputation in middle ages, being praised thus: "In the morning, he was gathering mulberry leaves on the mountain, and by midday, he showed us a painting of that mountain." His style influenced many later painters, including Wen Zhengming, Tang Yin, Chen Huan, Zong Zhou, Chen Duo and Shen Hao.

Wen Zhengming's paintings are fresh, soft, wild but delicate. His early works are elegant and beautiful, while his midlife works are more profound and full of extensive strokes. Most of Wen's works recorded his travels, thus they are full of vitality. Wen had many followers, such as famous painters Qian Gu, Lu Shidao and Qian Gong. Tang Yin was a versatile artist universally praised inside the Wu School. He took up more from the Tang paintings, formed a style of long-and-thin, tall-and-graceful brushwork, and combined *Pima* and *Luanchai* techniques. His works are vivid and full of spirit. Among the works of the four renowned Wu School masters, Qiu Ying's are the neatest and most carefully done. Many of them are painted with mineral blue and mineral green colour.

In addition to these masters, there were many other painters in the Wu School. Before Shen and Wen, there were Zhao Yuan, Wang Fu, Xu Ben, Chen Ruyan, Liu Jue, Du Qiong, Shen Hengji and Shen Zhenji; after Shen and Wen came Qian Gu, Lu Shidao, Lu Shixing, Song Jue, Xie Shichen, Wen Zhenheng, Mi Wanzhong, Bian Wenyu and Li Liufang.

Huating School, Four masters, Four Monks

Gu Zhengyi established the Huating School, also known as the Songjiang School. Dong Qichang is the most representative Huating painter, who followed his predecessors' techniques. His sophisticated but natural brushwork, light but delicate colouring, and lustrous style are typical of the Huating style, unlike the refined works of the Wu School.

Dong created his own theories based on his painting practise, and proposed the "Nanzong and Beizong" theory, which aroused debate in later ages. Dong advocated a scholarly style in literati painting, and emphasised in his book that the Nanzong painting system should be the legitimate form. Noted Huating School painters included Song Xu, Chen Jiru, Zhao Zuo (*Susong* Style) and Shen Shichong (*Yunjian* Style).

In fact, Dong built an orthodox school with his theories. Wang Shimin, a painter of the early Qing Dynasty, put this concept of orthodoxy into practise and influenced his peers, followers and families. Eventually they formed an orthodox painting system that copied the works of the ancient painters: the Four Masters.

Following in the vein of Dong's theories in the development of the literati painting, the Four Masters found themselves a main target: Song and Yuan painters. They copied their works constantly and learned along the way. In this way, they continued to grow the genre of literati painting.

Wang Shimin was the originator of the "Four Masters," as well as the Louxian School. He diligently and constantly copied the paintings of Huang Gongwang, but his strict and neat strokes and elegance in colour mainly came from Dong Qichang. The works of another of the Four Masters, Wang Jian, are very similar to those of Wang Shimin, but more skilful in copying the ancient artists, especially Dong and Ju, and more subtle in the use of the mineral green and blue colours. Of the Four Masters, perhaps, Wang Yuanqi contributed most in building their reputation as he served long in an official position, and possessed a more individualised style formed on the basis of Huang Gongwang's *qianjiang* technique of landscape painting. A critic once commented that Wang Yuanqi's paintings were "ripe but not honeyed, crude but not difficult, light but thick, solid but clear."

We should say the Four Masters spared no effort in developing landscape painting, which was meaningful, especially at a time when the ancient techniques were fading away. Their later followers greatly stressed copying the ancients and regarded de-individualised and invariable courses as canon, which, to some extent, ignored the creative spirit of art. There is always a reason for the spread of such abuses, but we should take more notice of the qualitative change that takes place during an evolutionary process.

The Four Masters' rivals in the painting world are the Four Monks, which brought a refreshing breeze to the Qing art circles, shrouded as they were by the ancient air. They established diverse artistic ideas and upheld individual style. Though they were not the main trend in a time when alternative painters tended to be marginalized, they were definitely an indispensible supplement to painting.

Shi Tao is most notable among the Four Monks. He travelled across mountains and waters for half of his life in search of fantastic subjects. What he painted often broke away from the norms of the day. He liked indulgent strokes and spraying colours at will, and his works are natural and unrestrained. Shi's book, *Words on Paint,* revealed his profound philosophy about painting, especially the "one stroke" theory, and was handed down and read by many later generations. Unlike Shi Tao, Zhu Da's works are bizarre; he never followed routines and created landscape works in the way others painted flowers and birds. His wild and pretty brushwork swept away the vulgar air of the art world. Shi Xi, always mentioned with Shi Tao, stayed outside the main painting trends, too. He used a dry brush to crack the finished strokes, which created a kind of calligraphic beauty. Hong Ren, Zha Shibiao, Sun Yi and Wang Zhirui are collectively known as the "Xin'an Four Masters." With their style tracing Ni Zan, they used long strokes to build fine structures, creating neat and powerful landscapes on paper.

With the waft of a brush on paper, Chinese painters have created wonderful landscapes accompanied by charming verses. Their creativity and brilliant thinking were sprayed across their paintings as well as through their writings on art theory, building a lively and sparkling art circle in China. Traditional Chinese painting has a unique artistry and is increasingly absorbed and employed by modern artists.

Work of Inventive Minds

The Parthenon in Greece, the Roman Forum, the Eiffel Tower in Paris, the *Chang Cheng* (the Great Wall) of China, and countless ancient cities, towns and villages around the world carry profound historical meaning. They are huge edifices of art in both the physical and spiritual sense, reminding people of the great eras and achievements of humanity.

People, whether folk craftsmen, kings and emperors, have always prized grand architectural art. They contributed to the development of ancient Chinese architectural arts and helped create China's architecture.

Unique system of art

Traditional Chinese architecture takes human feelings into account. This humanistic method has an origin that lies deep within the Chinese cultural tradition. Characteristics of traditional Chinese architecture permeate all levels, from external shapes to the internal design of the buildings and their decorations. This is where the charm of ancient Chinese architectural art lies.

The ingenious tower structure is the most important structural feature of ancient Chinese architecture. Symmetry is important architecture around the world, but Chinese architecture excelled in axis-symmetry, which was influenced heavily by an ancient thought, the rites of Zhou Dynasty (1045–221 BC). All plans for ancient capital cities set their main palaces on a central axis, with other buildings along the two sides. The left and right parts of capital cities were symmetrical. This was the case in Chang'an, the capital city of the Tang Dynasty (AD 618–907), and in Beijing, the capital during the Ming (1368–1644) and Qing (1644–1911) dynasties. This pattern is also seen in many ancient Chinese temples. Usually, the prime palace was located on an axis, the key position, with accessory palaces surrounding it. The space is laid out layer by layer, with a large courtyard in the centre.

Decorations on ancient Chinese buildings were colourful and included coloured paintings and carvings. The paintings served the functions of decoration, protection, signs and symbols. The themes on carved decorations were rich in content, and included plant and animal decorative patterns, human figures, dramatic scenes and historical anecdotes. There were many carvings inside and outside the rooms of ancient buildings, such as Buddha statues in temples, and stone statues of men, and beasts in front of tombs. There are still decorative patterns of dragons and phoenixes on a stone sculpture on the steps of the Hall of Preserving Harmony in Gugong (The Forbidden City) in Beijing, weighing 200 tons.

5,000 kilometres long, 2,000 years old

In the vast lands of northern China, a long magnificent wall stretches more than 5,000 kilometres (km) from west to east: the Great Wall. It was built in ancient times as a military defense, but it also embodied the persistence and intelligence of ancient Chinese people, their technical achievements and their long history as a nation.

The Great Wall remains the largest project constructed over the longest time in world history. Work began in the seventh century BC and continued for more than 2,000 years. The wall stretched across the vast lands of northern and Central China, and was listed as a World Cultural Heritage List site in December 1987. On July 7, 2007, it became one of the New Seven Wonders. Such an enormous project is unique not only to China, but also the world.

The story of Lady Meng Jiang finding her husband embodies the chastity, bravery and wisdom of ancient Chinese women, still known today. The building of the Great Wall was achieved by the hard work and cleverness of generations of Chinese people. It is the greatest miracle created by China alongsided Tian'anmen Square and Xi'an's Terracotta Warriors.

Eighth wonder of World

The Qin Shi Huang Mausoleum, or the tomb of First Emperor of Qin (Qinshihuang Ling), is located five kilometres south of Lintong County, Shaanxi Province. Behind it is Mount Li, in front of it is the Wei River, to its left is the Xi River, and to its right is the Ba River. High-quality jade is found to its south and gold to its north. It is truly a land of treasure, fulfilling the will of Emperor Qin Shihuang (lived: 259–210 BC) that his children and their descendants would enjoy happiness and longevity forever.

To arrange his resting place after his death, Qin Shihuang planned the construction of the Mount Li tomb. The building materials mainly came from Sichuan and Hubei provinces, with as many as 700,000 labourers conscripted to build the tomb. The tomb was not finished when Qin Shihuang died, so his son had the tomb finished two years later. So the project took 39 years to complete.

The cemetery stretches east to west over nearly eight square kilometres and includes an inner area, an outer area and a gate opening towards the east. The burial mound is in the southern part of the inner area and is shaped like an upside-down funnel that is 76 metres high and with a square base. It is supposed that Qin Shihuang's resting place must be behind the tomb on the west side.

The classic history book *Shiji (Historical Records)* by Sima Qian reads: "The tomb was dug until it met deep spring water…it was consolidated by copper, with the inner and outer coffins added later. Inside the tomb were palaces and pavilions full of treasures, and a crossbow mechanism to protect it. If someone dug the tomb, he would have become a new human sacrifice. Painted on the roof of the tomb was a sky with stars made of pearls. There was a mercury lake symbolising rivers and seas. There was a candle made of hellbender salamanders' fat, symbolising eternal illumination. After the burial, Qin Shihuang's son ordered that all imperial maids without children and the craftsmen who built the tomb should be buried alive.

Later generations were dubious about Sima Qian's colourful writing, but recent archaeological discoveries prove that his work was credible. The pit containing the Terracotta Warriors was discovered east of the tomb. Inside were about 7,000 statues of warriors, more than 100 chariots, more than 100 warhorses and thousands of weapons. It has become known as the Eighth Wonder of the World.

Model of bridge construction

China has been known as a country of bridges since ancient times. As a quote from an ancient Chinese book says, "Communication couldn't go beyond mountains or rivers if there were no bridges." Across China, bridges weave a traffic web extending in all directions. The ancient art of Chinese bridge construction developed quickly during the Sui Dynasty (AD 581–618), and flourished during the Song Dynasty (AD 960–1279), with many of those bridges now considered landmarks in the history of bridge building.

The technique of the arched bridge created during the Sui Dynasty was a first for China. Zhaozhou Bridge is one of the miracles of China's architectural history, dating back 1,400 years. It is the earliest and best-preserved open-shoulder stone-arch bridge in the world, an iconic structure embodying the creativity of the Chinese. Li Chun, the designer of the single-arch Zhaozhou Bridge, broke new ground in architecture, and made a huge contribution to the development of China's bridge technology.

Zhaozhou Bridge, also called Anji Bridge, crosses the Jiao River 2.5 kilometres south of the urban area of Zhao County in Hebei Province. The span of the stone arch is 37.7 m and the total length of the bridge is 50.82 m. Its long arch span made it an unprecedented and pioneering work of architecture. A brilliant feature is the addition of two small side arches, which replaced the traditional style of filling the space above the arch with a sand and stone mixture, and therefore created the world's first open-spandrel bridge design. This was a great invention. Such a big open-spandrel stone bridge was unique for a long time in the world's history. In Europe, a similar bridge on the River Touques in France was not built until the 14th century, 700 years later than Zhaozhou Bridge. The French bridge and was damaged in 1809.

The great contributions of Li Chun, the famous stone craftsman of the Sui Dynasty, will be remembered forever in the history of world architecture. In 1961, Zhaozhou Bridge was included in the first selection of National Key Cultural Relics Protection Units.

Lugou Bridge (Lugou Qiao) located in western Beijing, also known as the Marco Polo Bridge, enjoys a reputation both inside and outside China for its exquisite stone carvings. *The Travels of Marco Polo*, written by Marco Polo, records the bridge in detail. Its stone lions became well known due to the article, *The World-Famous Lugou Bridge*, by renowned architect Luo Zhewen.

During the reign of the sixth emperor of the Jin Dynasty (1115–1234), Emperor Zhangzong, the empire was in full bloom, creating closer political, economic and military connections with Central China. Earlier ways of crossing the river, whether by ferry, floating bridges and seasonal wood bridges, could no longer cope with the volume of traffic. In 1189, the emperor ordered that a large stone bridge be built across the Lugou River. The bridge was completed in 1192, and the emperor named it Guangli Bridge. But people have always called it Lugou Bridge after the Lugou River.

The bridge was renovated during the Yuan and Ming dynasties, and was rebuilt in 1698. The bridge is 212.2-m long, with 11 arches. Each of its stone balustrades is 1.4-m high, with stone lions carved on their tops. The lions are posed in various gestures: crouching, bending over and a big one touching a smaller one. At the ends are ornamental columns, Imperial Tablets Pavilions and inscriptions. There is also a square white marble pavilion housing a tablet at both ends, with exquisite carvings of dragons on the pavilion columns.

Lugou Xiao Yue, which means "there is a beautiful moon above the Marco Polo Bridge," is one of the Eight Great Sights of Yanjing (Yanjing is an old name of Beijing). Lugou Bridge means a lot to Chinese because the Lugou Bridge Incident provoked by Japan marked the beginning of the war of aggression against China on July 7, 1937. Therefore, the bridge is also a commemorative work of architecture with historical significance.

Top among all towers

Inside the Fogong Temple in the northwest corner of Yingxian County, Shanxi Province, there is a wooden pagoda dating back to the Liao Dynasty (AD 907–1125). Due to the enshrining of Sakyamuni relics in the pagoda, it is called the Sakyamuni Pagoda. Because all its components are made of wood, it is also called Yingxian Wooden Pagoda. The Yingxian Wooden Pagoda joins the Eiffel Tower in Paris and the Leaning Tower of Pisa as the world's three great towers.

The Fogong Temple has been renovated through generations. The existing Memorial Archway, the Bell and Drum Towers, the Great Buddha's Hall and the side halls were all modified during the Ming and Qing dynasties. Only the Sakyamuni Pagoda remains the same as it was in 1056 when it was built. It was consolidated several years later, but kept its original shape. It is the oldest, biggest and highest of wooden towers in the world.

The outside of the pagoda is an octagon. It has five floors and six eaves if seen from the outside. It is 67.31-m high. From the outside, it seems that it only has five floors, but actually has nine, due to the hidden floors that cannot be seen from the outside. The tower stands on a large two-layered stone base. The base layer is square and the top layer is a 4.4-m-high octagon. There are sculptures on each floor. The Sakyamuni sculpture on the ground floor is 11-m high with wall paintings around it. The caissons in the bottom layer are laid out exquisitely and made of high-quality wood from the Liao Dynasty. On the second floor is a Buddhist altar featuring a Bodhisattva sculpture. There is an octagonal Buddhist altar on the third floor and sculptures of one Buddha and two Bodhisattvas on the fourth floor. On the fifth floor are sculptures of one Buddha and eight Bodhisattvas. They were made between 1190 and 1195.

The iron decoration on the top of the tower is spectacular and exquisite. It is 9.91-m high and has a lotus-shaped brick base; eight chains wrapped around it hold it together through rain and storms.

The Shanxi Yingxian Wooden Pagoda is the only existing all-wood tower in China. It was listed as a National Key Cultural Relic in 1961.

'Carpenter Emperor' of Ming Dynasty

The Ming and Qing dynasties were a period of great prosperity for the development of China's construction industry, with the Ming's Great Wall and Forbidden Palace the greatest examples.

The Yongle Emperor (1360–1424) was highly gifted in military and architectural matters. He was a legendary figure of the Ming Dynasty, designing Beijing and building the Forbidden City, which he based on the great capital of the Yuan Dynasty. Among the 800,000 craftsmen who built Beijing, the most famous wood craftsman was Kuai Xiang, who was known as "Kuai Luban" (a *luban* is a Chinese master carpenter).

The centralisation of authority reached its peak during the Ming Dynasty, and this was embodied in its architecture. Beijing had three structured and orderly layers: the capital city, the imperial city and the Forbidden City. The most significant buildings were set along the Central Axis, with the main government offices concentrated in the south. The

Zhonglou (the Bell Tower) and Gulou (the Drum Tower) were in the north of the city. In ancient times, people beat drums at the first watch at 8 p.m. They struck drums and bells regularly to mark the time.

Zhu Youxiao (1605–27), the Tianqi Emperor of the Ming Dynasty, loved architectural art. As an emperor, he was busy with military matters, because at that time there were peasant uprisings and invasions by northern nomadic people. But he only paid attention to the making of woodenware.

As with some emperors before him—the last emperor of the Northern Song Dynasty was obsessed with calligraphy and drawing, and the last emperor of the Southern Tang Dynasty was obsessed by poetry—Zhu Youxiao didn't focus on politics but on literature and technology. His obsession with his hobbies meant that he ignored the governance of the country, and this led to the decline of his rule.

At that time, these emperors were considered to be sapping their will through excessive attention to trivialities. But from an objective perspective, their contributions to Chinese literature and technology were indelible.

Exquisite craftsmanship, Luxuriant Qing Dynasty architecture

The architecture of the Qing palaces and mausoleums followed the regulations of the Ming Dynasty. Gardens and religious buildings took a great leap forward, as characteristic temples and civilian buildings were now being designed and built.

The Qing emperors inherited the Forbidden City from the Ming, and made some revisions and additions. To prepare for life after retirement, Emperor Qianlong built a group of systematic palaces on the eastern side of the Forbidden Palace. The three consecutive emperors Kangxi, Yongzheng and Qianlong, all built extensions to the West Garden and took into form the structure of "three hills and five gardens." Some buildings in Zhongnanhai and Beihai to the west of the Forbidden Palace bear the imperial style.

The Western and Eastern Qing Tombs follow the layout of the Ming Tombs. But the underground palace of Emperor Qianlong's time is full of stone carvings with Buddhist themes. The three palaces at Empress Dowager Cixi's (regency: 1861–1908) tomb have 64 copper gilt columns decorated with Chinese dragons. Their exquisite craftsmanship goes far beyond that of the Ming Tombs.

The scale and quality of the imperial and private gardens of the Qing Dynasty were the best since the Song Dynasty. Religious buildings such as the Potala Palace in Lhasa, the Labrang Lamasery in Gansu Province, the Emin Minaret Mosque in Turpan and the Jingzhen Octagonal Pavilion in Yunnan Province demonstrate the extraordinary architectural techniques and unique style of China's ethnicities.

People can endure life without music, drama, paintings or literature, but they cannot live without shelter. Once a house is built, it is hard for people to forget or abandon it. Architecture is a monument to an age and a nation.

Reading classical Chinese works inspires one to give their respect and admiration to generations of masters and scholars who devoted their lives to Chinese cultural studies. They recorded a collective memory of the Chinese nation with their delicate words and created cultural legends by "applying innovation to reality" and "contributing to the nation and benefitting the people."

Preface

Just as China's gorgeous scenery and landscapes are a sight to behold, ancient Chinese civilisation is a breathtaking realm to study.

The rich wealth of Chinese civilisation is embodied in the numerous romantic characters and words. The word *"xingtan"* (apricot altar) evokes an image of an academy built on an altar surrounded by apricot trees. In spring light, apricot flowers silhouetted against fluffy clouds flutter. The word *"jiangzhang"* (red canopy) reflects the solemnity of traditional education in China. It summons an image of a teacher, sitting on high under a red canopy in the hall. His students sit in front of him, while women play music behind him, a pleasant scene from antiquity. The word *"jinshi"* (metal and stone), for a commemorative epigraph, brings out the tinkling sounds of metal and stone, as well as invoking their solid nature. Words engraved on tablets in ancient China recorded a person's virtues and achievements, so they needed to last into posterity. Words such as such as "brush and ink," "red and green," "red copper" and "red pigment" stimulate colourful imagery once used to record the exotic, yet splendid Chinese civilisation and to reflect the Chinese people's respect and admiration for their traditional culture. The word "firewood and fire" means that the flame of Chinese civilisation will continue to burn bright for generation after generation.

These cultural highlights, which continue to be a source of pride for the Chinese people, have been handed down through the writings and lectures of sages and erudite scholars who aspired to "establish and consolidate fundamentals for the people in the world, carry forward knowledge and pave the way for everlasting peace." The Chinese will never forget Zhang Taiyan, a master of Chinese studies who preached wisdom and tolerance, the essence of the Chinese civilisation, in Tokyo; nor will they forget Zhao Yuanren, the founder of Chinese linguistics, who demonstrated his erudition by interpreting the lectures of British philosopher Bertrand Russell into many dialects of China in 1920; nor will they forget the master of Chinese studies Nan Huaijin, who put forward the proposal and raised US$45.68 million to build the first joint-venture railway line in China on December 18, 1992. Today, the railway still winds its way through the hilly areas of southwestern Zhejiang Province, while this master of a generation has retired from the spotlight. Throughout Chinese civilisation, each generation has practised their knowledge and skills in advancing the nation.

Over the last 5,000 years, the study of Chinese civilisation has enhanced people's folklore, permeating the everyday lives of Chinese. It has produced distinct symbols of the Chinese culture, such as the red and green costumes at festivals, the brush and ink-based styles of painting and calligraphy, the gold and silver decorations on the stage of Beijing Opera, and the unique styles of letters as correspondence. Each of them reflects the delicacy and elegance of Chinese culture and symbolise the virtues and spirit of the Chinese nation.

While Chinese aspire to realise the dream of rejuvenating their nation, the study of Chinese culture is attracting attention from all over the world.

Scholars of Profound Knowledge Paragons of Human Virtue

It is said in the *Liji (Book of Rites)*, an ancient Chinese classic, "If he wishes to transform the people and to perfect their manners and customs, must he not start from lessons in school? Uncut jade will not form a vessel for use, and if men do not learn, they will not know the way to go.

What was said of ancient rulers could be said of any ruling authority: it must enlighten people through education to succeed. Since education is an essential foundation for people, traditional Chinese culture should be understood through development and spreading of knowledge.

Chinese education was characterised by unprecedented freedom of thought and cultural prosperity during the pre-Qin period (before 221 BC). In this atmosphere of academic thought and development, many talented people received their training, including Confucius (551–479 BC), Laozi (571–471 BC), Mozi (468–376 BC), Mencius (372–289 BC), Xunzi (313–238 BC) and Han Feizi (280–233 BC).

Confucius ran private schools and gave ordinary people access to education, ending local authorities' control of learning. Confucius taught more than 3,000 disciples throughout his life; 72 became distinguished scholars. He upheld the principle of "teaching students in accordance with their aptitude." This teacher-student relationship established by Confucius and his disciple Yan Hui (521–481 BC) became an ideal conception in Chinese thinking about education.

The followers of Confucianism summarised educational principles and teaching experiences during the Spring and Autumn Period (770–476 BC) and wrote the *Xueji (On Learning)*, *Daxue (Great Learning)* and the *Zhongyong (Doctrine of the Golden Mean)*. They expounded on the role of education, the educational system, morality, teaching principles and methods, the teacher's position and other theories. These books laid a theoretical foundation for ancient Chinese education.

After his unification of China, Emperor Shihuang (reign: 221–210 BC) of the Qin Dynasty (221–206 BC) took a series of measures consolidating the unification and strengthening his centralised authority. He unified the written script and issued edicts to prohibit private schools, burn books and persecute Confucian scholars. As a result, only books on medicine, fortune-telling and tree-planting were left. In addition, he said that only government officials could serve as teachers. The edicts restricted people's right to think and resulted in the destruction of many ancient classics, causing irreparable damage to the development of ideas and culture in ancient China.

The Qin's oppressive cultural policies changed with the Han Dynasty (206 BC–AD 220). During the reign of Emperor Wudi from 156–87 BC, the policy of "proscribing all non-Confucian schools of thought and espousing Confucianism as the orthodox state ideology" was promoted. This made Confucianism the ruling ethos and the official school system was soon established. This included an imperial college and the Hongdumen Academy where New Text Confucianism was taught. Official schools and private schools coexisted. Towards the end of the Eastern Han Dynasty (AD 25–220), private schools developed to the point where they were considered superior to official schools. In private schools run by masters of Old Text Confucianism, such as Ma Rong (AD 79–166) and Zheng Xuan (AD 127–200), there were more than 1,000 students. In his class, Ma Rong, the "knows-all scholar," would sit in a high-ceilinged hall decorated with red curtains, teaching his students while female musicians song behind him.

Because of the country's long division because of war and chaos, official schools fell into decline during the Kingdom of Wei (AD 220–265), the Jin Dynasty (AD 265–420) and the Southern and Northern Dynasties (AD 420–589). Still, this created favourable conditions for the development and prosperity of private schools, where what was taught was enriched by the emergence of metaphysics, Buddhism and Taoism in addition to traditional Confucianism. Progress was made in the development of family education. Yan Zhitui (531–circa 595 AD) summarised his experiences and philosophy in *Yanshi Jiaxun (Admonitions of Master Yan)*, a book intended to give admonitions to his offspring, and the first book of its kind in Chinese history.

The Sui Dynasty (AD 581–618) instituted the imperial civil examination system, whereby the government selected talented men from among ordinary people to improve local administrations by putting an end to the aristocratic hereditary system. The imperial civil examination system was a fair, open and just method that improved the use of personnel and offered the promise of social mobility. From 607 AD during the Sui Dynasty to 1905 during the Qing Dynasty (1644–1911), the system had a profound social, political, educational and humanistic influence in China.

School-based education expanded rapidly during the Tang Dynasty (AD 618–907). The educational system was regarded by scholars of later generations as complex, complete and typical of China's feudal society. It rose and declined within society and could be roughly divided into two periods of development. Before the rebellion led by An Lushan and

Shi Siming from 755–763 AD, official schools at the central and local levels dominated education across the country and formed a complete system. The saying, "Even a child would feel ashamed of not being able to compose a poem or write prose," appeared here. Official schools, however, gradually declined during the mid- to late-Tang Dynasty, when private schools became dominant. This is when the *shuyuan* (academies of classical learning) appeared.

An academy was an independent learning institution that emerged during the Tang and Qing dynasties. Private people or governments set them up, allowing students to gather, attend lectures and to study, and had a far-reaching influence on China's feudal society's educational and cultural development.

Many eminent educators appeared, including Han Yu (AD 768–824) and Liu Zongyuan (AD 773–819). As advocates of *guwen*, the classical prose style, both were called "Han-Liu." In addition, Han Yu was described by Su Shi, a great writer of the Song Dynasty (AD 960–1279), as a writer whose prose "raised the standards after eight dynasties of literary weakness." *Jinxue Jie (Progress in Learning)*, a prose work by Han Yu, became a renowned essay on teaching methods, which mentions the saying, "Progress in studing comes from diligence and is delayed by indolence; success comes from forethought, while thoughtlessness leads to failure."

After the Song Dynasty, official schools were quite complete in terms of their organisation from the central to local levels. They played roles in training talented people to varying degrees over successive dynasties, thanks to emperors who attached importance to education. In particular, official schools emphasised selecting talented students through the imperial civil examination, while private schools focused on cultivating talented students.

Another peak in the development of Chinese culture and philosophy came during the Song, Yuan (1271–1368) and Ming dynasties (1368–1644). As Neo-Confucianism became the main representative form of Chinese philosophy, this approach was called "Neo-Confucianism of the Song and Ming period." Neo-Confucianism dominated philosophical thinking of this era. Following the modification of Confucianism under the influence of metaphysical thinking during the Kingdom of Wei and the Jin Dynasty, Confucianism was influenced by Buddhist and Taoist thinking, representing a revival of Confucianism, which gradually declined since the Sui and Tang dynasties.

Wang Shouren (1472–1529) was a well-known philosopher, educator and military strategist. Born into an intellectual family of officials, his intelligence came early in life, and he developed a bold and unrestrained character. As he had a good command of the doctrines of Confucianism, Buddhism and Taoism and extraordinary talent in military and political affairs, he was one of the very few thinkers in ancient China who could develop his virtues, perform meritorious deeds and expound on his ideas in writing. He inherited and developed the philosophical proposition of "mind is principle" put forward by Lu Jiuyuan (1139–93), and founded the Yangming School of Mind, which later had a powerful influence on Confucian thought.

Neo-Confucianism reflected the philosophical wisdom summarised by the Chinese people who had pondered and resolved social and cultural problems. It had a profound influence on the social and cultural development of the later period of Chinese society. Even today the Chinese people still have to reckon with the social and cultural consequences of Neo-Confucianism, which responded to challenges arising from Buddhism and Taoism and enabled Confucianism to regain its orthodox position.

But the decline of Neo-Confucianism towards the end of the Ming Dynasty opened a door to social transition, enlivening thinkers such as Huang Zongxi (1610–95), Gu Yanwu (1613–82) and Wang Fuzhi (1619–92). These thinkers, along with their followers, advocated innovative thinking and the creative inheritance of the traditional Confucian canon.

Huang Zongxi was an erudite scholar and a master of classical and historical works, who was also knowledgeable in astronomy, calendars, mathematics and music. Philosophically, he was deeply influenced by the Yangming School of Mind. He proposed "putting knowledge to practical use for society" and criticised the empty and impractical style of study common at the end of the Ming Dynasty. Such propositions on education and learning focused on attaching equal importance to theory and practise. They embodied and developed the propositions put forward by the Yangming School of Mind.

Modern Chinese educational history is one of conflict between a blend of Chinese and western and ideas, between the old and new, and the traditional and the modern. Modern Chinese education system was established, improved and developed step by step through social transition.

Influenced by democracy and science, advocated during the May Fourth New Culture Movement in 1919, Chinese education became more active. Progressive ideas emerged, such as education for the masses, work-study and vocational education. Cai Yuanpei (1868–1940), Tao Xingzhi (1891–1946) and Huang Yanpei (1878–1965) advocated these ideas.

When Cai Yuanpei assumed the post of minister of education in 1912, when the Republic of China was founded, he proposed that developing the sound character of people should be the objective of education. He proposed a principle of attaching equal importance to education in five areas: military/citizenship, utilitarianism, citizen morality, world outlook and aesthetics. While serving as president of Peking University, he believed that a university should be a venue for studying knowledge by "collecting classics of various disciplines and gathering scholars of different schools." He advanced the concept of "abiding by the principle of freedom of thought and adopting an all-embracing attitude" towards various doctrines. When it comes to different schools of thought, he was convinced that, "So long as they are reasonable and well grounded and will not be eliminated by themselves, they should be allowed to enjoy freedom of development even if they may conflict with each other."

As a great democratic educator, Cai left a rich legacy of ideas on education. He attached importance to and advocated mass education; he worked to get others to operate universities in a spirit of democracy by organising appraisals and faculty meetings. All these are part of his educational legacy.

Many eminent scholars emerged in Modern China such as Liang Qichao (1873–1929), Tang Yongtong (1893–1964) and Lü Simian (1884–1957). These scholars earned their reputations by undertaking the cultural mission of "continuing lost teachings for past sages." In China today, there are great scholars like Rao Zongyi (born 1917), who is well versed in both Chinese and western cultures and has achieved both academic and artistic accomplishments. Despite his achievements in academic research and his prolific writings, Rao is still dedicated to his exploration in both academic and artistic areas in creative ways.

When the revival of the humanistic spirit and traditional Chinese culture is urgently needed, the "fever of Chinese studies" is in full swing. It will benefit China by inheriting the spirit and thoughts of many erudite scholars, extolling their virtues and propagating their articles, and awakening affection and respect for the modern and traditional Chinese cultures.

Confucius, Yan Hui as Model Scholars of Spring and Autumn Period

Education in China originated during the Spring and Autumn and the Warring States periods (475–221 BC). Confucius (551–479 BC) was the first to open private schools. He taught his students a wealth of ideas and knowledge in unique ways. In the West, Confucius is regarded as comparable to the ancient Greek philosophers Socrates (469–399 BC) and Plato (427–347 BC). He is ranked first among "the top-ten cultural figures in the world." Today, there are more than 400 Confucius Institutes in the world, which is evidence of the popularity of his educational theories.

Scholars Shall Be Strong-Minded, Shoulder Responsibilities

"I made up my mind to study at 15. By 30, I had established myself. By 40, I had dispelled all my doubts. At 50, I knew the revelation of Heaven. At 60, my ears were obedient to the reception of truth. At 70, I could do whatever I liked without violating any rules." This is how Confucius summarised his own life.

Confucius's ancestors were nobles in the Kingdom of Song (Song state) in Spring and Autumn Periods. Later, the family fell into decline and migrated to the Kingdom of Lu (Lu state). When Confucius was 3, his father died and his mother Yan Zheng (568–535 BC) moved to Queli in Qufu City, Shandong Province, and began to educate the boy by herself. As a boy, Confucius practised rites with his playmates and, after an impoverished childhood, he made up his mind to study at 15. When he grew up, he worked as a junior official in charge of warehouses and livestock. He was always ready to learn from whomever he met. It is said he learned rites from Laodan (571–471 BC), music from Changhong and played instruments from Shixiang.

At 30, Confucius was already an erudite scholar with fame and prestige in his hometown. He started his private school in Queli, the first in China. His core philosophy was "benevolence" *(ren)*, which implies "loving the people." Benevolence, as a code of conduct and aim of actions, interacts with righteousness in a mutually enhancing manner. According to Confucius, governors should preach virtue among the people and administer the country through rites and rituals, which would revive the heyday of the Western Zhou Dynasty (1100–771 BC), when both festivities and conquests were initiated through the goodwill of the monarch. That, according to Confucius, was the way towards the unity of the world.

In 500 BC, leaders of the Lu and Qi states held a meeting at Jiagu, where Confucius proposed the idea that diplomatic negotiations and military preparations were both necessary for a country. When King Jing of Qi (561–490 BC) planned to force Lu state into submission, Confucius reprimanded King Jing on the basis of rites. Finally, Confucius maintained the dignity of Lu state and persuaded Qi state to accept a peace deal and return Yun and Guiyin (in present Shandong Province) to Lu.

Confucius served as a local magistrate at Zhongdu in Lu state when he was 51; his administrative style was much envied and imitated by neighbouring regions. Later, he was promoted to the positions of chief prosecutor, chief justice and even the Lu state's premier. During his premiership, he sought to strengthen the authority of the king by undermining the power of three dukes, but the trio proved too strong and his plan was abandoned. Eventually, Confucius became dispirited with the king and ministers of Lu state, who indulged themselves with horses and beauties sent by the King of Qi, and left his position and his homeland. He led his disciples around the many kingdoms of that time, looking for opportunities to put his political-philosophical ideas into practise.

Confucius's wanderings lasted more than 10 years and covered thousands of miles. Although he endured many hardships and was turned down many times, he never gave up his aspirations. Many accounts of his perseverance and the education of his disciples remain to this day.

Anecdote *'Chencai Zhiwei'*

The famous anecdote *"Chencai Zhiwei"* reflects the unswerving aspiration of Confucius and his disciples. At the time, the Kingdom of Wu (Wu state) had invaded the Kingdom of Chen (Chen state), so Chu state came to Chen state's rescue and its troops were stationed at Chengfu (in today's Anhui Province). Chu state heard Confucius was staying on the border between the Chen and Cai states, so it sent a messenger with an invitation to Confucius. When the ministers of Chen and Cai states got the news, they had the following discussion: "As a virtuous sage, Confucius is always capable of pointing to the crucial failures of kings and dukes. Now, Chu state comes to invite Confucius. It he serves as a high official in Chu state, the governors of Chen and Cai states will be in peril." So the two kingdoms sent troops to encircle Confucius in the wilderness.

Confucius and his disciples were besieged and their food supply was running low. Some of his disciples became so feeble they could not stand up. However, Confucius continued to give lectures, recite poems, sing songs and play instruments. Zilu, one of his disciples, became furious and asked, "Will a man of integrity suffer poverty and destitution?" Confucius answered, "A man of integrity can maintain his integrity in the face of poverty and destitution, while a base person is capable of anything in such a situation."

Confucius spotted the discontent in his disciples, so he summoned Zilu (542–480 BC) and asked him, "Why have we fallen into such a quagmire? Is it because our teachings are wrong?" Zilu answered, "Probably our virtues are not strong enough, so we are not trusted by others. Or probably our wisdom is not sufficient, so we are refused access." Confucius said, "There's no truth in what you've said. If virtuous men could definitely win trust, why did Boyi and Shuqi die of hunger in Shouyang Mountain? If wise men could go wherever they want, why was Prince Bigan eviscerated?"

After Zilu left, Zigong (520–456 BC) came to see Confucius. He said to Confucius, "Master, you have such elevated teachings that no country in the world can understand you. Would you please lower your standards a little bit?" Confucius said, "Good farmers cannot guarantee good harvests. Good craftsmen cannot guarantee that people are satisfied with what they make. A man of integrity preaches his own teachings; still, he cannot guarantee the people will accept them. What you should do now is continue your study. Unfortunately, you intend to condescend to pander to others, which shows the limit of your aspirations."

After Zigong left, Yan Hui (521–481 BC) came to see Confucius. He said, "Master, you have supreme teachings so that no country in the world can accommodate you. However, you stick to the preaching of your own teachings, despite the lack of acceptance from the outside world. A man who does not cultivate his own teachings is a shame. A well-cultivated teaching that is not adopted and followed is a shame on the rulers. A man whose teachings are not accepted by the rulers is one with a distinctive character!" After hearing these words, Confucius was very satisfied and said, "You're right! If you were rich, I would like to be your steward and housekeeper."

Finally, Zigong went to Chu state and asked King Zhao of Chu (523 – 489 BC) to send troops to escort Confucius, which the King did.

Editing *Liujing (Six Classics)*, Composing Rites, Music

Until 484 BC, Confucius was invited back to his home country from Wei state by Ji Kangzi, a noble in Lu state, on the advice of Ranyou (522–489 BC), a disciple of Confucius. On his return, Confucius was honoured as the senior sage of the state, but he was not given any power. Confucius then focused his attention on education and the compilation of ancient documents.

Throughout his life, he had more than 3,000 students. Seventy-two of them were good at all the six core subjects, namely rites, music, archery, chariot driving, calligraphy and mathematics. From his teaching, he developed a whole set of educational theories, principles, qualities and attitudes, such as teaching students in accordance with their aptitude, balancing learning and thinking and drawing inferences about other cases from one instance, inspiration and induction. He edited, revised and compiled the *Book of Poems, Book of Documents, Book of Rites, Book of Music,* and the *Spring and Autumn Annals,* which constituted a complete summary of the ancient literature of China. As he got old, Confucius was keen on the *Yijing (Book of Changes).*

Teaching Students in Accordance with Their Aptitudes

In commenting on Confucius's achievements in education, the famous Song Dynasty historian Zhu Xi (1130–1200) said, "Confucius taught his students in accordance with their different aptitudes." Confucius stuck to that principle throughout his career as a teacher. He was completely familiar with his students' characters, so he could discern the differences in each and adjust his teaching accordingly. When different students asked the same question, Confucius usually gave different answers.

According to accounts in the *Lunyu,* when Meng Yizi, one of the three powerful nobles in Lu state, asked Confucius about filial piety, Confucius warned him to end his behaviour of violating rites. When Meng Wubo, the son of Meng Yizi, asked the same question, Confucius replied that filial piety implied children should care for the health of their parents. When Ziyou asked, Confucius replied he should show more respect to his parents.

This principle is also evidenced by another popular anecdote. Zilu asked Confucius, "Should I put a theory into practise as soon as I learn it?" Confucius replied, "You should consult your father and elder brothers before taking any actions." When Ranyou asked the same question, Confucius advised him to take action immediately. When Gong Xihua asked about the reason for the difference between the two answers, Confucius said, "Ranyou tends to flinch from action, so I need to give him some encouragement; Zilu tends to be bold and foolhardy, so he needs to be checked."

As a result of this method, disciples of Confucius acquired and cultivated various qualities and strengths.

Disciples of Confucius

Confucius (551–479 BC) divided his teachings into four subjects: virtue, speech, literature and politics. Each of his disciples had his own specialty among the four subjects, such as Yan Yuan, Min Ziqian, Ran Boniu and Zhong Gong in virtue; Zai Wo and Zigong in speech; Ran You and Jilu in politics; and Ziyou and Zixia in literature.

According to Confucius, the supreme achievement as a man is benevolence and the supreme achievement as a scholar is happiness. He stressed that a scholar should love knowledge and seek happiness in acquiring knowledge. Confucius said of his student Yan Hui: "Yan Hui is a man of integrity. He lived in abject poverty but retained his happiness." Yan Hui achieved happiness from his studies, so he could retain it even in extreme destitution. This level of happiness achieved by Confucius and Yan Hui became the ultimate goal of later scholars.

Zigong was another favourite disciple. Called "a capable man" by his master, Zigong was among the top-ten disciples. Being good at speaking and in administration, he was an excellent social activist and outstanding diplomat. He was also a successful businessman and became the wealthiest of all the disciples.

Zilu had the most forceful character. He was forthright and decisive, so he was good at politics. Zilu cared for his parents extremely well, which was highly regarded by Confucius.

When Confucius was 69, his only son Kong Li (532–481 BC) died. When he turned 71, his favourite disciple Yan Hui died. Confucius, in grief, exclaimed, "Heaven orders my demise!" In the same year, a strange beast was caught in the west of the Lu state and it soon died. Confucius thought the appearance and immediate death of an auspicious beast forebode turmoil, so he stopped his compilation of the *Chunqiu (History of Spring and Autumn Annals).* At 72, Confucius received the sad news his disciple Zhong You had sacrificed himself for the Wei state, which plunged him into grief. In the second lunar month of the following year (479 BC), Confucius was stricken with an illness for seven days and died. After his funeral, his disciples mourned for three years. After that, Zigong mourned at his tomb for three more years, which demonstrated his deep affection for his master.

Confucius's disciples, and the disciples of his disciples compiled the *Lunyu.* It is a collection of the dialogues and activities of Confucius and his disciples and the most direct and reliable source for the study of Confucianism.

Paying Homage to Three Sites of Confucius in Commemoration of Ancient Sage

The temple, tomb and former residence of Confucius are located in Qufu, Shandong Province. The three sites were included on the World Heritage List in December 1994. The World Heritage Committee noted, "Confucius is a great philosopher, politician and educator in the Period of Spring and Autumn from the sixth century BC to the fifth century BC."

The Confucius Temple was built in 478 BC in commemoration of the great scholar. Today, it is a cluster of more than 100 halls. The temple is famous for its stone carvings, including stone portraits from the Han Dynasty, engraved stone columns from the Ming and Qing dynasties and its images of holy deeds, which were carved during the Ming Dynasty. The stone engravings are a treasure trove of ancient Chinese calligraphy, and the temple has the largest collection of tablets from the Han Dynasty.

The scholar's former residence has been expanded into a grand mansion consisting of 152 halls. It has served as the official residence of the direct descendents of Confucius. Since his descendents have stuck to the rites and rituals of the traditional household, this residence is also governed by Confucian philosophy and ethics.

Confucius was buried at Sishang, north of Lucheng. Since then, his descendents have been buried in the same place, which gradually became today's Confucius Cemetery. Since the first tree was planted by Zigong near the tomb of Confucius, more than 10,000 trees have been planted nearby. Since the Han Dynasty, the cemetery's boundary has been expanded 13 times. Today, it covers 2 square kilometres (sq.m) and is surrounded by a 5.6-km-long, 3-metre-high and 1-metre-thick wall. Guo Moruo (1892–1978) said, "This is an excellent natural museum and a living chronicle of the family of Confucius."

In his lifetime, Confucius was honoured as "the divine sage." Since his death, he has been commemorated and respected as "the exemplary teacher for all ages." In education in China, he is regarded as "the supreme teacher," because he is the founder and master of ancient Chinese educational philosophies.

Academies with Thousands of Years of Glory

Academies were places of study established either by individuals or the government. They originated during the Tang Dynasty and matured during the Song Dynasty, but were abolished during the Qing Dynasty. Over a thousand years, academies exerted an important influence on the development of traditional Chinese culture and education. During the Kaiyuan Period (AD 713–741) of the Tang Dynasty, the Lizheng Academy was established in Luoyang. It was later renamed Jixiandian Academy (Talents-Soliciting Academy). After that, a number of private academies were established, such as the Wutong and Dongjia academies. During the Song Dynasty, academies and Neo-Confucianism were incorporated into an established educational system with distinctive structures and practises, representing the height of ancient Chinese education and learning.

During the Northern Song Dynasty, a batch of famous academies emerged. Bailudong, Yuelu, Suiyang (Yingtianfu) and Songyang academies are considered the four major academies of ancient China.

Yingtianfu Academy

The Yingtianfu Academy, aka the Suiyang Academy, was originally the Nandu School. It was located by South Lake in the ancient city of Shangqiu in today's Suiyang District, Shangqiu City, Henan Province. During the early Song Dynasty, academies were located in hilly resorts, with the exception of the Yingtianfu Academy, because this famous centre was located in a city.

This academy traced its history back to the Later Jin Dynasty (AD 936–947) of the Five Dynasties (AD 907–960). At the time, a local resident, Yang Que, was interested in education and gave lectures to his students. After he died, his student, Qi Tongwen (AD 904–976), continued to give lectures and cultivated a number of prominent historic figures, including Zong Du, Xu Xiang, Chen Xiangyu, Gao Xiangxian, Guo Chengfan and Wang Li.

Cao Cheng, a wealthy bibliophile in Yingtianfu, raised three million silver pieces, enough to build 150 classrooms and to buy thousands of books for Qi Tongwen's school. After this injection of funds, the school flourished and attracted many students. In 1009, Cao Cheng submitted a petition to the government requesting the school be incorporated into the state-education system. This was approved by Emperor Zhenzong (reign: AD 997–1022) of the Song Dynasty, who awarded it a tablet with the characters, "Yingtianfu Academy." During the reign of Emperor Renzong (1022–63), the Yingtianfu

Academy was transformed into the Nanjing Imperial College, which was the supreme academic institution of the Northern Song Dynasty (AD 960–1127). About 60 of 100 students from the academy who took imperial examinations passed, which brought the academy great fame and popularity among scholars in the country.

After several expansions, the Yingtianfu Academy acquired national fame and grew to be the centre of academic, cultural and educational exchanges. Fan Zhongyan (AD 989–1052), famous for his words, "A leader should plan and worry ahead of the people and enjoy the fruits after the people," studied at the academy when he was young and later taught there. Fan told his students the ultimate goal of study was shouldering responsibility for society. He stressed the importance of practising virtue and applying what one learned in real life.

As the only academy with the title of imperial college in China, Yingtianfu Academy was honoured as the first of the four major academies. During the early Song Dynasty, the academy promoted the transformation of academic culture from theoretical study to pragmatism and consolidated the position of masters in the development of academies.

Bailudong Academy

The Bailudong Academy was located at the southern foot of Wulao Peak in Mount Lu (in today's Jiujiang City, Jiangxi Province). It enjoyed fame as "the first academy in China." According to legend, its founder, Li Bo, who kept a white deer, was called Master White Deer. Since the winding Wulao Peak looked like a cave, the place where the academy stood was called White Deer's Cave (Bailudong). From AD 937–943, an academy named "National School of Mount Lu" was established. It was also called "National School of White Deer" and was Bailudong's predecessor.

During the early Song Dynasty, the school was expanded and became the Bailudong Academy but, in the late Northern Song Dynasty, Jin troops invaded southwards and destroyed the academy. It was rebuilt when the Neo-Confucism Zhu Xi (1130–1200) served as the magistrate of Nankang. Zhu Xi set the rules and regulations for the academy and gave lectures himself. Later, Lu Xiangshan (1139–93), a famous philosopher, came to teach at the academy. The meeting of Zhu Xi and Lu Xiangshan at the academy made it famous countrywide.

In philosophy, Zhu Xi accepted the idealistic ontology developed by Cheng Yi while absorbing various schools of thought dating back to the pre-Qin Period, including Buddhism; therefore, he epitomised the ancient Chinese philosophies. Lu Jiuyuan, another philosopher comparable to Zhu Xi, was the founder of the Philosophy of the Mind in the Song and Ming dynasties. His most famous theory was "truth comes from the mind," which contradicted Zhu Xi's philosophy. Their contradictions culminated in a face-to-face showdown at Ehu in 1176.

Lü Zuqian (1137–81) wanted to reconcile the contradiction between Zhu Xi and Lu Jiuyuan, so he invited Lu and his brother Lu Jiuling (1132–1180) to Ehu Temple for a meeting with Zhu Xi. The two philosophers conducted a heated three-day debate on academic methods and self-cultivation. Zhu Xi stressed the importance of knowledge in learning. He believed that if one wanted to be a sage, he should follow the steps listed in the *Daxue (Great Learning)* and start with the study of the physical world through reading and observation. Once he acquired the knowledge of the world, he could apply it as he preferred while conforming to heavenly principles. In contrast, the Brothers Lu thought virtue was most important and fundamental to learning, while reading for knowledge was secondary. They pointed out that Yao and Shun, two exemplary monarchs in ancient China, were universally regarded as sages, but they did not read any books. Later, Ehu Temple was also called Ehu Academy, in commemoration of this famous debate.

Despite their contradictions in philosophy, Zhu Xi and Lu Jiuyuan were good friends. They admired each other. After the debate at Ehu, Lu visited Zhu at Nankang and gave lectures at Bailudong Academy headed by Zhu. When Lu expounded on the chapter, "A gentleman sticks to righteousness while a villain sticks to interest" in the *Lunyu*, he gave a thorough explanation of his academic principles, which greatly moved the audience. After attending the lecture, Zhu felt ashamed he had not probed deeply enough into this chapter. This meeting at Nankang was also called "The Meeting at Bailudong Academy." The debate did not reconcile the differences between them. Later, Zhu popularised Song Dynasty-era Neo-Confucianism and was honoured as "the master of all ages" by posterity.

The Philosophy of the Mind, which was introduced by Lu Jiuyuan, was later developed into a systematic philosophy by Wang Yangming (1472–1529) and was also called "the Philosophy of the Mind by Lu and Wang." It exerted a profound effect on the development of Chinese philosophy during the Ming and Qing dynasties.

Yuelu Academy

Located on Yuelu Hill on the west bank of the Xiang River in Changsha, Hunan Province, the Yuelu Academy is a cluster of well-preserved buildings and is listed as a key national cultural relics protection site. The predecessor to the academy was a school built during the late Tang Dynasty and the Five Dynasties during which two monks gave lectures. The academy was established in AD 976. During its 1,000-year history, from the Song Dynasty through the Yuan, Ming and the Qing dynasties, it has cultivated many talented people.

During the Southern Song Dynasty, scholars of the Huxiang School, headed by Zhang Shi (1133–80), conducted academic research and teaching at the academy, which had a profound influence. In 1167, Zhu Xi came to Yuelu Academy to give lectures with Zhang Shi for two months. A number of historic figures, such as Wang Fuzhi, Zeng Guofan (1811–72) and Guo Songtao (1818–91), studied at the academy. Yuelu has always been a cradle for talent, as shown by the sentence, "The Kingdom of Chu is famous for its numerous talented people, and most of them come from the academy." During educational reform of the late-Qing Dynasty, the academy was transformed into the Hunan Institute of Higher Learning, which, in turn, became Hunan University in 1926.

The academy still operates as an institute directly under Hunan University. It is a leader in the study of Song and Ming Dynasty Neo-Confucianism, the history of China's academies, the cultural history of Hunan and the history of China's rites and rituals.

Songyang Academy

Emperor Qianlong (reign: 1736–95) praised the Songyang Academy when he visited the academy on October 1, 1750.

The academy was first built in AD 484 at the southern foot of Mount Song in Dengfeng City, Henan Province. It was originally a Buddhist temple called the Songyang Temple. During the reign of Sui Emperor Yang (AD 605–618), it was transformed into the Taoist Songyang Temple. When Tang Emperor Gaozong (reign: AD 649–683) visited Mount Song in AD 683, it was requisitioned as a temporary palace and renamed Fengtian Palace. During the Later Zhou Dynasty (AD 951–960) of the Five Dynasties, it was converted to the educational Taiyi Academy. In 1035, it was renamed the Songyang Academy, where prominent scholars taught philosophical works/literature.

The academy was famous for its research of Neo-Confucianism and its collection of cultural relics. Cheng Hao (1032–85) and Cheng Yi (1033–1107) were prominent Neo-Confucianism figures of the Southern Song Dynasty. They were learned scholars and very good at teaching through inspiration. Zhu Xi once studied under them.

The Datang Tablet in the academy was engraved and erected in AD 744 during the Tang Dynasty. It is 9.02-metres high, 2.04-metres wide and 1.05-metres thick. This large yet delicate tablet has long been honoured as the "First Tablet on Mount Song." It has been engraved with 1,078 characters, which recount the story of the Taoist Sun Taichong's practise of alchemy for Emperor Xuanzong (reign: AD 721–756). The essay was drafted by Li Linfu (AD 683–752) and was handwritten by Xu Hao (AD 703–783). This tablet weighs more than 80 tons. The top of the tablet alone weighs more than 10 tons. One legend has it that Lu Ban used his wisdom to erect the tablet and put the top on it.

Another relic at the academy is a stone map of Dengfeng County engraved in 1593. It depicts the location of tourist attractions and the names of mountains, rivers, roads, towns and villages. This stone map is a very accurate portrayal of the relic sites in the county. It is both an artistic treasure and a historical record of local geography and history.

The Songyang Academy has undergone many renovations and extensions; still retains its Qing Dynasty layout. The 9,984-sq.m. academy grounds measure 128 metres from north to south and 78 metres from east to west. Buildings on the central axis are arranged as five yards, which are the gate, the Hall of Sages, the Lecture Hall, Daotong Shrine and the Library. Side rooms flank both sides of the central axis. There are 106 buildings in the academy, most fitted with gray tiles, which is unlike other temples in China. Because of its uniquely Confucian style, the academy is regarded as a good example for the study of ancient Chinese academies, educational systems and the Confucian culture. On August 1, 2010, the academy was officially included on the World Cultural Heritage Sites List by UNESCO.

From the late-Tang Dynasty to the late-Qing Dynasty, the Songyang Academy played an important role in the cultivation of scholars. It also played a role in the dissemination of religions due to its previous use as both a Buddhist and Taoist temple.

During the Yuan Dynasty, academies were encouraged and protected by laws, so they flourished. Academies and Neo-Confucianism, which had originated in South China, penetrated the north, which eased cultural exchanges between the south and north. However, governmental protection came with regulation, so academies gradually became state colleges and lost their academic freedom.

During the Ming Dynasty, the government took control of state colleges to strengthen ideological control. Academic freedom was banned; academies were demolished. Despite the restrictive political climate, there were far more academies during the Ming Dynasty than during the Song and Yuan dynasties. During the Ming Dynasty, the Philosophy of the Mind was developed by Wang Shouren, competing with the Neo-Confucianism of Cheng Yi and Zhu Xi. Several heavyweight educators and thinkers emerged, such as Huang Zongxi (1610–95), Gu Yanwu (1613–82) and Wang Fuzhi (1919–92).

During the late Qing Dynasty, imperial examinations were abolished and colleges were established. However, with the advent of a modern educational system, the academies have re-emerged as tourist attractions and venues of cultural research.

Master Educators of Modern Era

Many talented people in the field of humanities emerged in China during the 20th century. Four major masters—Liang Qichao, Wang Guowei, Chen Yinque and Zhao Yuanren—taught at the Academy of Chinese Learning, Tsinghua University. They made invaluable contributions to the preservation and development of the traditional Chinese culture and education in general.

Among the 20th century scholars, Liang Qichao was regarded as a great educator with encyclopaedic knowledge.

Liang Qichao: New Thinkers Emerge in China

Liang Qichao (1873–1929) was a famous politician and scholar in modern China. He scored achievements in a wide range of disciplines, including philosophy, literature, history, Confucianism, jurisprudence, ethics and theology. He was most accomplished in the field of historical studies. His writings were compiled into the *Collection of Yinbing Room*.

As a child, Liang was a prodigy who received a traditional education. He mastered the *Four Books (Great Learning, Doctrine of the Mean, Analects of Confucius,* and the *Works of Mencius)* and the *Shijing (Book of Songs)*. At 8, he learned to write, and well enough that he could write a 1,000-word essay. He also received instruction in history and the humanities from his grandfather, Liang Weiqing. During the Lantern Festival each year, Liang Weiqing would take his grandchildren to a local temple to view lanterns with images of stories painted on them. The stories usually centred on patriotism, which greatly inspired the young Liang.

In 1889, Liang passed the provincial examination in Guangdong and came to Beijing for the imperial examination, but he failed. On his way back to Guangdong, he read *A Brief Introduction to the World* compiled by Xu Jishe. The book contained information on world geography, customs and democracy in the West and had a strong influence on his thinking. In the same year, he began to follow Kang Youwei and the reform movement.

After Qing Dynasty forces were defeated in the first Sino-Japanese War in 1894, Kang and Liang organised thousands of examinees to file a petition against the resulting *Treaty of Shimonoseki* in 1895. Then the two actively promoted reform by publishing *News of China and the World*, establishing the Qiangxue Society in Beijing and by publishing *News on Current Affairs* in Shanghai. In 1898, Liang took part in the Reform Movement (Hundred Days' Reform) initiated by Kang. He was in charge of the Translation Bureau at the Imperial University of Peking. He drafted the *Regulations for Imperial University of Peking*, which backed "a combination of Chinese philosophy as the foundation and western study for practical use" as an academic educational principle. After the Reform Movement failed, Liang fled to Japan. All reform measures were abolished, except the newly established Imperial University of Peking, which was renamed Peking University after the 1911 Revolution, becoming the first state university in China.

In the early years of the Republic of China (1912–49), Liang supported Yuan Shikai (1859–1916). But he wrote an essay, *On the Issue of the State System*, calling on the people to oppose Yuan's attempt to restore monarchic rule. Liang then went to Guangdong and Guangxi provinces to take part in the movement in person. Later, he became an official in the government led by Duan Qirui (1865–1936). After this government was overthrown by the Constitution Protection Movement, led by Sun Yat-sen in 1917, Liang quit politics.

Liang then went to study in Europe. When he returned, he focused on academic research. In 1922, he began to teach at Tsinghua University and, in 1925, he was appointed as a tutor at the university's Academy of Chinese Learning. He adopted an approach of critical acceptance in the studies of China's ancient civilisations. He believed that, since the injection of western studies was inevitable, young people should understand the conditions of China before incorporating appropriate and practical elements of western studies into China. This view of a critical combination of Chinese civilisation and western studies exerted an enormous influence on youths of that time.

Throughout his life, Liang remained an intellectual and politician of integrity, as was written in a couplet for his funeral by the educator Hu Shi (1891–1962).

Wang Guowei: Initiator of Modern Education

Wang Guowei (1877–1927) was a lifelong educator with a unique educational theory. He was also an outstanding scholar in modern China, an expert on ancient Chinese characters and relics, and he was a poet.

Wang Guowei was also involved in the Reform Movement in 1898, so he did not take the imperial examination. When he worked for *The News on Current Affairs*, he proposed normal colleges and primary schools should be established in Haining, Zhejiang Province, but this plan was never put into practise. After the failure of the Reform Movement, he wrote a letter to Wang Kangnian in which he said education would be paramount for the future of China.

In 1901, Wang Guowei went to study in Japan with the financial assistance of Luo Zhenyu (1866–1940). After he returned to China, he went to teach at Tongzhou Normal School and then at Jiangsu Normal College, where he taught western philosophy, psychology, ethics and sociology. He translated textbooks for those subjects, which was a pioneering move at the time.

In 1906, Wang Guowei moved to Beijing with Luo Zhenyu. First he served in the Department of Education and the Bureau of Translation, where he began to study Chinese literature, theatre and poetry and where he completed his masterpieces, *Collection of Yuan Qu*, *On The Theatre of Song and Yuan* and *Commentaries on Lyrical Works*. After the 1911 Revolution, Wang Guowei went to Japan with Luo Zhenyu. After he returned in 1916, Silas Hardoon, a Jewish businessman, invited him to teach at a university and conduct archaeological research on ancient characters of the Shang Dynasty. In 1922, he was appointed a correspondent tutor by Peking University. In 1925, he joined Liang Qichao as a professor at the Academy of Chinese Learning at Tsinghua University.

As a result of expanded contact with western cultural influences, education in China went through an enormous change. Wang was eager to absorb western culture. He believed the most urgent task for education in China was to develop higher education so as to cultivate "heroes" and "talent" for the country. He identified a shortage of teachers as the bottleneck to the development of higher education. He proposed to assist emerging disciplines in China, overseas teachers could be invited, while outstanding talent from China could be sent to study abroad to develop their capacity to teach at universities.

Wang stressed the importance of philosophy in life. He believed philosophy, as the source of all knowledge, was the methodological guideline for all other disciplines; therefore, he proposed an academic structure with philosophy as the core.

Wang Guowei's emphasis on humanism and philosophy represents an advanced educational theory that is still relevant to the reform and development of education in China today.

As the National Revolutionary Army marched toward North China in June 1927, Wang ended his life by jumping into Kunming Lake in the Summer Palace. Since he was still at the height of his academic career, his suicide became the most tragic mystery in the field of Chinese ancient civilisation research.

Chen Yinque wrote the epitaph for Wang Guowei in 1929, saying: "Throughout his life, he stuck to academic freedom and national independence, as shown by his work, *Biography of Liu Rushi*." That has become the spirit for all intellectuals in China.

Chen Yinque: Independence and Freedom

Chen Yinque (1890–1969) was the grandson of Chen Baozhen (1831–1900), the former governor of Hunan Province, and the son of Chen Sanli (1859–1937), a famous poet of the late Qing Dynasty. Chen was a well-educated and outstanding scholar. When he taught at Tsinghua University, he was honoured as a "professor of all professors." He was the most prominent historian, linguist and researcher of classical literature in modern China.

In his childhood, Chen learned the *Four Books and Five Classics (Book of Songs, Book of History, Book of Changes, Book of Rites* and the *Spring and Autumn Annals)* at home and read widely in history, philosophy and Buddhism. At 11, he entered Siyi School, which helped him consolidate his knowledge of Chinese culture and prepared him for the overseas study of modern western civilisation.

During his overseas study, he worked diligently to acquire knowledge in many fields and to master more than a dozen languages, including Mongolian, Tibetan, Manchurian, Japanese, Sanskrit, English, French, German, Pali, Persian, Turk, Tangut, Latin and Greek, which laid a solid foundation for his research in history. In 1925, Chen was also appointed a tutor at Tsinghua's Academy of Chinese Learning. He was ranked with Liang Qichao and Wang Guowei as the "Big Three in Tsinghua." Later, he taught for 40 years at Tsinghua University, Peking University, Guangxi University, Southwest United and at the Sun Yat-sen universities.

He was noted for using a variety of methods in his lectures and for the clarity of his explanations. His erudition attracted other professors at Tsinghua University such as Wu Mi (1894–1978) and Zhu Ziqing (1898–1948), who attended his lectures. He married Tang Yun, the granddaughter of Tang Jingsong, the former governor of Taiwan, in 1928 after meeting her at Tsinghua University. She was also a teacher.

Though he enjoyed great fame, Chen remained modest, forthright, down-to-earth and confident. As a master scholar, he had a dry sense of humour. When he and his students hid in a shelter during a Japanese air raid, he wrote a couplet: "Flee at the sight of planes / Hide in the shelter for safety," which demonstrated his optimism in the face of Japanese aggression.

During his academic career, Chen covered a variety of subjects, including history, literature, philosophy, religion and language. In the field of historical research, he switched from the history of minorities in China and the translation of

Buddhist scriptures to the study of ancient Chinese history. His 30 years studying the histories of the Wei, Jin, Southern and Northern, Sui and Tang dynasties culminated in *Study on the Origins of Systems in the Sui and Tang Dynasties* and the *Study of the Political History of the Tang Dynasty*, which paved the way for later researchers.

In his old age, Chen Yinque became blind, which was a tragedy for a diligent scholar. However, despite the disability, he continued his academic research, which won him everlasting respect from later scholars.

Zhao Yuanren: Father of Linguistics of Chinese Language

When the Academy of Chinese Learning was established at Tsinghua University, Liang Qichao, Wang Guowei, Chen Yinque and Zhao Yuanren (1892–1982) were appointed tutors and they were honoured as the "Four Major Tutors at Tsinghua." Among the four, Zhao Yuanren was the youngest. He had a rare genius for language learning and was able to speak 33 dialects, in addition to many foreign languages. He was the founder of linguistics in China and also made great achievements in the study of music.

Zhao was born to a prestigious family. He was a direct descendent of Zhao Kuangyin (Emperor Taizu, reign: AD 960–976), the first emperor of the Song Dynasty, and Zhao Yi (1727–1814), a famous historian. His father passed the provincial examination and was skilled in flute playing. His mother was adept at poetry and Kunqu Opera.

During his childhood, Zhao lived with his parents and grandfather in various places in Hebei Province. Frequent moves exposed the young boy to various dialects, which he picked up easily. As a prodigy, he was adept at imitating the accents of others, which prepared him for his later achievements in linguistics.

Zhao's intelligence and diligence led to him ranking second in the second batch of overseas students sent by the government to the United States. He accompanied Hu Shi and studied at Cornell and Harvard universities and was conferred a bachelor's degree in mathematics and a doctorate in philosophy. At the Research Institute of Harvard, he attended many language lectures in addition to his philosophical tasks. As Hu Shi said, Zhao was good at philosophy, physics and mathematics, while also a high achiever in linguistics and music.

After 10 years of overseas study, Zhao Yuanren returned to China in 1920 and taught mathematics, physics, Chinese phonology, general linguistics, modern Chinese dialects, Chinese music and western music at Tsinghua University. When the British philosopher Bertrand Russell came to China for a lecture tour that year, Zhao worked as his interpreter. Wherever they went, he interpreted the lectures into the local dialect of the audience. He picked up Changsha Dialect while on the trip and used it to translate one of the lectures. It seemed as if he was a native of Changsha.

In 1920, he met Yang Buwei whom he married later. Both were already engaged to others, but they were both open-minded so they forced their respective parents to call off the engagements. After their marriage, Zhao returned to Harvard for further study in linguistic theories.

Zhao took up his post as tutor at the Academy of Chinese Learning when it was established in Tsinghua University in 1925, and in 1928, he conducted extensive field research of local dialects and folk music. He was always eager to learn dialects from local residents wherever he went. He wrote a very clever story "The History of Shi Eating Lions" to depict the difference between sounds and characters. In the story, there is only one sound, *"shi"*; Zhao used various homophonic characters to tell the story.

In 1938, Zhao was invited to teach in Hawaii. Later he moved to Yale University, Harvard University and the University of California, where he finally retired. After the normalisation of Sino-US relations, the Zhaos returned to China in 1973 and were invited to meet Premier Zhou Enlai. Zhao mentioned his research into the reform of Chinese characters during their meeting. In 1981, Zhao came back to China at the invitation of the Institute of Linguistics in the Chinese Academy of Social Sciences. This time, he met Deng Xiaoping and was conferred the honorary title of professor by Peking University.

Zhao is honoured as the "Father of Linguistics of the Chinese Language," because he laid the foundation for the study of modern linguistics in China. His academic system is a shining chapter in the history of education and culture in China.

In modern times, many patriotic scholars have carried forward the ancient Chinese civilisation through education.

Carrying Traditions Forward

Masters of *guoxue* devoted their lives to the development of traditional Chinese culture in the modern era. In doing so, they expanded the scope of education and developed new academic perspectives. By expanding the scope and reach of the traditional Chinese culture, they have strongly influenced thinking and thought in the Chinese world but also in the world at large.

Zhang Taiyan: Introduced Concept of '*Guoxue*'

Traditional Chinese culture was severely challenged by the introduction of western thought during the transition from the 19th to the 20th century. Against this background, Zhang Taiyan (1869–1936) proposed to carry forward the study of traditional culture so as to boost patriotism.

After his involvement in the 1911 Xinhai Revolution, Zhang returned to his studies. Throughout his life, he had students all over China, so he was honoured as a master of Chinese studies.

During his life, Zhang went through the Reform Movement in 1898 and the Xinhai Revolution. He was arrested seven times and imprisoned three times, but he never gave up. He believed the study of traditional civilisation, including history, culture, characters and customs, was fundamental to the fate of the nation.

Zhang introduced the concept of "*guoxue*," the study of ancient Chinese civilisations. He believed patriotism came from the study of philosophical classics and history, so *guoxue* was fundamental to the rejuvenation of the Chinese nation.

Zhang was a rigorous scholar and a strong-minded fighter. When he received an invitation from Yuan Shikai, he wrote "Excuse me for not keeping you company," on the invitation and posted it back. When Yuan Shikai proclaimed himself emperor in December 1915, Zhang Taiyan was put under house arrest, which lasted until Yuan's death in March 1916.

In private, Zhang was by no means punctilious. He was a heavy smoker. Sometimes he mistook his cigarettes for chalk, which aroused laughter from his audience.

Zhang was devoted to *guoxue* throughout his life. He left works totalling more than four million characters on literature, history and linguistics. These works were later compiled into three collections.

Qian Mu: Last Master of *Guoxue*

Qian Mu (1895–1990) was a famous *guoxue* master in modern China, and his achievements in traditional Chinese history, literature and philosophy were substantial. At Peking University, he was as esteemed as Hu Shi. Both were popular professors at the time.

Qian studied at a private school during his childhood, but he quit middle school because his family was poor. He was disappointed at not being able to go to college, so he made up his mind to educate himself. In 1930, he was recommended by Gu Jiegang (1893–1980) to work as a lecturer in Chinese at Yanjing University. Later, he became a professor in the Department of Chinese at Yenching University. Simultaneously, he also taught at Tsinghua University and Beiping Normal University.

His lectures on history were based on historical facts and were elegantly organised around themes, so they always attracted large audiences, with more than 300 students often packed into a big lecture theatre, completely captivated by his lectures.

When the War of Resistance against Japan broke out in 1937, he moved south and taught at Southwest United University, Cheeloo University and West China Union University. He wrote *Outline of Chinese History*, a highly regarded general history of China.

Qian later moved to Hong Kong to establish the Xinya Academy for exiled students. In October 1963, the academy was combined with several other academies to form the Chinese University of Hong Kong. In October 1967, he moved to Taipei and became dean of the Institute of History and director of the first group of doctoral students at the Chinese College of Literature (later renamed Chinese Culture University). By 1986, when he stopped teaching, he had been a teacher for three quarters of a century. He had taught at all levels of schools from elementary schools all the way up to graduate schools. As a teacher, he had experienced his life as few others in the world.

Based on Confucian humanism, Qian probed into the essence of traditional education in China. He stressed the importance of fostering talented people and the cultivation of their patriotism. In his old age, he continued his academic research. After his death, his ashes were spread across Tai Lake (Taihu, near Suzhou, Jiangsu Province), symbolising his return to his hometown.

Throughout his life, Qian Mu wrote more than 17 million characters in works on history and culture. He is honoured as "the master of a generation" by the academic sphere in China. Some scholars considered him the last master of *guoxue* in China. His lifelong aspiration and most prominent achievement is still education.

Ji Xianlin: Master Scholar without a Crown

Ji Xianlin (1911–2009), an influential master scholar, said, "Wisdom begets happiness, and benevolence begets longevity. I am just an ordinary man of integrity. I stick to my virtues and principles. I follow the traditions, and I love my homeland."

Ji was born into a poor family in Shandong Province. At 6, he left home to live with his uncle in Jinan. His uncle was very strict with him, hoping the boy would amount to something in the future. When he graduated from middle school in 1930, he entered Tsinghua University to study German. In 1935, he moved to Germany to study Hinduism at Georg–August–University of Göttingen, during which time he experienced severe deprivation. In 1946, he returned to China after 11 years in Germany and was appointed a professor at Peking University. In 1978, he became the vice-president of the university and remained a professor there until his death in July 2009.

Ji summarised his academic research as a combination of Sanskrit, Buddhism and Tocharian (an extinct language from the Tarim Basin in the modern day Xinjiang Uygur Autonomous Region) and the integration of Chinese literature, comparative literature and literary theory. He was a master of 12 languages including English, German, Sanskrit and Pali. He was especially fluent in Tocharian and was one of the few in the world who could speak this language. Although he was generally regarded as a master of *guoxue* in modern China, he was modest. He wrote an essay to renounce the title. He also renounced other titles people had conferred on him: "leader of the academic sphere" and "national treasure." These three renunciations demonstrated not only his modesty, but also his respect for traditional culture.

Ji was keenly drawn to the development of human culture. He believed the cultures of the East and the West would alternate in world dominance. He said cultural exchanges could not be stopped and were essential for human progress. The various peoples of the world must learn from one another to develop. The ultimate goal of human progress would be a certain form of unity. The cultures of the East and the West were complementary, so cultural exchanges should be a two-way process. Through his research of cultural exchanges, he determined the East and the West were two distinct cultural systems, with the eastern culture following an analytical approach and western culture following a holistic approach.

In education, Ji promoted the concept of "macro *guoxue*," which consisted of the cultures of all the 56 nationalities in China. Many of his essays are used in mandatory textbooks, including *In Commemoration of Mother and Rosebay*. He established the Department of Eastern Languages, which expanded the scope of the discipline, and he completed more than 100 works, which have been compiled into the 24-volume *Collection of Ji Xianlin*.

Ji Xianlin was committed throughout his life to education and academic research. He put forward many theories on culture and education and made a major contribution to reviving Chinese culture and bridging the cultural gap between the East and the West.

Nan Huaijin: Carrying Forward Lost Knowledge

Nan Huaijin (1918–2012) was educated at a private school in his childhood. Later, he studied Buddhism, Confucianism, Taoism and other Chinese philosophies. He was also adept in traditional Chinese martial arts, literature and history, and he got great pleasure from his studies. Since he devoted his life to the spreading of traditional Chinese culture, he is honoured as a master of *guoxue*.

As a boy, he enjoyed reading kung fu novels. He admired the heroes in the novels, so he practised dropping to the floor from the beam in his study. When his parents discovered his interest in kung fu, they found a coach for him. In 1935, Nan turned 17 and began studying kung fu at the Zhejiang Academy of Kung Fu, near West Lake in Hangzhou, and he graduated at the top of his class after two years.

When the War of Resistance against Japan began, Nan joined the army and went to the southwest to teach kung fu at the Central Military Academy. During this period, he visited many scholars. He studied Buddhism and Chan (Zen) practises from Yuan Huanxian (1887–1966), a Chan master from northern Sichuan Province. He eventually left the military academy and shut himself away at the Daping Temple on Emei Mountain in Sichuan to study Buddhism. After three years in solitude, he went to Xikang and Tibet to visit various denominations of Tantra. After his extensive study of Buddhism, he began to teach at Yunnan University and Sichuan University.

At the end of 1947, Nan returned to his hometown and lived as a hermit. During that turbulent period, he focused his attention on *The Complete Library in the Four Branches of Literature* and *The Complete Collection of Ancient and Modern Books*, which were stored in the Wenlan Chamber of Zhejiang Provincial Library. That extensive reading paved the way for his later achievements.

In 1949, Nan migrated to Taiwan, where he was to stay for the next 36 years. He arrived there impoverished, but he remained optimistic. Later, he taught at the Culture University and at the Fu Jen Catholic University. He also went to the United States to disseminate culture and won fame around the world with his erudition, vivid speech and high moral character.

After returning from the United States, he migrated to Hong Kong and funded the construction of the Jinhua–Wenzhou Railway, the first joint-venture railway in China. After the line was completed, Nan handed it over to the people living in southwestern Zhejiang Province.

Nan regarded culture as fundamental to the survival of a nation, so he aspired to uphold traditional Chinese culture. In Taiwan, he established the Association of the Essence of the East and the West and published a magazine, *Humanistic World*. His book *Sitting Still to Cultivate Oneself for Longevity* was published in instalments from the first issue of *Humanistic World*. A separate edition of the book was published later, and the book was also translated into other languages. In 1990, Shanghai Fudan University Press published his books, including *An Explanation of Analects*. This book is his most influential among the public, because it explains the *Analects of Confucius* from a modern perspective and using simple language, integrating the philosophical texts and history. It aroused fervour for Nan's books that has lasted to today.

Quintessence of Chinese Culture
Folk Customs

The Chinese and their culture have produced a civilisation like no other. Its refined, humanistic spirit and its valuation of the importance of harmony, its artfulness in living, its poetry in motion is everywhere evident, whether in delicate miniature boats carved from walnuts, in refined eggshell porcelain made in Jingdezhen, in the ancient scriptures and frescoes in Dunhuang or in its creation of institutions such as the 1,000-year-old Yuelu Academy.

Throughout history, Chinese have sought spiritual happiness and comfort of the soul via culture and art. Traditional culture and art, such as music, games, calligraphy, painting, tea ceremonies, poems, its wine culture, costumes, gardens and architectural wonders, have been incorporated into the everyday lives of the Chinese, culminating in a lifestyle unique to them alone, although the value of this cultural phenomenon is widely recognised and has been shared.

China has long been famous for its fashion. In history, each dynasty had its unique style of fashion, such as the separate upper and lower pieces of clothing of the Shang Dynasty (1600–1100 BC), the headgear and robes of the Zhou Dynasty (1100–221 BC), the robes and skirts of the Qin (221–106 BC) and Han dynasties (206 BC–AD 220), the large sleeves and pleats in the Wei (AD 220–265), Jin (AD 265–420) and the Southern and Northern dynasties (AD 420–589), the turbans of the Tang (AD 618–907) and Song (AD 960–1279) dynasties, the cloaks of the Ming Dynasty, the cheongsam (*qipao*) of the Qing Dynasty and the Sun Yat-sen uniform jackets of the Republic of China (1912–49).

Some may be surprised to learn that Chinese fashion exhibitions were held as early as the 1970s and 1980s in the modern era. Chinese elements—stand collars and embroidery—have influenced the world's fashion industry. In recent years, a growing number of Chinese fashion designers have ventured abroad to market their products on the international stage.

In fashion, the most obvious Chinese elements are stand collars, threaded buttons and Chinese knots. Silk is the most typical material from the western perspective. Chinese fashion, with some modern details incorporated, has appeared in some famous international brands, as exemplified by the Chinese-style stand-collar jacket of Alessandro Dell'Acqua, the images of flowers and bamboo in Dries Van Noten's creations, the shining fuchsia colour of Celine dresses, the black tassels on Versace strappy sandals and Dior high heels, and the stand collar and threaded buttons down the fronts of Chanel jackets.

As the birthplace of tea, China has a long history of drinking tea, which originated with the legendary "Divine Farmer" Shennong about 5,000 years ago and became popular at the time of Luzhougong, a respected noble during in the Kingdom of Lu (1042–249 BC). Everything about tea, from the cultivation of its various types to its preparation, ceremonies, rituals and customs, originated in China, whether directly or indirectly.

In China, drinking tea is a cultural activity depicted in traditional Chinese paintings that incorporate various elements, such as the quality of tea leaves, clear spring water, a sunny day, pleasant scenery, a couple of confidants and a happy get-together. The tea culture can be enjoyed by the learned or the ordinary. Since ancient times, scholars have composed poems to describe tea-drinking scenes. The tea culture's ultimate achievement is the sense of physical and spiritual harmony it engenders between man and nature. Gradually, tea drinkers can achieve the supreme level of "tasting the tea with one's heart" and feel "the transition from bitterness to sweetness," which brings one to the ultimate stage of rapture.

Many places in China are famous, not coincidentally, for their beautiful scenery and quality teas. West Lake Longjing Tea is cultivated in Hangzhou, Zhejiang Province, a city dubbed as "Paradise on Earth." Taihu Lake Biluochun is cultivated on Dongting Island, in Jiangsu Province, which is covered with luxuriant plants; Putuo Buddha Tea is cultivated on Mount Buddha on Putuo Island, surrounded by the tidal waves of the sea; Mount Jun Yinzhen Tea is cultivated on Mount Jun in Yueyang, Hunan Province. A tour of these places often includes sightseeing, tea drinking, leisure and shopping.

Today, China's cities and towns are dotted with teahouses. The combination of quiet rooms, elegant paintings, pleasant music and tea ceremonies make teahouses ideal places to meet.

China also has a long tradition of wine making. Numerous local varieties of wine and spirits have become an important part of daily life, so activities surrounding the drinking of alcohol have grown to become customs.

Numerous kinds of banquets have been developed, for receptions, departures, enjoyment and entertainment. There are official State banquets and there are also banquets for festivals such as Tomb-Sweeping Day, the Dragon Boat Festival and the Mid-Autumn Festival. There are also banquets in honour of the elderly. These various banquets have fostered an extensive alcohol culture in China.

Over thousands of years, festivals in China have grown to form a philosophy of life in harmony with the environment. These festivals reflect our ancestors' knowledge of astronomy, geography and biology. The popularity of China's traditional culture finds its most vivid expression when celebrating festivals.

The formation of festivals is usually a long process. Festivals are an important part of the cultural tradition that dates back to the ancient times. The concepts of *"sui"* and *"shi"* reflect the understanding of time through experiencing life. *"Sui"* refers to the period of one year, while *"shi"* refers to the various seasons. They were both markers of time in ancient China. They have been in use throughout traditional Chinese society and have inspired a range of cultural activities.

In China, festivals integrate life and culture in wonderful ways. Today, Chinese retain and consult their traditional calendars that hang side by side with the Gregorian calendar, because traditional festivals are marked on the old calendar.

The distinctive features of the Chinese culture mean that, even in the face of modern prosperity, the Chinese still retain their time-honoured concepts, ideas, ethics, virtues and customs, especially filial piety and harmony with nature.

Fashion in China

In the prehistoric era, fashion emerged because people desired to cover their bodies for warmth, dignity and beauty. With the development of civilisation, fashion has developed from plain and simple clothes to a complex cultural element. It has grown to be an important expression of traditional Chinese culture.

A Review: History of 'The Kingdom of Fashion'

There is a legend in China about the invention of clothes. It was recorded in *Huainanzi*, that "Boyu invented clothes by weaving cloth." Boyu, who lived during the era of the legendary Huangdi (circa 2698–2598 BC), was the first man who made clothes. He described the process of weaving cloth in great detail. With the emergence of silkworm cultivation and silk, fashion in China entered a completely new era.

Grand Costumes of Pre-Qin Era

During the Shang Dynasty (1600–1046 BC), splendid clothes were made with delicate textiles. At the time, the popular costume consisted of two pieces: an upper coat that opened on the right that was fitted with narrow sleeves, and a short lower skirt fastened by a wide belt around the waist. There was a long axe-shaped decoration called *"fu"* hanging down in the front from the belt. There were geometrical patterns on the collar, sleeves, rims and the *fu*. Hats were also very popular at the time.

According to the *Zhouli (Rites of Zhou)*, "*Sifu* was an official in charge of the king's wardrobe. He chose clothes for various functions and occasions," giving fashion a political significance. During the Zhou Dynasty (1045–221 BC), headwear and suits were the typical formal attire for ceremonies. The design of headgear and suits incorporated traditional Chinese culture and expressed their ideas of ethics and rites. There were six types of headgear and suits for the kings of the Zhou Dynasty, and for the six levels of nobles.

The headgear was the most respected part of Zhou Dynasty formal attire. It consisted of a crown and a hat. The headgear and suit as a whole set was used from the Zhou Dynasty until the advent of the Republic of China (1912–49), with minor changes and additions. When Gen. Yuan Shikai proclaimed himself the Hongxian emperor (December 1915–March 1916), he had headgear made. That was the last official headgear in Chinese imperial history and it is now exhibited in the National Museum of China.

During the Zhou Dynasty, there was also an official position called the footwear man. At the time, when a courtier had an audience with the monarch, he was supposed to take off his shoes and socks and present himself barefoot to the monarch to show respect. This rite continued through the Han Dynasty (206 BC–AD 220) but was abolished during the Tang Dynasty (AD 618–907).

In the Spring and Autumn (770–476 BC) and the Warring States (475–221 BC) periods, *shenyi*, an overall that connected the upper coat and the lower piece, were popular. The chapter *"Shenyi"* in the *Liji (Book of Rites)* detailed specifications for its making and expressed the cultural pursuit for harmony between man and nature. *Shenyi* had a profound influence on ancient Chinese fashion and inspired the robes, long gowns and cheongsams of the Qing Dynasty (1644–1911) and even modern dress.

The transition from the Spring and Autumn to the Warring States periods was a time of great conflict among kingdoms. King Wuling of Zhao (circa 310–295 BC) adopted the fashion of the Hu people as well as equitation and archery. Hu people were nomadic tribes living in the northern grasslands. Their dress was short and close fitting, suited to fighting. To enhance the quality of his army, King Wuling reformed the uniform. He discarded the lower piece and replaced it with a pair of long trousers. The new footwear was a pair of long boots. The upper coat was transformed into a short, close-fitting robe that opened on the left. This was the first fashion reform in Chinese history.

Qin Dynasty Military Uniforms, Han Dynasty Formal Attire

In fashion, the Qin Dynasty (221–207 BC) followed the styles of the Warring States kingdoms. Robes and *shenyi* were the mainstream attire. Armoured coats, which were made in various forms, were the most distinctive attire during the Qin Dynasty. They served to boost morale and projected the power of the mighty empire. The neatly arranged Terracotta soldiers and horses excavated in Xi'an, Shaanxi Province, are an authentic representation of Qin Dynasty apparel.

During the Han Dynasty, the system of fashion reached a stage of maturity. The traditional system of headgear and suits was restored. Specific styles of fashion were designated for various levels of officials, the emperors, empresses and courtiers.

Shenyi continued to be used as the formal attire for official occasions. It still incorporated Zhou Dynasty designs, except the sleeves were looser. The government designated different colours for *shenyi* worn seasonally, with green for spring, red for summer, yellow for late summer, white for autumn and black for winter. Therefore, *shenyi* was also called "the five-colour attire for five seasons."

Han Dynasty robes followed the style of the Qin Dynasty. They were worn at court, without distinction for people of different ranks. Robes were made in a simple process and at a low cost; they were comfortable to wear, demonstrating a balance between social function and practicality.

Ru (a short jacket) was a coat shorter than a robe. It was usually worn together with a lower piece such as a kilt and skirt. Yan Shigu (AD 581–645) wrote in the *Jijiu Pian*, an enlightening book for children: "A long coat is called a robe, which reaches the ankles, while a short coat is called *"ru,"* which reaches above the knees." During the Han Dynasty, *ru* and skirts worn by nobles were made of high-quality textiles, while *ru* worn by the working class was made of linen and was shorter than most robes, facilitating working in the field.

During the Qin and Han dynasties, the headgear of women had distinctive styles and decorations that were regulated by a system of rules.

During the Han Dynasty, it was customary for women, whether the empress or noblewomen and dancers, to have headgear as part of their costume. According to *Account of Exotic Things* written by Li Quan during the Qing Dynasty, "The headgear was a wig made of decorations and hairs fitted on an iron ring." It could be fitted on the head with a ribbon. It looked like a garland and highlighted the women's beauty. Later, the name of this headgear was used as the general term for women.

Loose Clothes of Wei and Jin Dynasties

During the Wei (AD 220–265), Jin (AD 265–420) and the Southern and Northern dynasties (AD 420–589), ethnic integration accelerated the development of fashion. On the basis of traditional fashion of the Han people, various ethnic groups learned from one another and created fashions reflecting the distinctive characteristics of the time.

Emperor Xiaowen of the Northern Wei Dynasty (AD 386–534) spotted the cultural differences between Xianbei, the ruling class of Northern Wei Dynasty, and the Han, the people in Central China. As he was a great admirer of the culture and rites of China, he promoted the cultural assimilation of the Xianbei into the Han. The fashion of the Han replaced that of the Xianbei, which facilitated the development and transformation of ethnic fashion.

During the Wei and Jin Dynasties, the traditional *shenyi* gradually disappeared, replaced by the robe. Loose-fitting clothes came into fashion, as represented in paintings by the Jin painter Gu Kaizhi (AD 346–407) and the frescoes in Dunhuang. Women's dress was characterised by a scanty upper piece and a richly decorated lower piece.

According to the accounts in the *History of Song, Biography of Xie Lingyun*, Xie Lingyun (AD 385–433), a famous Southern Dynasties (AD 420–589) poet, enjoyed tours around mountains and rivers as a way to ease political pressures. He invented clogs with removable spikes. He removed the spikes on the front while climbing up and removed the spikes on the back while climbing down inclines. This invention inspired the great poet Li Bai (AD 701–762) to write the famous line "Climbing up the cloudy ladder wearing the clogs of Xie Lingyun." Clogs were also used in the army. When Sima Yi (AD 179–251) invaded Shu (AD 221–263), his troops wore clogs with flat bottoms, which protected their feet against thorns. Clogs were popular with the public, however, shoes were still the formal footwear for emperors and ministers.

On the basis of boots used during the Eastern Han Dynasty (AD 25–220), various types of boots became popular at the time. Some new styles emerged. According to *The Encyclopaedia of Dream Stream* by Shen Kuo (1033–1097), boots were extremely popular among officials and the public during the Northern Qi Dynasty (AD 550–577). During the Southern and Northern Dynasties, boots were usually knee-length. They were made of skins of sheep, horses and cattle. Some people even intentionally made the boots look worn out.

Tang Dynasty Elegant Dress

During the Tang Dynasty, the maturity of the traditional culture and the integration of domestic and foreign cultures injected unprecedented vitality into fashion.

During the Sui (AD 581–618), Tang and the Five Dynasties (AD 907–960), various types of well-designed round-collared robes were popular. During the reign of Emperor Taizong (reign: AD 627–649) a fold was added to the robe to carry forward the traditional combination of the upper and lower pieces. This new style combined the cultural elements of various ethnic groups and paved the way for a unified fashion in China.

During the early Tang Dynasty, Emperor Gaozu (reign: AD 618–626) stipulated yellow robes were for the exclusive use of emperors. He also made detailed rules for the colours of different levels of officials. Purple was for princes and senior officials, followed by red, green and cyan for lower-ranking officials. On the basis of that, Emperor Gaozong (reign: AD 649–683) made further regulations for the colours of official costumes. This system exerted a direct influence on the fashion during the Song (AD 960–1229), Liao (AD 916–1125) and Yuan (1271–1368) dynasties.

During the Sui and Tang dynasties, women's fashion followed an open style inspired by ethnic groups from northwestern China. Popular dresses at the time included a combination of a short blouse and a long dress, as well as low-cut strapless dresses. As depicted by Zhou Ben in his poem "Encounter with the Neighbouring Girl," women of the Tang Dynasty were very daring in their pursuit of happiness.

Women even wore the clothes of men, which was another prominent feature during the Tang Dynasty. That demonstrated female independence and open-mindedness. In the painting "Spring Tour by Madam Guo" by Zhang Xuan, five of the nine women are wearing round-collar robes, long trousers and boots, the typical costume of men at the time.

Song Dynasty Style: Elegant, Simple, Ancient

During the Song Dynasty, the textile industry continued to develop, and brocade making reached its heyday. Famous brocades included the Song brocade in Suzhou, Yun brocade in Nanjing and Shu brocade in Sichuan Province. Textiles were elegant and refined, which reflected a pursuit of elegance and simplicity.

Owing to the emergence of Neo-Confucianism, fashion developed towards an ancient, simple, regulated and complicated style, especially for official attire and men's costumes. Emperor Taizu (reign: AD 960–976) set out the basic system of official attire according to *The Pictures of Three Rites*. Official attire followed the elegant and formal style of the Zhou and Han dynasties. Positions and levels of officials were more obviously marked on their costumes. The basic form of an official costume consisted of headgear, a long-sleeved robe, a belt at the waist, a fish-shaped decoration and a pair of leather boots.

In folk fashion, various colours and new techniques such as embroidery and hand dyeing were applied. Simple and bright-blue-cloth costumes and clothes with embroidery gradually became the mainstream folk fashion in China. At the time, silk with patterns and textiles with gold thread woven into them were used for making headwear and clothes.

Women's dresses were tailored to demonstrate the beauty of the human body. Foot binding, which originated during the Five Dynasties among dancers in the palaces, was customary, since rites and rituals had a strong influence during the Song Dynasty. Arc-shaped shoes made especially for women with bound feet appeared.

Colourful Costumes of Ethnic Groups

During the Liao, Jin, Western Xia (1038–1227) and Yuan dynasties, nomadic people entered Central China, which brought new and different styles of fashion together, revitalising the fashion culture at the time. While carrying forward the traditions of Confucianism, Chinese fashion gradually moved towards simplicity and comfort.

Liao Dynasty fashion was influenced by the Han culture. The emperor and the southern officials who were in charge of the Han people wore Han fashions. At major ceremonies, people wore gold hats, white robes, red belts and fish-shaped decorations. At minor ceremonies, people wore hard hats and red robes with tortoise images. The empress dowager and the northern officials wore Liao fashions. In addition, the Qidan (an ancient nationality in China), the ruling class of the Liao Dynasty, and its subsidiary tribes were not allowed to don any headgear.

The Nüchen tribe (an ancient nationality in China) was originally a subsidiary of the Liao Dynasty. Later it grew powerful and established the Kingdom of Jin. From the start, Jin imitated Liao in fashion. Later, it adopted the system of official attire from the Song Dynasty. This official attire was characterised by narrow sleeves and round collars.

During the Yuan Dynasty, long robes were in fashion. These robes were larger and looser than those of the Liao Dynasty. Ceremonial costumes were Han styled, while other costumes were still in the traditional Mongolian style. According to historical records, men's costumes consisted of *shenyi*, coats, shirts, belts, turbans, hats and boots. Women's costumes were classified into two styles: the northern style consisting of necklaces and blouses, and the southern style consisting of capes, earrings, long dresses and blouses.

Flourishing Fashion of Ming Dynasty

During the Ming Dynasty, cotton was planted all over the country, and various types of silk and cotton textiles emerged. The costumes of the emperors, ministers, officials and noblewomen were made of specially woven, colourful textiles. These costumes were decorated with complex images of dragons, phoenixes, clouds, water, flowers, birds and beasts, demonstrating the advanced Ming techniques.

Ming Emperor Hongwu (reign: 1367–98) established new regulations for fashion on the basis of the customs of the Han. He initiated a complete fashion system that consisted of headgear and costumes for the emperor, the formal attire and dresses for empresses and concubines, costumes for officials and generals and clothes for commoners. According to *Accounts* by Yao Tinglin, "During the Ming Dynasty, officials and the gentry normally wore silk or satin robes at home. Wealthy people were allowed to wear whatever they could buy on the market." During the late Ming Dynasty, officials, the gentry and commoners could wear whatever they liked without sticking to rigid rules and regulations.

Ming Dynasty men's headgear came in many styles. The black gauze cap was a round-top hat worn by officials. Since the Ming Dynasty, these have symbolized official posts.

Qing Dynasty Manchurian Fashion

The Qing Dynasty had the most complicated fashion system, reflecting a combination of Han and Manchurian customs. Before the Manchurians invaded Central China, they had made detailed regulations concerning official attire. After establishing their rule in Beijing, this system was revised. In 1652, the Ministry of Rites issued the *Regulations on Attire*, which was a comprehensive and detailed set of rules for the styles, colours, textures and designs of official attire for ministers and generals. It also included regulations for the costumes worn by ordinary people such as merchants and labourers.

As depicted in films and television series, princes and nobles of the Qing Dynasty wore a splendid crown with a peacock feather attached. In the Qing Dynasty hierarchy, the peacock feature was used to show the status of a man. When an official was punished, he would be stripped of his peacock feather.

The emergence and dissemination of cheongsams was a significant event in the history of fashion in China. Manchurian women usually wore long gowns derived from official attire. These long gowns were collectively called cheongsams. Cheongsams were normally cut in straight lines. The sleeves were wide and the rims reached the ground and covered the shoes, hilighting the tall and slim stature of Manchurian women.

Combined Chinese, Western Fashions of Republic of China

During the Republic of China, traditional fashion went through a major reform. In the late 1920s, the government issued the new *Regulations on Fashion*, which stipulated the styles of formal attire for men and women and the official attire for civil servants. The fashion in this period reflected a western influence.

In the early years of the Republic of China, it was fashionable for women to wear the revised cheongsams, which acquired the status of "national costume." The 1930s were the heyday of cheongsams, which experienced various changes, such as higher hems, tighter waists and shoulder folds. Cheongsams became closer fitting and better demonstrated the beauty of women.

At the time, western-style suits and Chinese-style long gowns were both worn. Sun Yat-sen (1866–1925), the father of the democratic revolution in China, created a style of suit and named it the Sun Yat-sen uniform. It gradually became popular in cities. At formal occasions, officials and intellectuals normally wore either western suits or Sun Yat-sen uniforms.

Chinese fashion reflects the history, culture, rites, customs and arts of the Chinese nation. From the prehistoric era to the modern era, fashion has always symbolised the aesthetic pursuits and living philosophies of the Chinese.

The Charm of Chinese Tea

The tea ceremony reflects the Chinese cultures spirit. Tea drinking is an art of self-cultivation and great spiritual enjoyment. With the emerging custom of drinking tea, teahouses became popular places for socialising. This culture around teahouses has long been an important element in the life of the Chinese.

History of Tea Drinking Culture

The Chinese were the first to cultivate and drink tea. There were numerous books on the planting of tea and the customs surrounding tea drinking in China.

Tea was discovered and regarded as a kind of herbal drug in early China. According to *Shennong Discovering the Curative Virtues of Plants*, "Shennong tasted hundreds of plants, including 72 noxious herbs. He took some tea leaves to repel the toxicants." Gradually, tea grew from an herbal drug to a food, and finally became an everyday drink. During the Jin and Song dynasties, the people in Wu picked tea leaves and boiled them in porridge. At the time tea leaves were eaten as a kind of vegetable. In the Qin and Han dynasties, tea leaves were processed and cooked with onions, ginger and oranges.

During the Wei, Jin, Southern and Northern dynasties, the custom of tea drinking was highly refined. Scholars of metaphysics in particular, who pursued elegance and simplicity, favoured tea. For Buddhists, tea drinking was useful for entering into a state of deep meditation. Chan Buddhists promoted their ideas through tea drinking, while literati and officialdom approached and practised Chan by drinking tea. Tea was no longer an ordinary drink, it became a culture.

During the Tang Dynasty, tea was widely planted in China and tea drinking became a fashion among various classes of people. During the mid-Tang period, tea gatherings and tea banquets emerged as new forms of activities surrounding tea drinking. During the late-Tang Dynasty, tea banquets at the Qingming Festival emerged at the imperial palace. Monographs on tea also appeared at the time. *The Classic of Tea* was written by Lu Yu (AD 733–804) during the eighth century. It is the first and the most complete monograph on tea. It marked an important stage in the development of the tea culture, as it generalised all the knowledge about tea at the time. It was also then that tea ceremonies took shape. Tea leaves and water were carefully selected and followed a refined process.

During the Northern Song Dynasty, Chen Shidao (1053–1102) made a distinction between the tea ceremony and tea art. He thought the tea ceremony, as an art, was inferior to tea art, which was a virtue. Tea drinking was connected with the spirits of serenity, naturalism, modesty and thrift. During the Song Dynasty, tea processing improved, exerting a profound influence on tea drinking. With the emergence of more varieties of tea leaves, the authentic flavour and taste of tea was favoured, so tea leaves were boiled alone in hot water without any other ingredients. This became a major simplification in the preparation of tea. Tea drinking was subject to a gradual change that lasted from the Song Dynasty to the Ming and Qing dynasties.

Today, all the various forms of tea drinking can be classified into three categories. The first category is to drink tea alone without any other ingredients, which is in line with the traditional pursuit of peace and quietude; second, is to boil tea with other ingredients, such as milk, salt and lemon; the third, is to enjoy cakes, dancing, singing, music, painting, calligraphy and theatre while drinking tea. Teahouses are usually the place for enjoying such entertainment.

Various Teahouse Cultures

With the growing popularity of tea drinking, teahouses have developed into venues for public activities.While scholars pursued spiritual fulfilment in tea drinking, ordinary people tried to enjoy simpler pleasures.

The earliest teahouses appeared during the reign of Emperor Yuan (reign: AD 317–322) of the Jin Dynasty. During the Tang Dynasty, teahouses began to emerge, particularly in Chang'an (the Tang capital). Normally, the statue of Lu Yu was enshrined in the teahouses. At the time, teahouses were not independent businesses but part of hotels and restaurants. After further development during the Song Dynasty, teahouses finally became the fashionable places for leisure in the Ming and Qing dynasties.

Teahouses in Chengdu, Sichuan Province, have become an integral part of the traditional city culture. Local residents in Chengdu feel proud of their teahouse culture. Tea sets, consisting of three pieces, a cup, lid and saucer, and furniture, a little wooden table and bamboo armchairs, in the teahouses are the most distinctive features. Waiters are the souls of the teahouse. The waiter holds the teapot and fills the cup while standing a few feet away. The water spurts from the teapot directly into the cup and fills the cup to the brim, amazing goests and customers.

In the past, teahouses were everywhere Beijing and served various functions. At some teahouses, storytellers gave performances that were both entertaining and enlightening, disseminating the traditional virtues of benevolence, righteousness, courtesy, wisdom and trust. At other teahouses, customers sat chatting over current affairs and exchanging views. The most interesting teahouses were open-air ones at the springs in northwestern Beijing, where scholars sat down to enjoy tea while appreciating the scenery.

The famous modern Chinese writer Lao She (1881–1936) was an expert on tea culture. He wrote the dramatic play *Teahouse*. Since teahouses were an arena of various social activities frequented by various characters from different social classes, Lao She used the teahouse to reflect the social transformation taking place around him. *Teahouse* reflected on how social turmoil affected the teahouse economy, its culture and patrons.

Today, teahouses are still relevant to everyday life. They are places for entertainment and gatherings.

Tea is indispensable in the life of the Chinese. People in Guangdong drink tea at breakfast; in Hangzhou, people drink tea three times a day; in Chengdu tea is consumed at numerous teahouses; in Beijing people are known to drink tea from big bowls. Tea ceremonies and tea culture in China reflect a natural life philosophy. Tea culture, as an integral part of Chinese culture, has permeated every part of the world with its flavours.

Flavourful Tea: Appreciated Around the Worldwide

Tea was introduced to Japan during the Han Dynasty and became fashionable there during the Tang and Song dynasties. In AD 805, a Japanese Buddhist returned to Japan after finishing his studies in China bearing tea seeds that he planted in Shiga-ken. Later, tea planting spread to other places in Japan. During the Song Dynasty, another Japanese Buddhist returned to Japan after studying in China and wrote *Drinking Tea for Health*, based on his observations of tea drinking in China. The book was the first concerning tea published in Japan. In the early 15th century, Murata Jyukou, a Japanese Buddhist, established the distinctive tea ceremony in Japan. In fact, when Chinese tea culture entered Japan, it was transformed into a kind of tea ceremony, which was rather entertaining and technical, but it did not reflect the original spirit of tea culture.

During the Ming Dynasty, tea leaves became an important export from China. When Zheng He (1371–1433) led his fleet to the South China Sea and the Indian Ocean, he visited Southeast Asia, the Arabian Peninsula and the eastern coast of Africa. With expanded trading connections, tea leaves were exported in large volumes. In 1607, Dutch ships from Java arrived in Macau to pick up tea to take to Europe, which was the first documented export of Chinese tea to Europe. Tea soon became a top luxury item for Dutch nobles. By the 18th century, tea drinking had become a fashion in other European countries such as Great Britain and France.

In Britain, tea drinking was first introduced by the Thomas Garvey coffeehouse in London. During the 1650s, the owner of the cafe promoted Chinese tea on posters. The British preferred black tea, which has a strong flavour. Milk and sugar cubes were added to the drink, which enhanced its taste. Today, the practises continue; afternoon tea is customary in Britain. In Cambridge, scholars conduct academic exchanges over tea, called "the Cambridge Spirit."

Americans drink various types of tea: black, green, scented and oolong teas. TenRen Tea Shop in New York's Chinatown always has many customers.

From the Islamic style teahouses in Turkey to the deserts of Arabia and North Africa to the distinctive method of tea preparation by the Germans, tea drinking has been incorporated into the lifestyles of people all over the world.

Famous Teas

Chinese teas are most often classified as black, green, oolong, yellow, white and dark teas. There are more than 2,000 varieties, each with diverse shapes, flavours and tastes. Famous varieties, such as West Lake Longjing, Mount Huangshan Maofeng, Mount Lushan Yunwu and Dongting Biluochun, are usually planted in beautiful places, which have enhanced their reputations.

Longjing Tea: Excellent Colour, Flavour, Taste

Longjing belongs to the green tea family, with flat leaves that look like the tongues of larks. Tea water used to prepare it is clear and delicious. This variety is famous for its green colour, strong flavour, soft taste and beautiful shape. There are four origins of Longjing: Shifeng, Longjing, Wuyunshan and Hupaoshan, of which Longjing yields the best tea leaves.

The cultivation of tea at Longjing was recorded during the Tang Dynasty. During the Song Dynasty, Longjing was already very famous. Song Dynasty poet Su Dongpo described the shapes of the leaves of Longjing tea by comparing them to banners and spears, hence the tea's nickname "banner spear." During the Qing Dynasty, Emperor Qianlong applauded Longjing as "the golden shoot" and "the unparalleled." It is said that when the emperor came to Hugong Temple at the foot of Mount Shifeng, he picked tea leaves himself. At this moment, news arrived that the empress dowager had been stricken with illness. The emperor put the newly picked tea shoots into his sleeves and hurried back to Beijing. When he was with the empress dowager, she smelt the fragrance and her son told her that it was the shoots of Longjing tea. The empress dowager drank the tea for several days and gradually recovered from her illness. Therefore, the emperor issued an order that the 18 tea trees in front of Hugong Temple at the foot of Mount Shifeng would be used exclusively for the use of the imperial family, and tributes of tea shoots should be made each year. Today, the 18 trees are a famous tourist attraction.

High-quality tea leaves must be prepared in high-quality water. The water from Hupao Spring contains organic nitrites and small amounts of soluble minerals, so that it aids in releasing the flavour and enhancing its taste. Combining Longjing Tea and Hupao Water is an excellent choice in Hangzhou.

Biluochun: Amazing Fragrance

Biluochun is green in colour and curled in shape. As it was first harvested on Mount Biluo in the spring, it was named Biluochun (Mount Biluo in Spring). According to legend, on West Dongting Hill (Lake Tai, Jiangsu Province near Suzhou), there lived a beautiful girl named Biluo, who fell in love with a young man. The man fought the demon of the lake to save the local residents, and was severely wounded. Biluo saved him by healing his wound with a variety of tea leaves. Sadly, Biluo was so exhausted that she died. The tea was thus called Biluochun in her memory.

Processing Biluochun is technically difficult, because a fine balance must be achieved to guarantee the quality of the tea leaves. Half a kilogramme (kg) of high-quality dried Biluochun tea contains 60,000–70,000 tea leaves. The dried leaves are green. After drawing in water, the tea water is clear and bright; the flavour and taste are strong, with a sweet, fruity smell. The tea can energise the brain and the heart. It can also nourish the throat and eyes. Therefore, it is regarded as a high-quality gift in China.

Maofeng Tea: From Cloud-Capped Mount Huangshan

As the gem of green teas, this variety got its name from Mount Huangshan. According to *Chronicles of Huizhou*, the tea was famous about early as 300 years ago. During the reign of Qing Emperor Guangxu (1875–1908), first-class Maofeng was cultivated, which made the tea even more famous around China. After drawing, the fragrance spreads into the air with the evaporation of the water. Its flavour and taste can linger for a long time, even when the water has cooled off. First-class Maofeng is harvested between the Qing Ming Festival and Guyu (mid-April) and then carefully processed.

Tieguanyin Tea: Lasting Taste

Tieguanyin Tea refers to oolong tea made of the leaves called the Tieguanyin tea tree. It is cultivated in Anxi County in southern Fujian Province. The processed tea leaves look like dragonflies with tails of tadpoles tinged with red rims; this is first-class oolong tea. In Anxi County, Tieguanyin Tea is made through a complex process consisting of many stages. The drawing of Tieguanyin is still in the traditional kung fu tea style, at least in Quanzhou, Zhangzhou and Xiamen in Fujian Province as well as in Chaozhou, Shantou and Taiwan. The tea leaves are put into a pottery teapot before boiled water is poured in. The smell, the flavour and taste is sublime.

"As the tea water swirls in the teapot, the fragrance spreads to the nose." When you drink it, the flavour and taste lingers in the mouth.

Wine: Elegance of Rites at Banquets

In China, there is a long history of wine brewing. It was first recorded in the history books of the Shang and Zhou dynasties 3,000 years ago. Over this long period, wine went through complex changes. There have also been numerous legends, tales and anecdotes about winemaking and drinking.

Probing the Origin of Wine

Legend has it that as early as 15 million years ago, a group of primitive men lived by Hongze Lake along the Huaihe River. At dusk one day, they smelt a strange but sweet fragrance that came from the trunk of a big tree. It was the juice of a fruit. After drinking it, the men got drunk and fell asleep. Fast forward to 1953, the fossils of these primitive men were excavated and traces of the wine that had permeated their bodies and bones were found. These fossils found in Xiacaowan by Hongze Lake are by far the earliest evidence of the origin of wine. It proved that natural fruit wine existed long before the emergence of modern humans.

Wine brewing originated during the Neolithic Age, when human beings had sufficient stocks of grain and refined pottery containers. Humans learned to make wine from fermented grains, which marked the beginning of brewing. Archaeological excavations of pottery wine containers at the Longshan site from 2,800–2,300 BC, proved that brewing was advanced at the time.

The period from the Xia Dynasty to the Zhou Dynasty was the development phase of traditional Chinese wine. The discovery of yeast means that the brewing technology was already advanced. More varieties of wine were created. According to a record by Jiang Tong of the Jin Dynasty, "The origin of wine could be traced back to the earliest kings of China Dukang [dates unknown]. When there was a surplus of grain, the grain was put into empty containers for fermentation until it became fragrant." Dukang has become a household name and the legendary figure is honoured as the father of wine in China.

During the Spring and Autumn and Warring States periods, wine was more popular than before. There were many anecdotes about military and political issues in connection with wine. King Mugong of the Kingdom of Qin was a politician of the Warring States Period. Once, two of his cherished horses were stolen and slaughtered by slaves labouring at the foot of Mount Qi. When the king hurried to the mountain, more than 300 slaves were sitting around a pot of boiled horsemeat. His troops were about to arrest the slaves when the king stopped them and said, "I heard that eating horsemeat without drinking wine is unhealthy, so I'm rather worried for them." The king then gave wine to the slaves, who were moved by the benevolence of the king. When the king was later encircled by the troops of the Kingdom of Jin, these slaves hurried from Mount Qi to the battlefield and rescued the king, returning his favour.

There are many other anecdotes in the history of these two periods, so it can be said that history is soaked in wine.

Hongmen Banquet, Encounter of Heroes over Plum Wine

Throughout the history of wine, banquets recorded the heroism of soldiers, the leisure of country life, the complaints of concubines and the murderous atmosphere of political assassinations.

In 206 BC, two rebellious leaders, Xiang Yu (232–202 BC) and Liu Bang (256–195 BC), emerged. Liu Bang led his troops from Pei County and marched into Xianyang, the capital of the Qin Dynasty, with 100,000 men. Xiang Yu, who had just defeated the main army of the Qin Dynasty, was surprised by the news. He suspected that Liu Bang wanted to claim the throne as emperor, so he decided to invite Liu Bang to a banquet at Hongmen and finish him off at the dinner. Liu Bang came with his followers and made clarifications and apologies. At the dinner, Xiang Zhuang, a general of Xiang Yu, practised fencing with the aim of killing Liu Bang. At this crucial juncture, Fan Kuai, Liu Bang's follower, broke into the banquet to protect Liu Bang. Liu Bang pretended to be drunk and left the banquet. This was the well-known "Hongmen Banquet."

Another famous banquet in history was "The encounter of heroes over plum wine," which was first recorded in *History of the Three Kingdoms, History of the Kingdom of Shu, Biography of Liu Bei* by Chen Shou. When Liu Bei lost Xuzhou, he had nowhere to go, so he submitted himself to Cao Cao. He pretended to be without any aspirations by growing vegetables at home. Cao Cao saw through Liu Bei and invited him to dinner in order to probe into his mind. At the table, the two talked about history and current affairs. Cao Cao said, "Heroes shall have both great aspirations and wisdom." Liu Bei continued to pretend to be a fool and asked, "Who can be a hero?" Cao Cao then pointed to Liu Bei and himself and replied, "The only heroes today are you and me!" Just at this moment, a thunder came, so Liu Bei pretended to be frightened by it and dropped his chopsticks. He explained, "I was just so frightened by the thunderbolt." Cao Cao laughed and asked, "How can a man fear thunder?" Liu Bei replied, "Even Confucius was made to grimace at thunderbolts and gales." He cleverly concealed his fear and gave a plausible explanation. This dinner was the encounter of two heroes. The self-confidence of Cao Cao and the resourcefulness and versatility of Liu Bei were vividly demonstrated at the dinner, so this banquet ranks among the top three in ancient China.

Eight Drunken Talents Expressing Aspirations with Poems

"The Eight Drunken Talents" refer to eight talents of the Tang Dynasty. All of the eight were heavy drinkers. They lived in the same era in Chang'an (today's Xi'an). They were similar to one another in terms of drinking and aspirations. Du Fu, a famous poet, wrote "The Song for the Eight Drunken Talents" to describe them.

Du Fu adeptly described them in one poem, constituting a vivid picture of the eight drunken talents. Each of the eight was famous at the time and each of them expressed his aspirations through drinking wine.

More than 7,700 poems about wine were written during the Tang Dynasty, with more than 14 percent of all poems written during the dynasty. Famous poets, such as Wang Zhihuan, Chen Ziang, Meng Haoran and Bai Juyi, were all heavy drinkers.

Wine Flavours Poetry of Ouyang Xiu, Su Dongpo

Ouyang Xiu, a famous scholar of the Northern Song Dynasty, was nicknamed *"Zuiwong"* (Drunken Man). He wrote a famous essay entitled *Story of the Drunken Man's Pavilion*, which described joyful banquets at the pavilion. Ouyang Xiu even built a hall for banquets. In summer, he had lotuses picked and invited his friends to the hall for drinking sprees that lasted into the evening.

Su Dongpo, one of the Eight Master Essayists of the Tang and Song dynasties, was also a heavy drinker. He was also good at brewing and wrote a monograph entitled *Book of Wine*. His poetry was inevitably connected with wine. According to the scholar Lin Yutang, Su Dongpo "was more resourceful, versatile and humorous than other poets in China." He must have been inspired by wine.

Entertainment, Performances at Dinner

There can be found four categories of banquets throughout history. The first category was the folk dinner where family members, relatives and neighbours got together; second was the literary banquet organised by scholars and literati, the purpose of which was academic exchanges; third were the banquets of officials and the emperor; the fourth were official banquets either awarded by the emperor or held in connection with various state affairs. Such banquets were usually large in scope and ritually complex.

Wine drinking was closely connected with rites. As early as during the Western Zhou Dynasty, there were rites for archery. There were archery competitions held at banquets, where the losers were punished by drinking wine. Another custom that originated from archery was called throwing. Each of the diners tried to throw arrows into a pot; the losers were punished by drinking wine.

Drinkers' wagers were popular at banquets. They originated during the Western Zhou Dynasty and matured during the Sui and Tang dynasties. The wager game was played among literati and gentries. One man was appointed as a "dealer" who gave the first part of a poem or the upper half of a couplet. Then, the other participants were required to follow up with their own verses through improvisation. The wager game was mainly played by casting dice, drawing lots, finger-guessing and number-guessing. Like a catalyst, these wager games revived the atmosphere at the table, part of the complex wine culture of China.

Famous Liquors

Over thousands of years, numerous regional wines have been cultivated. Among them, Guizhou Maotai, Shaanxi Xifeng, Shanxi Fenjiu and Luzhou Laojiao are honoured as the top four oldest liquors in China.

Luzhou Laojiao: 'Good wine needs no bush'

A long and deep lane at Yinggoutou, south of Luzhou City in Sichuan Province was famous for its eight winemaking workshops during the Ming and Qing dynasties. The Shu Family Workshop set up there in 1573 was the predecessor of the Luzhou Laojiao.

The Shu Family Workshop had mature local winemaking skills. The pit mud was cultured with wine, which aided winemaking. Microorganisms penetrated into the liquor through wine lees, rendering the wine fresh and mellow. A poem, "Luzhou," by Zhang Chuanshan of the Qing Dynasty described people's love for Luzhou-flavoured liquor.

At the first Panama Pacific International Exposition (the expo) in the United States in 1915, Luzhou Laojiao won a gold medal. Today, the traditional technique of mixed steaming for continuous fermentation is still used in production. This liquor has a fragrant taste that lingers in the mouth.

That twisted lane and its time-honoured winemaking workshops no longer exist. The aroma of Luzhou Laojiao remains and is growing in popularity worldwide.

Guizhou Maotai: 'National Liquor'

Maotai is brewed in Maotai Town, Renhuai City, Guizhou Province, in southwestern China. It is honoured as one of the top-three liquors in the world, the other two being Scotch whisky and French brandy.

Maotai Town produced high-quality liquor during the Northern Song Dynasty, which was recorded in the book *Jiuming Ji (Record of Wine Names)*. Maotai's great taste is inseparable from its fine local water.

Before 1949, there were three breweries that produced Huamao, Wangmao and Laimao liqour. "Huamao" is the predecessor of today's Maotai.

Maotai liquor packed in dark-brown clay pots did not attract visitors' attention at the expo in 1915. Chinese officials came up with an idea. They broke the pots and the overwhelming fragrance spread every where. Participating delegations competed to order Maotai liquor and it was awarded a gold medal.

The making of a bottle of Maotai liquor takes five years. Maotai is regarded as the national liquor of China due to its soft and mellow flavour.

130

Shaanxi Xifeng: Pervasive Fragrance

Shaanxi Province is famous for its fine winemaking ingredients and clean water. As the oldest liquor in China with 3,000 years of history, Shaanxi Xifeng liquor originated during the Shang Dynasty, maturing during the Tang and Song dynasties. The liquor is brewed in Fengxiang County, Shaanxi Province. Fengxiang was called Yong in ancient China. It is considered the place of origin of Chinese culture, in particular the Zhou and Qin cultures.

The allusion of Mugong in the Kingdom of Qin throwing bottles of wine into the river to reward a victorious army after they won a battle against the State of Jin was written in the *Historical Record*.

During the reign of Emperor Zhenguan (AD 627–649), Shaanxi Xifeng won fame for its "fragrance extending 10 miles." It maintains a delicate balance of the five taste sensations: sour, sweet, bitter, hot and fragrance.

Liulinzhen in Fengxiang County has long been famous for its liquor. During the Ming Dynasty, brewing became a prosperous activity.

Shanxi Fenjiu: 'Wine in Poem'

The History of Fenyang County says: "The best liquor in Fenyang County is from Xinghua Village." From wineware unearthed in Fenyang County, Fenyang County has a 4,000-year-history of winemaking. During the late-Tang Dynasty, Du Mu wrote a poem "Qingming" with the famous line, "If you ask where the nearest pub is, shepherds will show you the way to Apricot Village."

In 1915, Shanxi Fenjiu won the first-level gold medal at the expo. Today, the liquor is sold in more than 40 countries and regions. The popularity of Shanxi Fenjiu is connected with its special brewing procedures, ingredients and water from deep wells.

The time-honoured wells for winemaking remains in Xinghua Village. Qing Dynasty scholar Fu Shan inscribed: "De Zao Huaxiang" for the well, which means, "refreshing wine made from the spring in an ancient well."

Festivals and Customs

The Chinese calendar is the common intellectual property of the whole nation, reflecting Chinese customs. Chinese had great fun in observing nature and astronomical phenomena. They created festivals that are components of Chinese culture and have been handed down, retaining much of their meaning to today.

Humanistic Source of Festivals

In ancient China, festivals were closely associated with primitive religions. Time was usually marked with ceremonies of worship. The concept of the year originated from agriculture, but it is shown in the cycle of worship ceremonies. Scheduled worship sessions became a natural part of life.

From the pre-Qin period to the early Western Han, the calendar originated from the universal belief in heavenly deities. During the mid-Western Han Dynasty, Emperor Wudi (141–87 BC) promoted the supreme authority of Confucianism and the concept of filial piety in Confucianism became the dominating ideology in China. The festivals in China went through a transition from being nature-orientated to being society-orientated.

After the mid-Han Dynasty, the festival system went through a process of secularisation. During the Eastern Han, Wei and Jin dynasties, a system of festivals gradually took shape. It was in line with nature and demonstrated the cultural beliefs of that time.

Spiritual Tradition of Festivals

In China, festivals are closely linked with everyday life. People in China still consult their traditional lunar calendars in addition to the Gregorian calendar. The Spring Festival, the Dragon Boat Festival, the Mid-Autumn Festival and the Double-Ninth Festival have always been an integral part of everyday life.

Chunjie (Spring Festival)

New Year's celebrations are a common custom worldwide. The Chinese Spring Festival is particularly important. According to the first Chinese book on festivals *Accounts of Festivals in Jingchu*, the whole family would get up at dawn on the first day of the year and set off firecrackers to dispel demons. Then people would change into new clothes and wish one another a happy New Year.

From the Spring Festival to the Lantern Festival, the sounds of firecrackers symbolise happiness and harmony. Ancient people believed that sounds could repel evil, so they burned bamboo. After gunpowder was invented, it was rolled into paper and burnt. During the Song Dynasty, the evening scene of setting off firecrackers was described by the idiom "burning trees and shining flowers." With new technology, auspicious decorations in the shape of firecrackers were made for the celebrations.

Couplets are indispensable. They originated from auspicious symbols made of mahogany. According to *Compendium of Materia Medica*, "Mahogany comes from the west and is capable of repelling evil." During the Han Dynasty, there was a custom of hanging it on the gates. Later, people drew the gate deities on mahogany boards. These were the predecessors of couplets. Ming Emperor Taizu hung couplets at the gate of the palace and ordered his ministers to do the same, which caused it to become a popular custom.

Yuanxiao Jie (Lantern Festival)

The Lantern Festival comes on the 15th day of the first lunar month. Since the Han Dynasty, this festival has been an overnight celebration with lanterns.

Apart from lanterns and riddles, the dragon and lion dance is also a splendid festival attraction. As the Chinese regard themselves as descendants of the dragon, the dragon dance is a unique scene on this carnival night for the Chinese.

Glutinous rice dumplings are a typical food for this festival. This custom originated during the Song Dynasty. This food symbolises family reunions and stands for good wishes for the whole family.

Qingming Jie (Qingming Festival)

The Qingming Festival originated during the Warring States Period, and the practise of tomb sweeping began during the Song Dynasty.

During the Tang Dynasty, the Qingming Festival (Pure Brightness Day) and the Cold Dish Day were combined. While people did not use fire on the Cold Dish Day to cook, they set up new fires for the Qingming Festival. Outings were another custom of the festival. Other activities on the day included kicking balls, tug of war and flying kites.

Willows play an important role during this festival, because they are the first plant to turn green in spring. In ancient China, willows were said to be able to carry the fire forward into the future and repel demons. Therefore, it is customary for people to put willow branches at the front of their gates and doors.

Duanwu Jie (Dragon Boat Festival)

The festival comes on the fifth day of the fifth month. It is a day for dragon boats, poets and *zongzi* (pyramid-shaped glutinous-rice-filled dumplings wrapped in bamboo or leaves), but this date has been a festival date since the Xia Dynasty, when it was a day for taking a bath to help repel illnesses.

Zongzi are the customary food of this festival. It is said that the food commemorates Qu Yuan, a patriotic poet of the Warring States Period. According to legend, he committed suicide in the Miluo River on the fifth day of the fifth month, as his political aspirations could not be fulfilled. The people of the Kingdom of Chu kept throwing dumplings into the river to feed the fish and shrimps to keep Qu's body from being devoured, thus creating this custom.

Dragon boat racing during this festival has a history of 1,000 years. It was for the purpose of praying for rain and it was also a kind of military training. Dragon boats are normally prepared before the festival. There is a range of detailed rules for the race, including the timing.

Today, dragon boat racing has acquired a much wider significance. It is now one of the carriers of traditional Chinese culture.

Qixi Jie (Double-Seventh Festival)

Double-Seventh Festival is the traditional lovers' day in China. The legend of the reunion of the shepherd boy and the weaver girl on the Magpie Bridge has remained a fascinating story. This romance between the immortal and the mortal is a love classic that has been replayed for thousands of years on the seventh day of the seventh month.

The day originated from the ancient calendar. According to *History of Han • Calendar*, the Star of the Weaver and the Star of the Shepherd are directly opposite each other across the Milky Way galaxy on this day. This astronomical phenomenon was later romanticised into the reunion of lovers, adding a romantic flavour to this purely astronomical phenomenon.

Yin Yun first recorded the love story during the Southern Dynasties era. According to *Novels by Yin Yun*, "East of the Milky Way is the Star of the Weaver, the daughter of the Heavenly Emperor. She was busy working at the loom all day long. Her father saw that she was lonely, so he married her to the Star of Shepherd west of the Milky Way. When she gave up weaving after the marriage, her father got angry and ordered her to come back to the east. He allowed the couple only one reunion per year."

With cultural development, the content of the story has changed from time to time. However, the reunion of the couple on this very day has encouraged lovers in China to pursue their own happiness.

In addition, Double-Seventh Day is also the birthday of the God of Literature and the Seventh Aunt who is in charge of peace. Various customs have been developed to celebrate this festival. It is a day for people to express their best wishes, for the reunion of lovers, and for the protection by the God of Literature and the Seventh Aunt.

Zhongqiu Jie (Mid-Autumn Festival)

Mid-Autumn Festival is in autumn when laurel trees are blossoming. The bright full moon on this date symbolises family reunions for the Chinese people.

This festival was closely linked with the worship of the sun and the moon. The worship of the moon was regulated in imperial codes. Mythologies involving the moon had undergone several major changes until the Tang Dynasty, when it was said to be the place for exiled deities. The moon was given a fairylike aesthetical connotation by people of the Tang. Chang'e took ambrosia and became the spirit of the moon, while Wu Gang was punished for his lapse at studying and was doomed to cutting trees in the Moon Palace. After the Song Dynasty, the custom of worshipping and appreciating the moon appeared. During the Ming and Qing dynasties, the festival was more secularised and elevated to become one of the three major traditional festivals, the other two being the Spring Festival and the Dragon Boat Festival.

The moon cake originated during the Song Dynasty, as recorded by Su Dongpo in his poems. During the Ming Dynasty, the moon cake became an essential food for the Mid-Autumn Festival. According to *Records of the Tour around West Lake* by Tian Rucheng of the Ming Dynasty, "On Mid-Autumn Day, people send one another moon cakes, which symbolise reunion." During the Qing Dynasty, special moon cakes for worshipping the moon were made. These moon cakes were larger than the ordinary ones. According to *Festivals in Yanjing*, "Large worship moon cakes measure over one *chi* [33.3 cm] in diameter. The images of the Moon Palace and the Jade Rabbit were painted on them." Family members shared these special worship moon cakes after worship, so they were also called "reunion cakes."

In China, there are various kinds of moon cakes with distinctive flavours and tastes. Among the varieties, the ones made in Beijing, Jiangsu, Guangdong and Chaozhou are the most famous. Recently, new shapes of moon cakes have been developed in addition to the traditional round-shaped cakes. There are now moon cakes in the shapes of flowers, pentagons and octagons with all kinds of fillings.

On the evening of the Mid-Autumn Day, the whole family sits down to smell the scent of laurel, drink laurel wine and to eat reunion moon cakes, the ultimate happiness for the Chinese.

Chongyang Jie (Chongyang Festival)

The Chongyang Festival (Double-Ninth Day) is regarded as the day when the elderly pray for longevity. The customs of this day, such as mountain climbing and drinking chrysanthemum wine, have long been a part of the Chinese culture.

Before Han Dynasty, there was an autumn ceremony for the dispelling of disasters. During the Wei, Jin, Southern and Northern Dynasties, mountain climbing and wine drinking for happiness became customs of this day. *The Letter to Zhong Yao* by Emperor Wendi of Wei (AD 535–551) gave an explanation for the significance of this day: "The number nine is the largest number and the double nine on the day symbolises longevity." Ascending to the mountaintop for picnic was the main activity that day, as described in a poem by Wang Wei.

Staying in a remote town as a stranger,
I miss my family particularly on festive days.
I see my brothers sitting on the mountaintop,
Planting cornels without me.

On this day, chrysanthemum wine is considered indispensable. The wine brewed on this particular day was usually regarded as good for health. It could ease the inner heat, relieve pressure and nourish the eyes and kidneys. This custom of brewing wine on this day has been kept in some places, such as Linyi and Rizhao in Shandong Province.

As a custom, people picked cornel on the Double-Ninth Day, because they thought that it could repel toxics and protect the body against the cold. They put cornel in small bags and carried them on the body, so they were always surrounded by the pleasant fragrance of the plant.

The ninth month is the time for harvesting, so the ancient Chinese made cakes out of the newly harvested grain. These cakes were shared among the family members before they were used to worship the ancestors.

All the people in the world have kept their festivals and customs alive in their beliefs and lives. Many distinctive cultural heritages have grown to be the pride of posterities. Today, people still need to absorb the vibrant elements of traditional festivals in order to embrace and restore the harmony between man and nature.

Promoting Chinese Studies, Preserving Moral Integrity

China's ever-increasing influence is generating greater interest in its culture around the world, a phenomenon that is provoking discussion and deep thinking in intellectual circles both nationally and internationally. In China, people are turning to Chinese studies *(guoxue)* to explore the influence of their cultural legacy on their contemporary social and cultural lives.

The *guoxue* concept emerged during the early 20th century as a major concern in academic circles of that time. Some supported the concept, while some opposed it; as a field of endeavour, it has experienced ups and downs. The recent boom in Chinese studies has expanded beyond academic thinking and discussion to become a conscious consideration in socio-economic thinking and of people's daily lives. The influence of Chinese studies has expanded, because of attention given it by the mass media and numerous people concerned with cultural development and its effects. Still, the true vitality of a culture or civilisation is not limited to small clusters of thinkers; it is rooted in social life and practise. This social concern for Chinese culture is reflected in the development of ancient Chinese studies, offering a way for these to better understand modern Chinese culture.

The Hongdao Fund and Hongdao Academy are non-governmental Chinese studies communities founded by Confucian scholars. The directors of the Hongdao Fund and its main participants are scholars. It is an influential Confucian community, created by experts of all fields, and although every expert has a different field of study, they consider Confucianism their common interest. By raising money and gathers resources for the revival of Confucianism, their accumulated resources are used to support Confucian charities, cultivating people, rehabilitating rites and music, promoting discussions of knowledge, training talents, the publishing of books, website maintenance and social relief activities.

Civil organisations and communities involved in ancient Chinese studies today include private academies such as the Pengcheng, Weihang, Qibaoge and the Jiguang academies, which contribute to spreading traditional Chinese culture and pre-school education for children. College associations and organisations of Chinese studies for university students also provide a platform for young scholars to gain access to Chinese studies and traditional culture.

Chinese studies were discussed widely and studied much in the 20th century on the Chinese mainland for their unique charm, despite pressures arising from the influence of western civilisation and integration resulting from globalisation.

The establishment of Confucius Institutes and increasing, higher-quality cultural-exchange activities are essential parts of the overseas propagation of Chinese studies.

The prospects for Confucius Institutes around the world are generally positive; their quality is improving. A journey of a thousand miles begins with a single step. It is believed that with the influence of Confucius Institutes, the overseas propagation of Chinese studies will develop an audience at home, as one day Chinese studies will be a part of people's everyday lives.

Humanistic Pragmatism

Only a strong national foundation can guarantee the long-standing existence of any kind of academic discipline or even an ethnic culture; only a culture that reaches out to the people can convey values and develop. Today's rise ancient Chinese studies refers to the influence of intellectual discussions extending into the daily lives of ordinary people. Due to the expansion of modern media, Chinese studies are now free from barriers, and beyond national boundaries they are closely linked to people's lives.

Chinese-Style Enterprise Culture

In recent years, the application of ancient Chinese studies has expanded to the management mode of enterprises and enterprise cultures. China has a unique socio-cultural environment, so it is crucial to ensure that the modern-enterprise system adapts to China's socio-economic environment, forming a modern-enterprise management mode and culture with Chinese characteristics. In recent years, some scholars and entrepreneurs have tried to solve this problem by turning to *guoxue*.

'Fotile' Phenomenon, *Sunzi Bingfa (Master Sun's Art of War)*

Ancient Chinese studies are being used in some specific enterprise's management. One of the most striking examples is the use of Chinese studies in the Ningbo Fotile Kitchen Ware Company Limited's management, an application called the "Fotile" phenomenon.

Fotile was established in the mid-1990s as a kitchenware company that grew to become one of the leading kitchenware manufacturers in China. In this time of rapid development, it also encountered many problems. Mao Zhongqun, Fotile's chairman, chose to approach these problems relying on *guoxue*.

Mao applied the Taoist philosophy of "doing nothing is doing everything" and Confucian doctrines of "benevolence" *(ren)* and "harmony" *(he)* to enterprise management. He built tight dialectical relations between "doing nothing" and "doing everything," referring to "non-action" *(wuwei)* in business expansion, manufacturing innovative products, in acquisitions and in the company's expansion and product development. Prudent expansion and management policies and seeking leading technologies was wise, but Mao felt that western enterprise management should not simply be copied, that China's enterprise management could and should be adapted to accommodate China's cultural background. On the basis of reality, Fotile highlighted the cultural image of "home." The company also combined benevolence with harmony, making a seemingly cold enterprise management more humane, improving the cultural connotation and cohesion of the company. Fotile proved that *guoxue* involved more than a scholarly discipline, and that its practical value should not be underestimated.

Guoxue contain a wealth of management lore. In keeping with the saying, "Business is war without bullets…" military doctrine among various schools of China, particularly *Master Sun's Art of War*, was combined with enterprise management early in Chinese history. The book's value for business operations has been well recognised: Konosuke Matsushita, who was known as "god of business management in Japan," once said: "The sage Sunzi in ancient China was a deity in the world; my company's staff must adore him and take memorising his book seriously, but also to use it flexibly. Only in this way can our company thrive." In recent years, domestic scholars have paid more attention to the value of *Master Sun's Art of War* in business management. They have explored the book's significance in the following respects: enterprise personnel training, decision-making, enterprise crises and daily management, as well as enterprise cultural shaping. There are many articles that discuss this, such as *Master Sun's Art of War and Ways of Business Operations* by Li Zhiming; *Intelligence of Tai Chi: Sun's Art of War and the Modern Enterprise Strategy Management* by Li Xuefeng; and *Sun's Art of War and Strategy Management* by Zhong Yongsen.

Mass Media: From *Lecture Room* to *Learn Chinese Studies Happily*

An important characteristic of the current boom in ancient Chinese studies is the influence of the mass media on the popularity and spread of Chinese studies. The mass media, newspapers, radio, television, and the Internet, have become an important channel to enhance the awareness of Chinese studies among the public.

The *Lecture Room* and *Learn Chinese Studies Happily* Television programmes, broadcast via China Central Television (CCTV), helped tp popularise Chinese studies. *Lecture Room*, which started broadcasting in 2001, is for the general public and focuses on history, literature, classics and traditional etiquette. Yi Zhongtian, Yu Dan, and Wang Liqun are star scholars in the programme. The works of these star scholars have become bestsellers. In 2007, *Confucius from the Heart* by Yu Dan and *Appreciation the Three Kingdoms (Volume 2)* by Yi Zhongtian ranked at the top on the national bestseller list, and generated huge cultural effects.

The other programme, *Learn Chinese Studies Happily* on CCTV, allowed ordinary people to take the scholar's microphone and participate in the spreading and promotion of Chinese studies. The programme was broadcast in 2009, and from the beginning, it has attracted thousands of applicants aged 4–60. Participants are fans from the Chinese mainland but also fans of Chinese studies from more than 30 countries and regions, including the United States, Russia, Japan, Australia and Germany. *Learn Chinese Studies Happily* combines a TV contest, a typical contemporary TV programme form and a knowledge of Chinese studies, with the programme trying its best to embody traditional culture and the Chinese style via the use of costumes, stage design and background music. Its intuitive form and friendly style guaranteed its success, greatly improving the public's "affinity" for Chinese studies.

But local TV programmes, films and TV series also have great influence on ordinary Chinese and their awareness of Chinese studies. The abundant reading materials in Chinese studies now available for teenagers have great educational significance in shaping children's characters and personalities.

Sanzi Jing (Three-Character Scripture), *Baijiaxing (The Book of China's Family Names)*, *Dizi Gui (Disciple Rules)*, *Qianzi Wen (Thousand Character Classic)*, *Youxue Qionglin (The Children's Knowledge Treasury)*, and *Zengguang Xianwen (Social Wisdom)* contain rich historical stories and are very easy to recite. They are helpful for children's moral cultivation and mental health.

Reading classes have also been organised to promote traditional Chinese culture among children for 10 years, including the Tongxue Class in Shenzhen, and Meng Mu Class (Meng Mu is the mother of Mencius) in Shanghai. They read the *Three-Character Scripture*, *The Book of China's Family Names*, *Lunyu (The Analects of Confucius)*, *Zhongyong (The Doctrine of the Golden Mean)* and *Daxue (Confucius- The Great Learning)*.

Using mass media to popularise Chinese studies is at a primary stage. More mass media are being explored to popularise Chinese studies.

Renaissance of Chinese Studies

The reawakened need for Chinese studies is an important phenomenon in community life. In 2011, Hangzhou held activities to enliven Chinese studies in that community. It held seminars, read classical works and organised performances. Similar activities have also been held in communities in Chengdu, Sichuan Province, and in Jinan and Qingdao, Shandong Province.

Ancient Chinese placed great value in their rich patriarchal clan life and the thought of filial piety. Over the past decade, the rebuilding of ancestral temples and revitalising clans in the coastal villages and towns in South China where the economy is relatively developed has become a common sight. The renaissance of the traditional social formation is a natural revelation of national sentiment and the people's instinctive desire for revitalising the traditional Chinese culture. Scholars alone cannot decide the fate of a given culture. Instead, the aspirations of the masses will decide whether a culture continues or fades away.

Chinese studies have had a profound social influence, even when applied to the development of an enterprise culture, but also in the mass media and all kinds of common publications and readings. Chinese studies represent an exploration of the lives of the Chinese people; it is a symbol of cultural vitality. Inheriting Chinese studies is a responsibility of scholars but it's also a mission for each Chinese descendant.

Unity of Knowing, Doing

As the influence of Chinese studies has grown in colleges and universities, activities in universities attract famous scholars and inquisitive students. Communication between social organisations and institutes in universities brings academic and social circle closer together driving Chinese studies to have a more extensive and profound effect.

Confucian Scholar Society:
Cultivating Selves, Pursuing Righteousness

The Confucian Scholar Society was established in 2001 in Fuquan, Guizhou Province. First named the "Zhushi Society" and relying heavily on the teachings of Wang Yangming (1472–1529), a philosopher, official, educator and general, who himself relied greatly on Mencius' (372–289 BC) teachings, the society's teaching emphasised "the unity of knowing and doing and having both morals and techniques." It pursues "holding a firm faith in one's own career, upholding morality and remaining curious until death to perfect one's virtues" as a person of integrity who upholds the traditional spirit of "justice, loyalty and lenience, filial piety and fraternal duty" and who stands as an advocate for the values of "filial piety and fraternal duty as a basis, for loyalty and lenience as an orientation and for justice as a final result." Alluring to young people, its influence has been growing.

The society has four groups: a chanting group, teaching club, shaping-the-righteousness group and the cultivating-oneself club.

The chanting group's main task is the collective reading of classics. Every day, there is a morning and night reading or party reading or long-distance group readings via multimedia channels. The shaping-the-righteousness group has a weekly meeting about daily life issues, while the cultivating-oneself club engages in morning exercises, studying traditional customs, playing the zither, copying the classics and archery. It emphasises the harmonious lives of its members. The teaching club is a kind of public welfare activity group. Its activities are to spread Confucian teaching among the poor, to engage in community chanting, environmental protection, taking care of the elderly and the childless.

In addition, the society holds sacrificial ceremonies every year, with sacrifices to heaven during the first month of the lunar year and worshiping ancestors on Tomb-Sweeping Day with the family. On October 6, 2013, the society held a large ceremony to worship Confucius in conjunction with a public lecturing activity in a Confucian temple in Beijing. It attracted college teachers and students from across the nation, along with social elites from Beijing and Guangzhou municipalities and Shandong and Heilongjiang provinces, and gained support and a positive response.

Now, the society has shifted its orientation to passing on and studying Confucianism and to promoting and popularising Confucian education. It also cultivates Confucian groups and organisations among the people, develops public Confucian benefit programmes and helps benevolent enterprises start businesses. It takes an open and natural attitude to welcoming people who are devoted to learning and practising the traditional culture and spares no effort in revitalising Chinese studies.

On the road of revitalising Chinese studies and passing on the Confucian culture, scholars are not confined to supporting and practising Chinese studies in higher educational institutions only, but also in everyday life.

Hongdao Fund: Preserving Practice, Expanding Doctrines

Confucian scholars such as Jiang Qing, Chen Ming, Kang Xiaoguang, Xu Zhangrun and Qiu Feng established the Hongdao Fund on June 18, 2012, raising money from people who study Confucianism in all fields and those who support the development of Confucianism and the Chinese culture. Their aim is to revive the idea of Confucian scholars, promoting and developing the values of Confucianism and reconstructing a lifestyle with Chinese characteristics.

In 2001, Jiang Qing obtained enlightenment from the great thinker Wang Yangming and established the Yang Ming Academy in Guizhou Province. His major works are *An Introduction to Gongyang School, Good to Good: A Dialogue Between Jiang Qing and Sheng Hong, The Value of Confucianism,* and *Confucian Society and Orthodox Revival—A Dialogue with Jiang Qing.* Jiang's academic opinions are relatively trenchant, being on the way to explore the true spirit and values of Confucianism. He is a real Confucian scholar.

Chen Ming is the author of *The Historical and Cultural Functions of Confucianism – Aristocratic Families: A Special Form of Intellectual Research, The Dimension of the Scholar,* and *The Culture of Confucianism: Critical Thinking and Argumentation.* He founded the magazine *Yuan Dao* in 1994 and set up the Chinese Academy of Social Sciences

Institute of World Religions and Confucianism Research Centre in 2005. He also worked as a director of the research centre of Confucianism, which was established in 2007. He was active in the fields of academics, print, and media and has become a representative of new Confucianism on the Chinese mainland.

Founder Yao Zhongqiu, who uses the pen name of Qiu Feng, was dean of Hongdao Academy. He is also a professor of the Institute of Advanced Studies of Humanities and Social Sciences of Beijing University of Aeronautics and Astronautics. His works, *The Skills of Constitutionalism, Ways of Change: The Governance Order and its Reform Plans in Contemporary China*, and *Rediscover Confucianism*, lead readers to find the truth of Confucian thought.

The Hongdao Fund seeks to raise money and gather material resources for the revival of Confucianism, using its funds for charity work, social cultivation, the rehabilitation of rites and music, the discussion of knowledge, talent training, the publishing of books, website maintenance, and social relief.

Private Academies: Open Lyceum, Shaping Minds

Civil organisations and communities involved in Chinese studies include many private academies educational institutions, such as the Pengcheng and Wei Hang academies.

Poet and writer Han Feng established the Pengcheng Academy in 2007. He wrote *The Lost Scenery*, a poetry collection; *Before the Summer Solstice*, a work of prose; and *To Buy Books that One Does Not Read*. Critics call him "a writer who stands under the eaves of history, and looks into the future." The academy features lectures on Chinese studies, classical readings for children and tea parties based on the 24 solar terms. The influence of the academy continues to grow among young students and scholars. Scholar Li Changji said: "The Pengcheng Academy represents a new direction in the cultural construction of the Chinese nation."

The Weihang Academy was established in Beijing in 2006. Yang Ruqing, its founder, worked for a long time at Tsinghua University, at a Buddhist Institute in Hebei Province, and at the International Youth University. She studied Confucian thought, pre-school education and the practise and exploration of public welfare for a long time. Her major activities include the establishment of reading clubs, annual speeches, and classics sorting. She also interpreted some classics as well as glossaries for pre-school education use, such as Disciple Rules and Three-Character Scripture.

Systematic schools for pre-school education began to appear among the academies, at Qibaoge, Global Confucius and Jiguang academies. These academies aimed at pre-school education, adhering to the traditional thoughts of Chinese culture. A lot of schools of Chinese studies for youths, for pre-school education and for children were set up. *Disciple Rules, Three-Character Scripture* and T*housand Character Classic* are the main teaching sources. They train children geniality through reading and via explanations of the classics and via training based on traditional etiquettes.

The spread of traditional reading materials for pre-school education, even the classes that help children in reading some classics and education in academies are at primary stage of shaping a child's personalities. These also serve as foundations for Chinese studies. In recent years, the Chinese studies institutions, communities and the activities in colleges and universities are conscious choices and positive responses for young students to take advantage of access to Chinese studies.

China Traditional Culture Institute

The China Traditional Culture Institute's establishment came at the right moment. It accords with historical trends in the great rejuvenation of the Chinese in the 21st century and has gotten widespread attention and support from all sectors of society.

Confucius Research Institute

Confucius, recognised worldwide as being among "the world's top-ten ancient philosophers," is admired and respected by many people. To discern the essence of Confucian thought, and to advance China's culture, China's State Council approved the establishment of the Confucius Research Institute in the sage's hometown, Qufu, Shandong Province, in September 1996.

The Confucius Research Institute's design uses "squares" and "circles" as its basic motif, metaphorically expressing Chinese cultural connotations, while incorporating the Confucian concepts of "benevolence" *(ren)* and "harmony" *(he)* in the institute's planning. The architectural form fully expresses the cultural connotations of Confucius life, thought and character, while also reflecting China's national character, modernity and its history.

The Confucius Research Institute has five function:

- Conducting academic research and exchange; compiling and publish monographs on Confucian studies and enhancing the popularity of these books, and organising various international and bilateral academic seminars.

- Organising exhibitions about Confucius and the Confucian heritage highlighting characteristics of the Asian culture.
- Collecting, sorting and preserving literary documents about Confucius and Confucianism, both ancient and modern, from China and abroad.
- Researching information exchange about Confucius and Confucianism; preserving achievements in research, relying on modern equipment and technology, and providing information for experts and scholars in China and abroad. Engaging in talent training; sets up training courses; and receiving national and international scholars.

Over the past 10 years, the Confucius Research Institute's achievements in academic research, exchange and in promoting traditional Chinese culture have been remarkable.

School of Chinese Classics of Renmin University of China

The School of Chinese Classics of Renmin University of China, in 2005, set up the first educational research institution that combined bachelor and master's degree programmes involved in the study and teaching of Chinese studies. The first president was Professor Feng Qiyong.

Some educational research institutes have been set up in the School of Chinese Classics, such as the Chinese Classical Literature Research Institute, Chinese Ancient History Research Institute, the Research Office of Classics and Classic Research Centre. The School of Chinese Classics also founded some academic journals, planned and organised the writing of various related books. And it also published some teaching materials to explain the Chinese classics. Now, some curricula are available that can be used to promote Chinese studies in society and let it take root in the hearts of the Chinese people.

Universities' Chinese Studies Community–Making Friends through Knowledge, Cultivating Virtue Together

Many universities in China have set up Chinese studies communities, including the Chinese Studies Community of Tsinghua, Academy of Southwest University and the Chinese Studies Morning-Reading Community of Jilin University. This is an important way for college students to learn more about this field of study. Universities in Hunan and Hubei provinces have established the Higher Education Chinese Studies Community Union.

The activities in Chinese Studies Community involve studying the classical Chinese culture, understanding the traditional Chinese culture and social-communication activities. In addition, they also hold Chinese studies salons, reading parties and competitions, exhibitions of Han Chinese clothing, etiquette, archery events, historical studies and tours of cultural and other attractions. The union aims at expanding the influence of Chinese studies in universities and convincing more university students to participate in promoting and developing an outstanding traditional Chinese culture and national spirit.

Chinese civilisation has a long history that brings the intelligence of self-cultivation, mature behaviour and a history of achievement to the Chinese. Contemporary Chinese should shoulder their historical responsibility to inherit the national culture and develop Chinese studies.

Overseas Inheritance

Cultural diversity in times of economic globalisation is a theme of cultural development in today's world. While Chinese culture's expansion is closely related to the revitalisation of China's traditional culture, the propagation of Chinese studies overseas contributes to establishing a more harmonious world.

Long History of Cultural Exchanges

The propagation of Chinese studies overseas did not begin yesterday. Ancient China had cultural exchanges with Central Asia, West Asia, North Africa, South Asia and Europe via the Silk Road and by sea. It had a lasting and profound cultural influence on Japan, the Korean Peninsula and on Southeast Asia, forming the so-called Chinese cultural circle.

With China as its centre, Chinese civilisation had sparkling collisions with western civilisations over time. There is a famous saying by the prophet Mohammed: "Knowledge must be purchased, though it is in remote China." At the end of the Ming (1368–1644) and the beginning of the Qing (1644–1911) dynasties, the West and the East learned much from each other. With the efforts of early missionaries from the West, some Chinese classics were translated and brought to the West where they had a great influence on western scholars of the Age of Enlightenment (late 17th century–18th century). Even in modern times, Western sinologists and overseas Chinese students made contributions to the influence of Chinese studies abroad.

Chinese studies have had a more far-reaching significance in East Asia. Early in the fourth and fifth centuries, the classics of Confucianism arrived in Japan while Chinese Buddhist thought reached Japan during the Sui (AD 581–618) and Tang (AD 618–907) dynasties. At the end of the Ming and beginning of the Qing dynasties, a host of adherents of the Qing Dynasty took an eastward sea voyage, taking the Neo-Confucian scholar Zhuxi's (1130–1200) thought to Japan. Since modern times, Japanese scholars have made an introspection and reorganisation of Chinese studies. Chinese studies have had an influence on the Korean Peninsula as early as during the Han Dynasty (206 BC–220 AD). Silla (57 BC–935 AD), one of the Three Kingdoms of Korea, was called *"junzi"* (the land of the virtuous) during the Tang Dynasty. Afterwards, Chinese studies with Confucianism's strong influence grew in popularity on the Korean Peninsula; Jeong Mong-ju and Yi Hwang were famous Confucian scholars on the Korean Peninsula. Even now, Korean Confucianism has a place in the world's Confucianism system, with famed scholars such as Dong-jun Lee.

In modern times, the overseas inheritance of Chinese studies has reached a new and remarkable level of attainment. The current craze for Chinese studies reflects the concentration on Chinese studies domestically, but this is also reflected in its spreading influence and discussions abroad, inspired, in part, by the establishment of numerous Confucius Institutes overseas.

Confucius Institutes: Advancing with Times

In 2004, the first overseas Confucius Institute was established in the Republic of Korea. According to data from www. people.com.cn, by the end of 2012, 400 Confucius Institutes and 500 Confucius Classrooms had been established in 108 countries. About 655,000 foreign students were studying Chinese in their own countries. In addition, there are more than 400 universities in 76 countries bidding to host Confucius Institutes. Despite the "visa storm" of Confucius Institutes in the United States in 2012, more than 30 new Confucius Institutes and 40 Confucius Classrooms were established there within that year.

With the rapid development of Confucius Institutes in Europe, their influence is gradually increasing. In France, there were 16 Confucius Institutes established by the end of June 2013. Confucius Institutes in France have flexible forms of education. There are joint ventures between colleges and universities, between French and Chinese local governments and between Chinese universities and the French local government or community organisations. In June 2012, the Central Conservatory of Music and the Royal Danish Academy of Music co-founded the world's first music-oriented Confucius Institute. It is a useful attempt to expand the activity's scope. European Confucius Institutes held a joint meeting in 2012, unanimously agreeing that making a long-term development plan is an important guarantee for sustainable development. This shows that the development of Confucius Institutes in Europe has entered a long-term stable phase.

Confucius Institutes have been welcomed in some Arab countries. By the end of March 2012, seven Arab countries had established nine Confucius Institutes that offered about 300 courses with 5,000 participants and one Confucius Classroom. Arab countries mainly rely on cooperation in the establishment of the Confucius Institutes. Their courses include Chinese language teaching and acupuncture. At the same time, the Confucius Institutes are also committed to the promotion of the Chinese culture. They held as many as 100 diverse international Chinese promotional activities with almost 20,000 participants.

Confucius Institutes have also made great achievements in Africa. By of the end of June 2012, at least 20 African countries had set up 17 Confucius Institutes and four Confucius Classrooms. In 2011, the African Confucius Institutes held nearly 600 cultural activities at local universities and communities, with more than 400,000 participants. As China-Africa cooperation and exchanges have been strengthened in recent years, Confucius Institutes in Africa will receive broad development, overcoming language and cultural barriers.

ASEAN (Association of Southeast Asian Nations) countries are China's neighbours and all have a long history and tradition in cultural exchanges with China, which has greatly influenced these countries' cultures. With the ever-increasing cooperation in economics and trade, Confucius Institutes will achieve even greater success in these regions, where the traditional Chinese culture once again has strong appeal.

Activities offered by Confucius Institutes are continuously expanding and deepening. Promoting the Chinese culture and enhancing China's cultural soft power will be the future task of the Confucius Institutes. As Xu Lin, director of Hanban and director-general of the Confucius Institute Headquarters, said: "The world is undergoing major developments, major changes and major adjustments. To develop Confucius Institutes on the world stage is important if we are to strengthen our cultural awareness and cultural self-confidence. It is our duty and mission."

In addition to the Confucius Institutes, official and folk visits and activities serve in spreading Chinese culture worldwide.

'Chinese Bridge'

The overseas continuation of Chinese studies is based on Chinese teaching and promotion. Language is the key to a culture. The global spread of the Chinese language has its own important basic value and significance in the overseas promotion of Chinese studies.

The programme *Chinese Star–'Chinese Bridge'*, a Chinese proficiency competition for foreign students in China, has been broadcast six times by CCTV and Hanban since 2008. A language competition, it also tests the contestants' comprehensive understanding of the Chinese culture, whether the classics, poetry, classical literature or traditional folk arts. It attracts the participation of foreign students in China and has significant implications in promoting Chinese studies. Moreover, this has affected promoting Chinese culture in students' home countries have taken place after their return home.

A Cultural Feast on World Stage

The overseas promotion of Chinese studies is closely connected with the global influence of Chinese culture, with its development is generally positive. From cultural products, cultural agencies and media to cultural art festivals, Chinese studies are excelling on the world cultural stage, bringing a spiritual, cultural feast to the people of the world.

The Jilin Yuping Technology Company Limited specialises in silk-figurine production, drawing inspiration from figures in classical Chinese literature and folklore. Its products are sold overseas in 27 countries and regions. Its annual sales amounted to hundreds of thousands of pieces, earning them the name "Asian Barbies."

The Chinese Culture Centre in Mexico, established in June 2013, is the 13th overseas Chinese cultural centre and also the first in the Americas. The Chinese culture centre is an official institution of the Chinese Government abroad and an important platform for foreign cultural exchanges and cooperation. It brings foreign cultures to China and accelerates the development and prosperity of culture. On Children's Day in 2013, Chinese cultural centres in Germany, Benin, Mauritius, Russia, the Republic of Korea and other countries held a variety of celebratory activities for local children, including traditional paper-cutting, a Chinese zodiac exhibition in Germany and a reading of the *Three-Character Scripture* in Russia.

The China (Qufu) International Confucius Cultural Festival opened on Confucius's birthday on September 28, 2013, and a solemn ceremony for Confucius was held. The funeral oration written by Tsinghua University professor Peng Lin was full of Confucian spirit: "Manners should always pay attention to harmony, no matter how big or small issues are. We should use manners to restrict ourselves and to pursue harmony." From the beginning of the first Confucius birthday activities in 1984 to today's China International Confucius Cultural Festival, the influence of the Confucius cultural festival has been growing. Various forms of commemorations were held on Confucius's birthday in Liuzhou, Quzhou, Tongan, Jianshui and Wenchang in China.

In recent years, the number of Chinese books available overseas has been increasing, and books on Chinese studies have earned a reputation. Statistics show there are 34 publishing companies in China, offering more than 100 kinds of their books that are available in 30 libraries around the world. The Zhong Hua Book Company and Shanghai Ancient Books Publishing House are the top-two publishing houses engaged in publishing Chinese studies books. Among all of the 34 "printing presses," there are nine ancient-book publishing houses for ancient books, accounting for 26 percent of the total. This proves that Chinese studies play a crucial role in promoting Chinese cultural. China Network Television presented a new programme, *Chinese Public Class*, that uses a network platform to promote the Chinese culture, covering broad subjects such as education, technology, history, philosophy, history, literature and art. The promotion of Chinese studies is the most important section. It is likely to become the overseas and online edition of *Lecture Room*.

Let's appreciate the beauty of the Chinese and other countries' cultures and combine them to achieve and develop complementary beauty. The overseas promotion of Chinese studies involves in the charm of Chinese civilisation, and will contribute to the development of the world culture. More importantly, only when combined with other world cultures will Chinese studies be integrated into the history of world civilisation.

References

A Brief History of Chinese Music (revised edition), Wu Zhao, Liu Dongsheng, People's Music Publishing House, December 1993

A Complete Interpretation of the Journey to the West, Huang Zhiqiao, Zhonghua Book Company, January 2012

A History of Chinese Philosophy, Feng Youlan, East China Normal University Press, 2000

A History of Chinese Philosophy, Ren Jiyu, People's Publishing House, 2003

Ancient Chinese Academies, Wang Bingzhao, China International Radio Press, 2009

Annotations of the Four Classical Confucian Books, Zhu Xi, Zhonghua Book Company, 2011

Annotation of Analects, Yang Bojun, Zhonghua Book Company, 2006

Annotation and Evaluation of Laozi (revised edition), Chen Guying, Zhonghua Book Company, 1984

An Outline of the History of Chinese Philosophy, Hu Shi, Yuelu Publishing House, 2009

A Pictorial History of Architecture of Ancient China, Hou Youbin, China Architecture & Building Press, November 2002

A Study on Zhu Xi's Philosophy, Chen Lai, East China Normal University Press, 2000

Comments on Chinese Poetry, Wang Guowei, Chanjiang Literature and Art Press, December 2008

Complete Works of Zhong Zhongjing, Liu Shi'en, China Ancient Books Press, September 1, 2007

Contention of Numerous Schools of Thought in Pre-Qin Period, Yi Zhongtian, Shanghai Literature and Art Publishing Group, 2009

Feng Ru, Huang Qingchang, Guangdong People's Publishing House, November 2009

Four Supervisors of Tsinghua University, Dongfang Publications, 2009

General History of Taiwan, Lian Heng, Jiuzhou Press, June 2008

Guan Zi, Li Shan, Zhonghua Book Company, March 2009

Historical Records, Sima Qian, Zhonghua Book Company, November 1982

History of Ancient China's Foreign Exchanges, Wang Xiaofu, Higher Education Press, May 2006

History of Han Dynasty, Zhonghua Book Company, June 1962

History of Jin Dynasty, Fang Xuanling, Zhonghua Book Company, March 2011

History of Song Dynasty, Tuotuo and some others, Zhonghua Book Company, December 2011

History of Yuan Dynasty, Song Lian, Zhonghua Book Company, April 1976

History of Ming Dynasty, Zhang Tingyu, Zhonghua Book Company, April 1974

Li Ji—Zhong Yong (The Book of Rites—Zhong Yong), Shanghai Gu Ji Publishing House, 2004

Lun Yu—Li Ren (The Analects—Li Ren), Zhonghua Book Company, 2006

Lun Yu—Tai Bo (The Analects—Tai Bo), Zhonghua Book Company, 2006

Lü's Spring and Autumn Annals, Lü Buwei, Shanghai Ancient Book Publishing House, 1995

Management Thinking of Chinese Military Strategists, Liu Yunbo, Shanghai People's Publishing House, 1993

Mengzi (Mencius), Zhonghua Book Company, 2006

Miscellanies of Xiaoting, Zhao Lian, Zhonghua Book Company, December 1980

Mozi, Li Xiaolong, Zhonghua Book Company, 2007

New Culture Movement, Jin Kaicheng, Jilin Literature and History Press, January 2012

New History of Tang Dynasty, Ouyang Xiu, Zhonghua Book Company, February 1975

Popular Chinese Medical History, Ren Yingqiu, Chongqing People's Press, 1959

Romance of the Three Kingdoms, Chen Shou, Zhonghua Book Company, July 1982

Seven Sages of the Bamboo Grove, Cao Xu, Ding Gongyi, Zhonghua Book Company, February 2010

Spirit of Martyrs: Deng Shichang and the Zhiyuan Fleet in the Sino-Japanese Sea War in 1894, Chen Mingfu, People's Literature Publishing House, October 2003

The Ancient Chinese Banquet Protocols, Lü Jianwen, Beijing Institute of Technology Press, 2007

The Autobiography of Liang Qichao, Liang Qichao, Jiangsu Wenyi Publishing House, 2012

The Chinese Drinking Customs, Guo Panxi, Shaanxi People's Press, 2006

The Confucian Analects Interpretation and Notes, Yang Bojun, Zhonghua Book Company, December 2006

The Festival Culture of Chinese, Hai Shang, Yuelu Publishing House, 2005

The Folk Customs of Wine, Tian Long, China Social Press, 2006

The History of Chinese Philosophy, Feng Youlan, East China Normal University Press, 2000

The History of Chinese Philosophy, Ren Jiyu, People's Publishing House, 2003

The Last Two Decades of Chen Yinque, Lu Jiandong, Sanlian Bookstore, 1995

The Lifetime, Ji Xianlin, Central Compilation and Translation Press, 2009

The Press and Politics in Modern China: starting from the reform movement of 1898, Liu Xinghao, Central Compilation and Translation Press, July 2011

The Tea Aroma, Hong Yu, Gansu Culture Press, 2004

Thought and Spirit of the Legalist School, Wu Shuchen, Li Li, China Radio and Television Publishing House, 2007

Three Caos and Chinese Poetry History, Sun Mingjun, Tsinghua University Press, September 1999

Translation of the History of Eleuthes Mongols, the Institute of Ethnology and Anthropology, Chinese Academy of Social Sciences, December 1981

Translation of the Analects of Confucius, Yang Bojun, Zhong Hua Book Company, 2006

Wu Mi and Chen Yinque, Wu Xuezhao, Tsinghua University Publications, 1992

Sponsors: Information Office of the Beijing Municipal Government
Compiled by: Beijing Foreign Cultural Exchanges Center
Beijing This Month Publications
General Planner: Wang Hui
Planners: Zhang Jinlin, Bai Jie
Editor in Chief: Bai Jie, Wang Lin
Writers: An Dun, Wang Wei, Zhang Jian, Du Yuqing, Wan Yunyun,
Si Meina, Zhang Rui
Managing Editors: An Dun, Huang Jinmin
Editors: Li Xiaoli, Yang Baohua, Jin Yan, Zhou Fujing, Wang Wei
English Language Consultant: Charles J. Dukes, Mark Zuiderveld
Photo Editors: Ma Ke, Sang Yi
Design and Production: Dong bo, Han Yü, Shen Jie, Liu Lili
Address: Bldg. 10, Fahuananli, Tiyuguan Lu, Dongcheng District,
Beijing 100061
Tel: +86 10 6715 2380
Fax: +86 10 6715 2381
Website: http://www.charmingbeijing.com
Publisher: China Intercontinental Press
Address: Huatian Plaza, 6 Beixiaomachang, Haidian District, Beijing

图书在版编目（ＣＩＰ）数据

国学撷要：汉英对照 / 安顿主编 . —— 北京：五洲
传播出版社，2016.3
ISBN 978-7-5085-3338-4

Ⅰ . ①国… Ⅱ . ①安… Ⅲ . ①国学－通俗读物－汉、
英 Ⅳ . ① Z126-49

中国版本图书馆 CIP 数据核字 (2016) 第 050586 号